Pitt Series in Policy and Institutional Studies

Policy Analysis by Design

**Davis B. Bobrow and
John S. Dryzek**

University of Pittsburgh Press

To

Gail and Peggy

Published by the University of Pittsburgh Press,
Pittsburgh, Pa., 15260
Copyright © 1987, University of Pittsburgh Press
All rights reserved
Baker & Taylor International, London
Manufactured in the United States of America
Second printing, 1989

Library of Congress Cataloging-in-Publication Data

Bobrow, Davis B.
  Policy analysis by design.

  (Pitt series in policy and institutional studies)
  Bibliography: p. 221.
  Includes index.
  1. Policy sciences.   I. Dryzek, John S., 1953–   .
II. Title.   III. Series.
H97.B6   1987   361.6'1   87-5974
ISBN 0-8229-3559-7
ISBN 0-8229-5392-7 (pbk.)

Contents

Preface

*E*ACH OF US teaches and writes about public policy, even occasionally trying to influence it (albeit on different issues and in different ways). While pursuing these tasks we decided to put our own thoughts in order concerning some recurring basic questions about one's stance in approaching public policy. Our main purpose here is to promote a clearer understanding of the menu of approaches available, the foundations adopted unreflectively by partisans of each approach, and the considerations that might guide intelligent acts of selection.

The choices we address are not about technical detail, and thus will not help the harried practitioner seeking a plausible product in a short time to fit a bureaucratic agenda. Our concern lies deeper, involving the questions that will be asked about public policy, the answers that will be found, and the social consequences of any resulting policy actions. We believe orderly examination of such basic choices can contribute to sound judgment among those who approach public policy from the social sciences. Such examination may not make policy problems any more soluble or the work on them less frustrating. But it may make this work more intellectually responsible and give those who labor a clearer compass.

We began with an awareness of the plethora of analytical options available to policy analysts. This awareness has led us to develop a framework for systematically comparing the possibilities, which appears in chapter 1. We apply this framework to the major contending frames of reference in part 2. Chapters 2 through 6 address, respectively, welfare economics, public choice, social structure, information processing, and political philosophy. While these dissections reveal differences and enable some judgments within and among approaches, they do not provide a sufficient basis for conclusive choice. To resolve remaining dilemmas about knowledge-based policy interventions, we turn to fundamental theories of knowledge in chapters 7 through 11. Once again, some important distinctions surface, and we can further refine our judgments. But no thoroughly conclusive strategy for policy inquiry emerges (though some fall by the wayside). Accordingly, we turn in part 4 to some modest suggestions about how policy analysts should proceed in the face of diversity and limited analytic capabilities.

Along the way we intermittently try to make our arguments a bit less abstract with reference to an imaginary policy case—air pollution in Smoke Valley. Bibliographical notes at the end of the text suggest further reading, which may help compensate for the brief treatment we sometimes accord to schools of thought worthy of more extended discussion.

The collaboration that produced this volume began in 1978, and we would like to thank Susan Wiley for introducing us then. In subsequent years we have had the benefit of suggestions from Kathy Peroff and David Segal, criticisms of draft chapters from Hayward Alker, Bob Bartlett, and Kenneth Shepsle, and research assistance from Rebeka Maples. Stephen Elkin deserves special thanks for reading the entire manuscript and suggesting improvements in organization and emphasis. Bob Goodin was a continuous source of encouragement for the whole venture. Finally, comments from several anonymous reviewers helped us improve the manuscript.

Part One

Prelude

Chapter 1

Reconsidering the Policy Field

Some THIRTY-five years ago, Daniel Lerner and Harold Lasswell (1951) issued a call for the "policy sciences." They sketched a program to meet the need for a wide range of social science contributions to "knowledge *of* and knowledge *in* the public decision process." The intervening decades have seen three developments important in their own right and curious in their coincidence. First, programs for training experts and producing knowledge for public policy have proliferated in departments of political science and public administration and in schools of public affairs. Second, techniques supposed to improve the quality of public policy have been invented, refined, and widely adopted. Third, a wave of optimism (at least in the Anglo-American world) concerning the potential contribution of government action to collective well-being has been replaced by a general scepticism—indeed, in many quarters, hostility—toward the very idea of public sector action. The positive developments one might have expected to improve the performance and credibility of the public sector have failed to arrest the growing doubts that purposeful governmental action can bear a good harvest.

We leave it to others to allot responsibility for this disappointing outcome. Nor do we intend to produce yet another tract about the limits of what government can do (interspersed with appropriate horror stories) or, from the other side, warn of the dire consequences of market sovereignty. We do, however, recognize a prima facie case that policy analysts should balance their attention to technique with a more reflective contemplation of the rationales underlying their interventions in the policy process. It is admirable to advocate "speaking truth to power" (Wildavsky 1979), but the lack of an intellectually coherent discipline under the "policy" umbrella after so many years suggests that such a homily will not suffice. We need to understand what sorts of truth might be spoken, in what languages, and to what ends.

The contemporary state of the policy field brings to mind a familiar story in which students from different cultures are asked to write an essay on the elephant. As the story goes, the Frenchman hands in an essay on the sex life of the elephant; the Jew, on the elephant and the Jewish problem; the Russian, on the role of the elephant in Marxist-Leninist thought; the Englishman, on the effect on elephants of the weather we've been having lately; the American, on the market in elephant futures, and so forth.

Discussions about public policy manifest the diversity in perspectives, which makes this story humorous, except that for matters of social importance the result is not always funny. As we listen to policy discussions going beyond those within "tribes" of experts, the participants seem not only to be talking about different matters but even to be speaking different languages. They fail to agree on the point of what they are discussing, the key parties they must consider, the set of means that can be brought to bear, the values that matter, and relationships of cause and effect. As a consequence, policy debates often come to resemble a babel of tongues, in which participants talk past rather than to one another. This book tries to sort out the babel.

The policy field includes work that seeks only to understand and explain the process of public policy making—"knowledge of," in Lasswell's terms. Little can be said about such work that is not also applicable to the social sciences more generally. Our concern here is different. We address the side of the policy field that distinguishes it from ordinary social science: the knowledge in (or, more precisely, the knowledge for) component. Accordingly, when we consider the analytical options open to the policy analyst we care less about their capacities to explain the past or predict the future than about how they strengthen the "propensity of thoughtful and reasonable persons to approach the threats and opportunities of the emerging world . . . in ways that satisfy and contribute to . . . human values" (Lasswell 1980: 516).

This "knowledge for" aspect of the policy field includes studies that clarify the consequences and attractiveness of one or more policy options, or canvass and invent policy means to some end.[1] Analysis that clarifies can be retrospective or prospective; that which canvasses and invents must be prospective and strategic. Both kinds can address the content and the process of public policy.

THE MANY LANGUAGES OF THE POLICY FIELD

If the field is currently home to a babel of tongues, the first step for any serious reconsideration is to characterize the principal languages spoken by the various tribes of experts. Just as an ordinary individual apprehends the world through the medium of language, so the expert interprets reality through the conceptual lens of a technical frame of reference. Any such frame is composed of theories, methods, rules of evidence and inference, and a set of entities deemed worthy of attention. Frames provide guidelines for interpretation, explanation, prediction, and evaluation. A frame is a source of comfort to its partisans as they adhere to its guidelines, a source of doubt if they stray further afield.

The policy field is currently marked by an extraordinary variety of technical approaches, reflecting the variety of research traditions in contemporary social science. That variety is likely to persist for the foreseeable future, for the reductionist dream of a unified social science under a single theoretical banner is dead. Indeed, the only social science discipline with anything approaching an internal consensus on a frame of reference is economics. Even here, the orthodox neoclassical synthesis is not without challenge from within the economics

---

1. We shall pay little attention to the kind of policy advocacy pervading real-world policy processes. Recommendation of courses of action clearly does have a place in the policy field, but its status therein depends on sound analytical backing. Real-world policy advocacy generally fails this test (see Bobrow and Stoker 1981).

profession (for example, by Marxist political economy and by energy economics) nor without strident external criticism.

The policy field magnifies the variety of technical approaches in contemporary social science inasmuch as the activity draws upon and cuts across a number of social science disciplines (and some nonsocial science ones, too). Policy problems do not respect entrenched disciplinary boundaries that owe their existence to the accidents of intellectual history and the rigidities of academic institutions.

The welter of contending frames, each of limited validity, does much to explain three of the more troubling problems policy analysts can encounter. First, many policies have consequences that surprise their intellectual parents by being different from what analysis had led their supporters or designers to expect. Second, critics of a particular piece of work often find that they must address the implicit premises of the work in question, rather than its execution, in order to locate the central grounds of their disagreement with it. In other words, analysts keep having to return to first principles, instead of refining and applying work already done. Third, retrospective policy studies can present several strikingly different yet equally compelling explanations for the same historically observed set of policy outcomes, without providing grounds for a choice between alternative explanations.[2] There is clearly a need to provide analysts with some better basis for making choices, or at least for managing diversity.

Part 2 of this study enumerates and assesses the various frames currently prominent in the policy field. Our profiles are inevitably incomplete, and perhaps do less than full justice to some of the nuances of each tradition. But, for the sake of brevity, they must suffice to capture the central tenets of each approach. The frames we address are those that have loomed particularly large in policy analysis in recent years. They do not exhaust the range of conceivable approaches, but together they cover most kinds of policy analysis currently undertaken,

---

2. For example, Allison (1971) provides an interpretation of decision making in the Cuban missile crisis in terms of three models: rational actor, organizational processes, and bureaucratic politics. Each of these explains different aspects of decision, yet each taken alone is not compelling.

and each is far more developed than any incipient competitor. The primary contenders are as follows.

Welfare economics has the greatest number of policy field practitioners. This approach is manifested in such familiar techniques as cost-benefit and cost-effectiveness analysis. *Public choice* straddles the disciplines of microeconomics, political science, and public administration, and concerns itself for the most part with the analysis and design of decision structures. *Social structure*, rooted in sociology, has some crucial subdivisions. We address its two principal strands, based respectively on individual endowments and group endowments. *Information processing* starts from a less sanguine view of individual capabilities than welfare economics and public choice. Optimistic practitioners of this approach seek to extend individual and organizational capabilities in the direction of better public policy. Their pessimistic colleagues seek only adaptation to the limits inherent upon any participant in the policy process. Finally, *political philosophy* applies moral reasoning to the content and process of policy.

Our setting forth of this set of profiles might suggest that we have before us a smorgasbord, in which each frame of reference resembles an available offering for one course of the meal, such that the diner can choose a selection for each course. However, each approach is really a relatively complete meal in itself; mixing approaches may cause indigestion by introducing incompatibilities in analysis and design. An inquiry that involves the systematic application of several approaches can, nevertheless, be particularly informative—though taxing on budgets of time, energy, and research resources. Those who opt for the multiple-framework strategy still need some grounds on which to choose among the frameworks available. Later on in this study, we explore possible ways of making intelligent choices.

These frames of reference are devices we simply cannot do without. It is perhaps possible to conceive of totally atheoretical work in the policy field; though one suspects this would be little more than applied common sense. If analysis is to have any flesh and power beyond common sense, then it must draw upon social science wisdom. If one seeks to explain the consequences of past policy actions and to predict those of future options, then one needs a theory of intervention, however tacit. Such theory is provided by frames of reference. To deny that such frameworks matter is to deny that social science has any role in social problem solving. Even partisans of such denial should allow a serious consideration of just how far social science as policy inquiry can be pushed.

We seek to show that the choice of a frame of reference matters a great deal in at least three ways. First, it makes some topics of inquiry more central and salient than others. Second, it makes some kinds of policy instruments look markedly more attractive than others. Third, it makes some social consequences more legitimate than others and thus affects the likelihood that public sector resources will be harnessed to their pursuit. Accordingly, in choosing a frame of reference for policy analysis and design we pick not only an agenda for research but also, de facto, an agenda for public policy. We are choosing among social values, whether we realize it or not. A minimal intellectual responsibility demands that we recognize that the choice of a policy analysis frame of reference is an ethical and not just a technical matter, and is in itself a major political decision.[3]

In practice, analysts often evade making this choice—and may indeed be unaware that there is a choice to be made—as a result of sheltering within the confines of their disciplinary socialization or residence. Some of those who are aware of the choice defend their own proclivities on sectarian grounds of inherent technical or normative superiority. Their defensiveness is manifested in acting as though their adopted frame provides an axiomatic, objective basis for judgments about the goals of public policy and the efficacy of policy alternatives. Yet there is ample evidence that even in economics (by far the

---

3. As Hirschman (1970: 338) points out, "without models, paradigms, ideal types and similar abstractions we cannot even start to think. But cognitive style, that is, the kinds of paradigms we search out, the way we put them together, and the ambitions we nurture for their powers—all this can make a great deal of difference." He goes on to point out how some paradigms make large-scale social and political change seem more unlikely than it really is, deny the open-endedness of history, and foster illusions about the predictability of revolutionary change.

most consensual and formalized of the relevant disciplines) there is substantial disagreement about "practical economic policy" (Frey et al. 1984: 986). This disagreement applies with equal force to macroeconomic and microeconomic policy measures, and can be explained in large measure by differences in historical and cultural experience among economists. No frame provides a closed system for the policy analyst, only different gaps to be filled by subjective judgment.

Our comparative dissection of major frames of reference can, we hope, facilitate reasoned choice among them. Further, this dissection should enable a distinction between the elements of any piece of policy analysis inherent in the frame applied and those elements whose origins must be sought elsewhere (possibly in the subjectivity of the analyst).

A FRAMEWORK FOR COMPARATIVE SCRUTINY

If we are to discourse intelligently about the various frames of reference abroad in the policy field, let alone provide a basis for their comparison, we must be selective and consistent in the questions we ask of each. Essentially, we need to identify the foundation on which the frame is erected, characterize what its practitioners actually do, summarize its contribution to the resolution of social problems (bearing in mind the practical intent of policy analysis), and pinpoint its perspective, especially with respect to normative issues. Four sets of questions can be put along these lines:

1. *Givens*
   Hard core (ontology and crude analogy)
   Realism of hard core assumptions
   Capabilities attributed to the policy process
2. *Contents*
   Theoretical themes
   Methodological principles
   Empirical content
3. *Practical Usefulness*
   Policy applicability
   Problem-solving adequacy
   Progressing or degenerating capabilities

4. *Perspective*
   Time
   Audience
   Normative stance
   Treatment of conflicting values

Givens

The first set of questions consists of the accepted and un-questioned givens in the practice of an approach. The most fundamental given is what Lakatos (1970) calls the hard core of an approach. The hard core in its turn reflects the entities and properties that populate the world perceived by practitioners. In the social sciences, the hard core typically involves some view of human nature reflecting a conception of human needs, capabilities, and modes of interaction (Ball 1976: 167). The nonfalsifiable hard core of an approach may also contain what Masterman (1970) calls a crude analogy. If a frame or research tradition is indeed a way of seeing, then as Masterman notes, it involves viewing phenomena through reference to something else—that is, by analogy. Examples of crude analogies are solar system models for the representation of atomic structure, the use of language structure to represent genetic codes, the particulate representation of light, and analogies drawn by sociobiologists between human beings and social insects.

Recognized properties and entities (together constituting the ontology of a frame) and crude analogy are clearly important delimiters of an approach—if they exist. But we should allow for the possibility that an approach may be lacking one or both. To the extent that ontology and crude analogy are missing, an approach will be ill defined and not readily distinguishable from other approaches. Hence it cannot easily be taught or applied. So, for example, systems analysis has fallen from favor in part because nobody can really describe what it is (see Wildavsky 1966). The research tradition of policy analysis as a whole currently lacks anything resembling an ontology or crude analogy, which is why a study of the kind we are undertaking here is necessary.

The practical intent of the policy field makes two further

givens important. The first concerns the realism of the basic assumptions and axioms in the hard core. The degree of realism is irrelevant in many areas of inquiry. Thus Friedman (1953) holds that the extent or seeming unreality of assumptions is of little importance, provided only that theories thus derived yield testable propositions. Nevertheless, in policy analysis plausible assumptions enhance the probability of the analysis being persuasive to its intended audience. This does not gainsay the adverse consequences for parsimony, clarity, and the ability to generalize caused by a proliferation of assumptions motivated by a desire to fit reality.

A final given has to do with the assumed capabilities of the policy process. Differing views on this score underlie the long-standing debate within the policy field between those who see instrumentally rational policy making as both possible and desirable (for example, Simon 1960; Dror 1964, 1971a; Goodin 1982) and those (notably Lindblom 1959, 1965, 1979; and Wildavsky 1966, 1974) who see incremental and interactive decision processes as an inevitable norm, which also happens to produce as desirable outcomes as can be achieved. Incrementalism refers not only to the modest extent of intended and feasible change but also to a style of decision making—"muddling through" or "partisan mutual adjustment" in Lindblom's terms—consistent with a disjointed and pluralistic process. If disjointed incremental decision making is indeed inevitable, then the prospects for useful policy analysis and design become dim. Their utility may be restricted to heuristic stimulation of partisan participants in the policy process.

In contrast, the rationalist view posits a policy process presided over by actors capable of rational and purposive action. Many pieces of policy analysis and policy analysis texts simply assume this to be the case (for example, Stokey and Zeckhauser 1978: 3). The rationalist model requires an awareness of alternative courses of action, knowledge of the likely consequences of each alternative, substantial theoretical understanding of causal mechanisms, and choice among alternatives on the basis of well-defined criteria.

The incremental-rationalist debate runs through major questions of choice of practical approach in policy analysis. Some approaches lend themselves well to rational analysis, some deny its possibility, and, as we shall see, at least one of the approaches we consider is internally divided on this question. If an approach has a thoroughly mistaken image of the policy process, then one should hesitate before employing it.

Contents

Our second set of questions attempts to capture the contents of an approach beyond its hard core. These contents are more open to modification and manipulation by practitioners. The kinds of contents most open to adjustment are the *theories* pursued, developed, and tested by practitioners. When it comes to the practical tasks of policy analysis, theories and models (think, for example, of the market model) are important elements in the analyst's tool kit. One should recognize, though, that theoretical content can be in a state of flux; hence any characterization of these theories applies only to a particular historical period.

Another element in the practitioner's tool kit consists of the methods intrinsic to an approach. Practitioners can adhere to fundamental methodological principles about observation, description, induction, deduction, experimentation (piecemeal or holistic), speculation, rhetoric, and interrogation. Some methods and techniques are approach-specific and hence less fundamental. Think, for example, of the retrodictive experiment of paleontology, the psychoanalytic encounter of Freudian psychology, or the methodological bag of tricks (shadow pricing, discounting, etc.) associated with cost-benefit analysis.

A final consideration is the degree to which an approach has empirical content. Most theories encounter empirical evidence sooner or later, but some are adept at avoiding the issue (Marxism is often charged with this sin). Other things being equal, an approach that yields propositions—and in the case of the policy field, prescriptions—amenable to empirical testing is preferable to one that does not. This recognition is not to downplay the role of theoretical speculation in social science but merely to note that the policy field faces some practical empirical tasks.

The empirical content an approach possesses or seeks can come in various forms—qualitative or quantitative, and subsets of both. The statistical fetishes of many contemporary social scientists notwithstanding, there is no intrinsic reason to prefer one kind of empirical content over another.

Practical Usefulness

Given the practical intent of the policy field, the questions under the rubric of practical usefulness constitute perhaps the most important aspect of any assessment of an approach. Our first aspect of practical usefulness is the extent to which analysis generated by a technical approach is applicable in the policy process rather than merely relevant to it. Relevance requires only that a piece of work increase our understanding of a policy problem. Applicability is more demanding. The results of the work must be capable of contributing to the resolution of problems. In general, work that is only relevant concentrates on attempting to understand causes of or influences upon real-world policy outcomes.[4] Work intended to be applicable seeks factors amenable to change by or in the policy process. The practical usefulness of each approach depends on the extent to which it can inspire policy-applicable and not just policy-relevant work.

Given that an approach is highly applicable, its practical usefulness can still vary in two important ways. First, the current *adequacy* of an approach in social problem solving can be assessed and compared, especially with respect to recurring social problems. Civil violence, inflation, recession, terrorism, war, poverty, and pollution are all hardy perennials. Second, and dynamically, the rate of progress (or, conversely, the rate of degeneration) in the social problem-solving capabilities of an approach can be ascertained. Any lack of progressiveness in an approach simply implies that theoretically inclined policy analysts should direct their attentions elsewhere. A static but useful approach still needs and merits a cadre of professionals to keep it in good order and to apply it skillfully.

Progressiveness matters in social problem solving because the world typically presents an array of seemingly intractable

---

4. Elkin (1974) finds political science traditions of analysis, such as policy output studies and case studies of policy processes, wanting for the very reason of their lack of prescriptive utility.

problems to the policy process. Anything remotely approaching complete adequacy is unlikely, even after the capabilities of all approaches in the policy field are summed. Hence we need to know what is happening at the margins of each approach. Has it encountered—or is it likely to encounter—absolute limits to its capabilities? Degeneration might be good reason to question an approach, if not to abandon it in favor of a more progressive competitor. Note, for example, the degeneration (in practical terms) of Keynesian economics in the 1970s. In retrospect, it is clear that Keynesian economics was unmatched by any competing approach in terms of adequacy, but it was displaced in several cases by approaches of (momentarily) superior progressiveness, such as monetarism and supply-side economics.

Judgments about the practical usefulness of an approach can be informed by successes and failures in actual applications in the policy process, though evidence of this sort alone is insufficient basis for appraisal. Lack of use of an approach is no proof of its failure. Approaches can be ignored because of uninformed judgments of potential users, intellectual prejudice, mobilization by proponents of alternative approaches, and a lack of propaganda skills or financial resources on the part of practitioners. Moreover, complex political decisions often defy attribution of praise or blame to any particular intellectual input. So the key to judging the practical usefulness of an approach is its potential: that is, the extent to which it is capable of yielding prescriptions for or in the policy process.

Perspective

Finally, we turn to a set of concerns grouped loosely under the heading of perspective—that is, the outlook an approach presents to its potential users or audience.

In its time perspective, an approach may lead to analysis that is forward or backward looking, dynamic or static. Static or backward-looking analysis has obvious limits in the context of variable and novel policy problems.

The audience for which analysis is intended can vary. That audience may consist, for example, of policy makers, social reformers, program administrators, local notables, ordinary citizens, or fellow practitioners of a technical approach.

The third—and perhaps most important—aspect of perspective concerns the normative disposition of an approach. This disposition has two distinguishable aspects. One concerns the normative stance inherent in the approach. As we shall see, each approach generally possesses some identifiable normative position. The other concerns the means by which the approach handles the conflicting values held by stakeholders in the policy process. The normal condition of any interesting policy issue is one of conflicting values (see Tribe, Schelling, and Voss 1976; Dryzek 1983a). Value conflict can be handled in a number of ways. Alternatives include (1) attempting to integrate conflicting values in some way—for example, with reference to a single metric provided by some higher value; (2) making explicit the performance of policy options according to a number of criteria and leaving the problem of value weighting to an external decision maker; (3) ignoring the problem; and (4) specifying rules for normative discourse.

In chapters 2–6 we apply the questions developed in this section to some major frames of reference in the policy field. If there are important and distinctive branches within a more general approach, we identify any different answers associated with each. Summary and dissection of the alternative approaches set the stage for the lingering question of appropriate choice among them.

APPEAL TO THE COURT OF EPISTEMOLOGY

If the various frames of reference extant in the policy field are languages, then one way to make sense of their comparative capabilities is through appeal to the metalanguage of social science: the philosophy of inquiry. Now, more practically minded policy analysts might greet this move to epistemology as tantamount to unnecessary wading in a quagmire of obscure and abstruse philosophy. After all, members of more established professions (such as engineers, architects, physicians, and lawyers) rarely attend to the origin, nature, and limits of *their* knowledge. Might not such metatheoretical introspection actually obstruct more practical tasks—or indeed, threaten paralysis in the policy field? Let us suggest that, far from causing paralysis, attention to epistemology may help overcome the stalemate resulting from the plethora of analytical frameworks discussed in part 2.

To begin with, the very essence of policy analysis lies in knowledge-based interventions in public policy making. Theories about the content, production, dissemination, and interpretation of knowledge may therefore be expected to have implications for the nature, content, and role of the policy field, and for the qualities demanded of the contributions of frames of reference. Moreover, even allowing that policy analysis is above all a practical activity, the very notion of practice is an epistemological question. If we can determine the appropriate role of theory in relation to this practice, then we can go far toward determining how to make good use of the various frames.

Unfortunately, there is no one philosophy of inquiry through which to adjudicate our multiplicity of frames. Though less extensive than the proliferation of frames of reference, variety exists in epistemological metalanguages, too. We will see in part 3 that each major epistemological position does yield a way of making firm comparative judgments among frames. But the means of judgment is variable. Hence, before we can make appeal to the court of epistemology we need to determine which philosophies of inquiry are defensible as orientations toward the policy field and which are indefensible. The basic four epistemological categories are positivism, piecemeal social engineering, relativism, and reasoned consensus.

Adherents of positivism in the policy field are generally schooled in mainstream, behavioral social science. They see policy analysis in terms of the application of behavioral procedures to a particular class of situations. Hence their intention is to develop a body of propositions about causal relationships between key variables. Once this knowledge is established, variables can be manipulated through public policy intervention, in confident expectation of the consequences for goal or target variables. Frames conducive to deductive reasoning and empirical verification of lawlike statements are likely to meet with positivist approval.

A number of policy analysts, consistent with the philosophical outlook associated with Popper, see no possibility of social science (or, for that matter, any science) ever producing a verified set of causal laws. Instead, they suggest that social engineering should be the focus of the policy field. Cognizant of the weaknesses in social science understanding, this school of thought sees limited, piecemeal, and experimental policy interventions as simultaneously increasing theoretical knowledge and moving toward the amelioration of social problems. Any frame must therefore allow for empirical testing of policies through controlled social experimentation.

Both hard science and piecemeal social engineering would have us treat policy analysis and public policy as eminently rational affairs. Yet the kinds of knowledge they would have us pursue often seem unattainable in the face of complex and dynamic policy environments, jumbles of policy problems, and multiple conflicting values. A relativist position commends the generation of (admittedly partial) perspectives on such situations. Several epistemological positions can be grouped under the relativist umbrella. One would have analysts take an eclectic stance toward technical approaches, theories, and methods. Another advocates a forensic posture in the development of arguments for or against particular policies or particular interpretations of a social problem. Eclectic and forensic orientations avoid complete relativism to the extent one believes some degree of rational comparison across perspectives can occur. If even a modicum of rational comparison is rejected, then any particular approach to the policy field is arbitrary—one more piece of ideological verbiage. In this light, the whole policy analysis enterprise becomes at best illusory, at worst fraudulent.

A fourth cluster of knowledge orientations targets the large set of cases where rationalism is unrealistic and relativism fruitless. The two positions in this cluster both seek reasoned consensus among policy stakeholders about policy problems, goals, and options. In most other respects, these two variants are direct opposites. The first, accommodation, would have policy analysts adjust their thinking to that of responsible public officials, thus effectively accepting the outlook prevailing at key points in the policy process. Accommodation takes as given the status quo in the distribution of policy-making capabilities, political resources, and interpretations of the world.

In contrast, critical enlightenment would have policy analysts shatter frame-bounded thinking about policy problems, goals, and options as a prelude to the establishment of a more defensible consensus. Policy analysts in critical clothes are provocative and reformist, if not actually revolutionary in intellectual terms. Critical policy inquiry plays on the tension between policy-making capabilities, political resource distribution, and ideas about policy as they are and visions of how they could be. Critical discourse rather than instrumental, purposive action is the order of the day.

Choice among these four sets of epistemological orientations is no simple matter. With the possible exception of positivism, these orientations are the topic of live debate among philosophers of science—a debate we make no attempt to resolve. While no clear and definitive resolution is possible, we do question the very possibility of positivist policy analysis, and find piecemeal social engineering and critical enlightenment the most defensible orientations.

The court of epistemology proves less than decisive, and it certainly yields no unambiguous ranking of the frames across the universe of policy problems. Moreover, our endorsements of piecemeal social engineering and critical enlightenment are highly qualified—and ultimately incompatible. In part 4 we attempt to move beyond this epistemological impasse and develop our own ideas about how to do policy analysis in the light of an only partially reducible plurality of analytical frameworks.

POLICY DESIGN

Underlying the difficulty in passing summary judgment on the absolute and relative merits of the various languages spoken in the policy field is the richness and diversity of the various settings within which policy problems arise. This context has major implications for the relative attractiveness of the various frames. In particular, each of the frames we discuss in part 2 implicitly assumes and hence requires a particular kind of context. For example, welfare economics demands stability in the environment in which policy is to take effect, substantial control on the part of some "policy engineer," minimal uncertainty concerning the future effects of policy, and a reasonably well-functioning market system to aid computation of monetary costs and benefits. The other frames we consider make equally stringent demands upon context. The key requirements of context will never be fully met and may be only rarely approximated. The fit between frame and context will always be imperfect. Thus we will rarely be in a position to confidently apply a single frame or to accept its results uncritically. Yet selection in context is more defensible than selection insensitive to context.

In the final chapter of this study we build on this theme of contextual selection to commend the idea of policy design as an integrative strategy for the policy field. A move from the philosophy of inquiry to the philosophy of design is more a shift in emphasis than a radical break, but it does enable us to bypass some epistemological tangles while indicating how to use frames intelligently.

Policy design, like any kind of design, involves the pursuit of valued outcomes through activities sensitive to the context of time and place. These activities revolve around factors that can be affected by the volitions of human beings. But policy design cannot always resemble more traditional design enterprises. Engineering and architecture, for example, generally pursue simple, uncontroversial goals in an unchanging environment through manipulation of highly controllable factors. Policy design faces a messier world of multiple, unclear, and conflicting values, complex problems, dispersed control, and the surprises that human agents are capable of springing. Design in the policy field must be sensitive to this reality (and not simply assume or demand that it can be coerced away).

Policy design requires three core elements. The first is clarification of *values* to the point where they can provide clear guidance for developing and weighing policy alternatives. The second is characterization of the *context* of policy (and policy analysis). The third involves ascertaining the proclivities of the *audience* of analysis—those in a position to further or hinder a policy, or those the policy will ostensibly serve.

The values informing policy design will rarely be few, fixed, and consistent. If they are, policy designers can confidently apply any frame encompassing the value or values in question. So if economic efficiency is clearly and solely at issue, welfare economics stands ready. But interesting policy problems normally feature multiple, changeable, and conflicting values. A rough consensus on values among the relevant actors is required at some point if policy design is to proceed—if not at the outset, then during the course of design. One task of the policy analyst may therefore be stimulation of critical debate about normative judgments. While alien to analysts schooled in dominant Western (social) science, reasoned deliberation over normative judgments can occur in political life and public policy.

The context to be captured is of two kinds. The first is external to the policy process, referring to the world "out there" in which policy will take effect. Important dimensions of this context include complexity, uncertainty, and the potential for rapid feedback about the effects of policies. The second aspect of context is the analyst's milieu within the policy process. Important here are the degree of control any actor has over the execution of policy and the stability of concern of various actors (interest groups, bureaucrats, elected officials, and so forth) with respect to the issue at hand.

Sensitivity to the audience of analysis does not mean that its proclivities, interests, and judgments be taken as given, immutable, and dominant. The audience is, however, composed of the people who will need to act if any policy is to move ahead. The idea here is not necessarily to generate analysis acceptable to the audience but simply to take its position as one starting point—if only for critical dialogue. The analyst does, of course, have some freedom to select an audience.

Identification of an audience, capturing of context, and apprehension of the values at issue can demand a great deal of analytical effort, especially if any critical dialogue is involved. Assuming that the audience has been identified, a rough consensus on values obtained, and the key aspects of context captured, the designer can proceed to select the technical frame or frames yielding a rough fit on these dimensions. Given that this fit will often be loose, there is a large element of art and craft (rather than automatic application) in shaping and modifying approaches to suit the case at hand. If even a loose fit is unobtainable, the analyst would best be occupied by trying to fill in the gaps in the policy field tool kit. Given the demanding requirements placed on context by the major contemporary policy analysis frames, plenty of opportunities along such lines should arise.

If one or more appropriate frames can indeed be located, the analyst can proceed to apply the approach to the operations at the heart of policy design. These operations involve interpretation of the social problem at hand, specification of goals for policy, identification of the information needed for intelligent policy choice, actual gathering of that information, development of policy alternatives, and assessment and comparison of alternatives.

Policy design as developed is not a rigid recipe. Initial attempts to capture context and clarify values may lead the analyst in the direction of certain kinds of technical approaches (or even epistemologies), which can inform the development of process and content alternatives. But this very activity may in its turn raise the need for further clarification of values and revised comprehension of contexts. Policy design is not mechanical; the intention is to provide catalysts that shape the character and content of policy debate. Critical dialogue is more appropriate than a cookbook. Hence a policy designer, unlike an architect or engineer, can expect continuing engagement in dialogue with human subjects. Like any participant in discourse, the designer must therefore attend to the construction of arguments, including arguments about the degree to which a technical approach is appropriate. Public policy in a democratic system is the product of debate; the task of the policy analyst is to raise the level of that debate and provide informed contributions to it. While modest in comparison to the utopian ambitions of some would-be policy architects, this conception of the place of policy analysis is consistent with the limitations and imperfections of the major analytical frameworks.

We do not expect that all our readers will agree with our judgments on all the points we raise. We are, though, hopeful that they will agree with us that the issues we address merit the most serious consideration.

INTRODUCING SMOKETOWN

In order to add some color to our comparative dissection of frames of reference in the policy field, each of the chapters in part 2 commences with a story about policy analysis aimed at one particular policy issue. For the sake of exposition, the issue in question is stylized in an imaginary case. We apologize in advance for the poetic license and allegory in our narrative. Each story we tell is, however, based on work that has actually been done by mainstream practitioners of the approach in question.

Our issue example concerns environmental pollution. Smoketown is a city of 300 thousand people nestled in a valley in the Misty Mountains. The local economy includes both heavy, smokestack industry (notably steel mills) and more modern, light industrial plants. Air pollution in Smoke Valley is severe. Aside from the emissions of manufacturing industry, Smoketown has two large coal-fired power stations (which burn the local high-sulfur coal). There is only a rudimentary public transportation system, hence most people travel by car, and automobile exhaust fumes contribute to pollution. In addition, many Smoke Valley residents have wood-burning stoves in their homes, the Misty Mountains being heavily forested. The topography of Smoke Valley facilitates frequent temperature inversions, which exacerbate air quality problems.

Smoketown's pollution problem has met with some governmental response. A number of local government ordinances cover polluting activities, but environmental policy is primarily the responsibility of the national government, and is administered through the Environmental Pollution Agency (EPA). The EPA is a regulatory agency that interprets, applies, and enforces national pollution control laws. These laws specify targets for ambient environmental quality and measures that polluters must take to reduce emissions. The regulations developed by the EPA detail how much of each pollutant each source (be it a factory smokestack or an automobile exhaust) may emit. There is a substantial financial penalty for violations of regulations. In addition, some government subsidy is available for the installation of pollution control equipment.

Hardly anyone is satisfied with environmental policy in

Smoketown. Local residents grumble about eye irritation, smog, and high morbidity and mortality rates from respiratory disease. Environmentalists add complaints about the export of acid rain from the use of high-sulfur coal. Industry is unhappy with the cost of compliance with regulations. Managers of the newer steel mills, on whom the burden of abatement falls, are envious of the older concerns, which are granted exemption from pollution control. Labor unions fear that excessive and costly regulation will drive industry away from Smoketown. The mayor and city council have mixed feelings: on the one hand, they do not want to lose the heavy industries; but on the other, they are aware that a pleasant environment is an important factor in attracting the high-technology industry they are trying to entice to the Silicon Smoke Industrial Park.

Both national and local governments are perplexed by the competing pressures on antipollution policy for Smoke Valley. How might policy analysis help?

Part Two

Frames of Reference

Chapter 2

Welfare Economics

SMOKE VALLEY WELFARE ECONOMICS

*T*HE PREVIOUS CHAPTER concludes with some perplexed Smoke Valley policy stakeholders. Fortunately, help is at hand. Located at Smoketown University is the prestigious Camelot School of Government. A team of Camelot School economists headed by Professor Frederick Uteil receives a grant from the Environmental Pollution Agency to determine the optimal air pollution control policy for Smoke Valley. These economists are happy to undertake this task, for they regard it as more tractable than the national-level studies they have carried out in the past, which generally ended up focusing on a single pollutant (for example, sulfur dioxide) for a single industry (such as electrical utilities).

A huge number of policy alternatives could conceivably be adopted to attack the Smoketown pollution problem. To make their task manageable, Uteil decides to restrict the analysis to policy options pertaining to industrial point source pollution. Thus automobile pollution (which can only be addressed credibly on a national basis, anyway) and residential wood smoke pollution (which is, as it happens, outside the current orbit of regulatory responsibilities) do not enter the analysis.

Our economists decide to further simplify their task by addressing only two types of policies. The first policy is essentially the regulatory status quo for point sources. Well read in the economic environmental policy literature, they decide to investigate a system of standards and charges as a second policy category. This approach involves the specification of a standard for the quality of the ambient environment (expressed, for example, in a ceiling on parts per million of car-

27

bon monoxide), together with the imposition of per-unit charges (measured in, say, dollars per kilogram) on pollutants discharged into the environment. The charge level can be varied in the interests of achieving the predetermined standard. The ceiling at which the standard is set is itself a manipulable policy variable.

The team first of all attempts to determine the costs and benefits of continuing with the existing regulatory policy. The direct financial costs to industry of this policy are readily calculated and duly noted. The administrative costs of the policy are also easily measured by examining the regulatory agency budget. Clearly, it is also necessary to measure both the benefits to Smoketown residents of any reductions in pollution levels achieved by existing policies and the continuing costs to residents of the degree of air pollution that still occurs.

Our economists have access to data on historical and current air pollution levels, but they need to interpret this data in terms of its impact upon human well-being. They decide this impact occurs with respect to the amenity of clean air and the health of individuals. Amenity effects can be ascertained through evidence linking variations in residential property values with differentials in air quality—these variations indicate how much people are prepared to pay for the amenity of clean air. Health effects can be measured by drawing upon epidemiological studies relating concentration of pollutants to morbidity and mortality rates, and combining this information with monetary estimates of the value of life and health to individuals. While the team would also like to take into account the effects of Smoketown's emissions on health and amenity in distant areas—for example, through the export of acid rain— and upon both local and regional ecosystems, such effects are too diffuse to be captured with any precision, and hence are excluded from the analysis.

Good information on the health and amenity effects of air quality proves to be hard to obtain, and no uncontroversial translation of these effects into monetary terms is possible. These difficulties hinder any attempt to calculate the monetary costs and benefits of continuing with current regulatory policy. Harder still is any monetary assessment of the benefits to be expected in the future from the imposition of various standard levels. Thus the Camelot team cannot come up with a persuasive single figure for the dollar benefits to compare with the cost associated with each standard. Hence they submit that the choice of standard is essentially a political decision, to be determined by some governmental authority.

Our team does find it easier to estimate the cost of each standard, which is calculated by summing administrative costs and the expense of installing pollution control devices, redesigning production processes, and curtailing production. Even here, though, the estimates are not conclusive, for the economists cannot predict the exact response of each polluter to various charge levels, as they lack good knowledge of the technological options open to each polluter. The enterprises in question are reluctant to divulge such information, and can be expected to give inflated estimates of likely costs.

What Uteil and the Camelot economists do know is that whatever level of abatement is desired, a system of standards and charges is the least-cost way to achieve it—even if these costs cannot be specified with any precision. Unlike regulation, a charges system leaves essential decisions in the hands of enterprises rather than regulators; managers themselves can decide on their own least-cost mix of emission treatment, production curtailment, and continued emission. Those for whom abatement is costly will prefer to pay the charge associated with pollution; those for whom abatement is cheap will cut back heavily on emissions. In this manner, pollution reduction will occur where it is cheapest. Regulation, in contrast, does not take cost of abatement into account. Moreover, a charges system involves lower administrative costs than regulation, for there are no time-consuming, case-by-case battles.

The Camelot team therefore makes a confident recommendation that a system of standards and charges be adopted in order to deal with pollution in Smoke Valley. They qualify this recommendation by noting they have ignored automobile and wood smoke pollution, and that they have addressed particular pollutants in isolation, rather than any synergistic interaction effects between different chemicals.

The Uteil Report gets a mixed reception. Government officials find it hard to figure out just how much abatement will result from any given charge level; the Camelot economists reply that charges will have to be adjusted on a trial-and-error basis until the desired level of air quality is achieved. The managers of polluting industries protest that any such adjustments would introduce intolerable uncertainty into their own decisions on investment in pollution control. New industries argue that the burden of cleanup is unfairly concentrated on their relatively efficient, lightly polluting production processes, rather than on the aging smokestack operations. Low-income residents in the vicinity of the smokestacks protest that abatement will not occur to any great extent in their immediate area. The president of the local chapter of Friends of the Environment (FOE) is unhappy on several counts. She interprets a system of charges as the moral equivalent of a license to pollute. Moreover, she stresses that long-term ecological effects were not addressed in the Camelot study; Uteil replies that any long-term effects are highly uncertain, and that they should be accorded little importance anyway because of the need to downweight future effects in proportion to their temporal distance in sound financial decisions. The EPA hierarchy regards the study as a threat to its regulatory authority and hence looks for ways of criticizing the analysis—or, if possible, quietly burying the Uteil Report. The EPA administrator reassigns the head of its Office of Contracts and Grants (which financed the study) to a new position, overseeing liaison with Albania. The local office of the EPA also points out that the report fails to deal with highly toxic pollutants or with the dangerously high concentrations of familiar pollutants that can occur during the sporadic temperature inversions in Smoke Valley.

THE WELFARE ECONOMICS APPROACH

Oscar Wilde's definition of a cynic is "one who knows the price of everything and the value of nothing." Welfare economics provides us with a set of methods and techniques for the analysis of public policy that treats values as prices. Does it therefore necessitate a lapse into cynicism?

More than any of the other approaches we discuss subsequently, welfare economics has been made use of by public agencies—and indeed, held to be in and of itself equivalent to policy analysis. Its policy applications take the form of techniques such as cost-benefit and cost-effectiveness analysis. As an approach to policy analysis, welfare economics has, at first sight, a number of attractive features. Microeconomists have a well-defined and accepted body of theory at their disposal. Moreover, they agree among themselves not only on certain technical matters as to what constitutes a "job well done" but also—more remarkably—on a broad range of policy prescriptions (such as systems of standards and charges for pollution control). The reliance on a measure (money) that is ostensibly objective and amenable to interval scaling adds to the attractiveness of the approach by endowing it with the appearance of value freedom and an ability to reach conclusions on technical rather than political grounds. In addition, the practical import of the conclusions that can be achieved can be linked readily to a major class of policy decisions—those involving expenditures and budgets—that all modern governments must make.

GIVENS

The welfare economics approach to public policy is an outgrowth of mainstream, neoclassical, microeconomic theory. The entire elaborate superstructure of microeconomics is built upon a hard core model of man as an instrumentally rational individual who always maximizes his self-interest (utility). Rational, self-interested individuals are the only inhabitants of the welfare economist's world, with the exception of one benevolent actor (the state), whose interest is only in the well-being of society as a whole.

Here, welfare economists apply a crude analogy between the state and a profit-maximizing firm making investment decisions. In this sense, economic analysis is simply an extension of financial appraisal, in which a governmental agency seeks to maximize profit—or net benefit—on behalf of society as a whole, rather than just to "stockholders."

Outside the state, individuals are seen as engaging in social relationships only through the market—that is, by generating and acting upon price signals. The fact that there might be community associations, a chamber of commerce, and a chapter of Friends of the Environment articulating citizens' concerns on pollution in Smoketown is ignored. Only market behavior—such as moving to a house in the suburbs away from polluting factories or paying for medical treatment for respiratory disease—is recognized.

The welfare economics view requires several substantial assumptions as to the capabilities of both the analysis itself and the policy process it targets. First of all, the analyst must be aware of all of the available policy options and must be able to quantify all the costs and benefits of each. Second, there should be no political constraints on the feasibility of whatever policy choices the conclusions of analysis suggest. Third, all costs must be commensurable and capable of expression in monetary terms. Fourth, all benefits must be commensurable and, if not reducible to a monetary metric, susceptible at least to ordinal and preferably interval-scale measurement.

One cannot but doubt the realism of the assumptions of the approach. In reality, much economic and political life "cannot be explained without recognizing that many individuals are motivated partly by noneconomic and/or nonegotistic motives" (Harsanyi 1969: 519). People often *do* behave in ways inconsistent with the rather unattractive personality of economic man—for example, in voting, or in voluntarily contributing to goods with widely shared benefits. The omniscience required of the analyst is a little hard to swallow. Further, as any student of the policy process will tell you, there are very real political constraints upon policy makers.

CONTENTS

Welfare economics policy analysis is an extension of conventional, neoclassical, microeconomic wisdom on the workings of the free market, which is therefore the source of its theoretical themes. This wisdom holds that a perfectly competitive market in which individuals have perfect information will normally produce an "efficient" solution—that is, a situation in which preference satisfaction across the individuals in society is maximized.[1]

---

1. See Bator (1957) for the derivation of this result. A particularly clear exposition of economic efficiency can be found in Dorfman and Dorfman (1977: 7–25).

Following logically from this view of the competitive market is a prescription for the proper role of governmental action: to correct for market failure. As Haveman and Weisbrod (1975: 171) put it, welfare economics as applied to public policy analysis is "an attempt to replicate for the public sector the decisions that would be made if private markets worked satisfactorily." Failure exists when a market falls short of optimality in welfare maximization. Possible causes of market failure include barriers to entry into the market, differential capacity to be informed, the exclusion of certain types of costs and benefits—especially externalities such as pollution—from market transactions, and, above all, the existence of public goods (such as air quality or national security) which no market can conceivably supply.[2] The role of the policy analyst is therefore to identify the nature and extent of market failure and to devise the best means for ameliorating it. This view embodies a normative theory of the state. However, few practitioners of the welfare economics approach would hold that government intervention will necessarily improve matters. Indeed, a growing minority is extraordinarily pessimistic on this score, as a perusal of almost any issue of the *Journal of Political Economy* or the *Journal of Law and Economics* will attest.

How, then, do welfare economists determine net benefit maximizing solutions for public policy? In principle, the first step is to construct a social welfare function. A social welfare function is simply a formula for aggregating net benefits (utilities) accruing to individuals (see Mueller 1979: 173–83). Any such formula requires distributive value judgments about the relative worth of individuals. Should we treat a rich man and a pauper identically? Or do we prefer that the poor should benefit most from our decisions? Most economists are uneasy about interpersonal utility comparisons and the value judgments they necessitate. The Pareto criterion is often advocated as an escape from this problem, in the belief that "if everyone agrees on a value judgment then it is not a value judgment at all" (Sen 1970: 57). The Pareto doctrine holds that a course of

---

2. See Bator (1958) for a taxonomy of the causes of market failure. A public good is characterized by the impossibility of excluding people from its benefits and the necessity of joint supply.

action should be followed only if there are individuals who will gain from it but none who will lose.

Given that there are losers in virtually all policy choices, the Pareto doctrine threatens sterility. Consider our pollution example: whatever policy is followed, somebody—be it a polluter or a victim of pollution—has to pay. To circumvent this incipient sterility, welfare economics turns to the "potential Pareto," or Kaldor-Hicks criterion, which specifies that a course of action is a correct one if potential gainers could compensate potential losers and retain a net benefit. *Could* is the key word—such compensation will not in general occur. Cost-benefit analysis is erected on this foundation. All the analyst need do for each policy alternative under consideration is sum costs and benefits. If the ratio of benefits to costs exceeds unity, then the action is more desirable than than status quo. The course of action with the highest expected net benefit (as opposed to the benefit-cost ratio) is the most desirable. When economists talk about economic efficiency, they are really referring to this quality.

The methodological substance of a practical cost-benefit analysis is therefore the assessment of costs and benefits. When competitive markets exist, net benefits are reflected in market prices of goods and services (for example, a new subway that generates business in downtown shops). Where such markets do not exist or are highly imperfect, the analyst's role is to determine how individuals would behave if a market did exist (Sugden and Williams 1978: 149). Numerous techniques have been developed by economists to quantify shadow prices for nonmarketed values. Even in the case of public goods, whose nonexcludability properties rule out a market, valuations can be inferred from market-related behavior in access to the good. For example, the value of a clean environment can be assessed through an examination of the statistical relationships between property values and ambient air quality (Ridker and Henning 1971). The value of a human life can be quantified by present value of expected future earnings of the individual. A natural environment such as the Grand Canyon can be valued by the amount people are willing to pay to travel to see it. Such valuations are of course impossible in the case of pure public goods, which have no element of privateness—but pure cases are in fact rare. Even national security occasionally lacks such purity (Zimmerman 1973).

Putting a money value on costs can be difficult. Britain's Roskill Commission quantified the cost of destroying a centuries-old church standing in the way of a new airport by the extra traveling costs churchgoers would have to incur in order to get to the nearest available substitute church. Formulations on the benefit side are more troubling still—valuing lives saved through pollution control is an obvious case. Tribe (1972: 84) has some of these formulations in mind when he likens some uses of cost-benefit analysis to comparing a Rembrandt and a Picasso by the quality of the paint used in each.

To skirt difficulties in monetizing benefits, one can take half a step outside the welfare economics frame of reference by shifting from cost-benefit to cost-effectiveness methodology.[3] Under cost-effectiveness analysis, benefits are measured in units of effectiveness rather than in units of utility or money. The most efficient solution is the one that achieves the goal at the least financial cost. This approach is especially appropriate in the provision of relatively pure public goods, such as national security, whose benefits are not easily translated into money. *Effectiveness* may refer to fractions of the Soviet population that will be destroyed, or to numbers of college degrees conferred, or to parts per million of carbon monoxide in Smoketown air. The approach itself provides no guidance on the choice of valid effectiveness measures.

The idea of cost effectiveness can be turned on its head in a determination of how to maximize the number of effectiveness units for a given cost. The benefit side now becomes the variable, to be maximized subject to some cost constraint. So, for example, one might ask how best a city could improve its air quality subject to a budgetary limitation (or total cost to the local economy) of x million dollars.

The empirical content of the welfare economics approach is substantial. The logic of shadow pricing tells economists

---

3. The reason cost-effectiveness analysis is half a step outside the frame of reference is that the only valid benefit measure within the approach is utility—or its proxy, money. The benefit measures in cost-effectiveness analysis have a more tenuous connection with utility.

exactly where to look for the requisite empirical evidence—and where next to look if at first it cannot be found. However, empirical analysis is blinkered in at least two ways. The first concerns a neglect of values that must forever remain intangible. Examples include factors such as environmental quality as it enters directly into the utility functions of individuals without being priced in any market (see Krutilla 1967). There is a possible escape from this problem: the analyst could simply compute the monetary costs and benefits of an action, calculate the net benefits, and present this result to decision makers, along with a list of intangible costs and benefits excluded from the calculation. The second way in which analysis is constricted involves the exclusion of information about all but revealed costs and benefits. Desires and abhorrences nurtured by individuals but not expressed in their observable, preferably market-related, behavior go unheeded.

Despite this general empirical strength, economists occasionally are frustrated by practical difficulties in gathering data and attaching monetary values. Clearly, economic techniques are most suited to well-structured policy problems in which goals and inputs are clear, quantifiable, and readily monetized. Absent such conditions, many economists turn to rhetorical or discursive analysis, often advocating market-type mechanisms (such as systems of standards and charges for pollution control) solely on their theoretical merits.

PRACTICAL USEFULNESS

Amacher, Tollison, and Willet (1976: 15) claim the papers in their volume on the economic approach to public policy "show that the economic approach provides a fundamentally 'correct' view of policy problems." Undeniably, welfare economics provides a set of tools for arriving at directly applicable knowledge and definitive prescriptions in the policy process. Applications encompass everything from preschool education to airport siting. Nevertheless, there are some very clear limits to the adequacy of the approach.

Let us start with a potentially fatal flaw: the well-known difficulty with distributional issues. Much of the substance of politics and policy concerns just who should get what, rather than how much of the good in question should be produced. The application of the Kaldor-Hicks criterion implies that a dollar's worth of benefit or cost is equivalent in utility terms for all individuals, be they millionaires or paupers. Any movement beyond Kaldor-Hicks to weight individuals differentially causes numerous practical problems. One way of making distributive judgments is through inference of the social welfare function implicit in the past decisions of the policy process, with respect to taxation and transfer policy specifically (Musgrave 1969) or to policies more generally (Weisbrod 1968). However, the distributional consequences of past policy decisions may have been unintended or merely reflective of the status quo in the distribution of political resources. Surely policy inquiry should inform choice, not automatically perpetuate past choices.

An intriguing approach to distribution in economic efficiency terms has been offered by Lerner (1944). Virtually all economists accept the law of diminishing marginal utility.[4] Lerner argues that if we accept this law and then assign utility functions to individuals in a group at random, total probable (not certain) satisfaction within the group will be maximized by a completely egalitarian distribution of income within the group. The negative incentive effects of this totally equal distribution may explain why most economists have chosen to ignore it.[5]

Economists are comfortable with distribution only when they treat it in efficiency terms. Thus any distribution has an effect on efficiency, and the most efficient means of achieving any given distribution can be determined.

The difficulty welfare economics has with distributional issues is a severe shortcoming, because interpersonal comparisons of utility must be made all the time in any political process. In fairness to economics, though, few practitioners of the approach would claim that techniques such as cost-benefit analysis should be authoritative in any decision with major

---

4. This law states that successive units of a good consumed will yield increasingly less satisfaction to the individual.

5. Lerner's formulation bears some similarity to a Rawlsian social contract (see chapter 6).

distributive implications. Rather, identification of the most efficient policy is simply the first step, which should be followed by lump-sum transfers of income to effect any redistribution deemed desirable. Such transfers will not, however, generally be made.

A second major limitation arises inasmuch as costs and benefits are often intangible and not amenable to expression in monetary form, despite the best efforts of shadow pricers. As Leman and Nelson (1981: 99) admit, "economists have not made much progress in determining the 'right' values to be placed on retaining an option, on saving human lives, or on avoiding a variety of risks." This difficulty persists for good reason: if the rationale for government intervention in the first instance is market failure (see above), then governments will be active in just those areas where markets are not working well, such that prices are poor indicators of values (see Haveman and Margolis 1977: 4). Even when costs and benefits are tangible and susceptible to measurement, they may well be incommensurable. Consider, for example, the comparison of human health and industrial health in Smoketown. As we shall see, welfare economics is not the only approach to policy analysis that finds multiple values highly problematical.

A third major limitation on the contribution of the welfare economics approach to public policy analysis stems from its treatment of policy adoption in terms of the calculus of a unitary actor and its treatment of implementation as mechanical execution. The approach has little to say about policy process and its alternatives. More precisely, the approach ignores inherently political phenomena and the subtleties of the political behavior of individuals, groups, and organizations. Accordingly, attempts to apply synoptic devices such as cost-benefit analysis, cost-effectiveness analysis, and program budgeting frequently run into political trouble. Participants in the policy process are unlikely to allow anonymous techniques insensitive to coalition building in policy adoption to usurp their role. For example, PPBS (planning, programming, budgeting systems) in the U.S. federal government failed largely because of political conflict over "whose utility function is to prevail" (Wildavsky 1966), since PPBS demanded a single utility schedule. Impatient economizers might at this point suggest changing political reality—a strategy we explore in the next chapter.

As far as policy implementation goes, the welfare economics approach implicity conceives of policies as directives that are automatically followed. In reality, implementation is highly uncertain, to the extent that some observers express surprise that any central government programs ever get implemented at all (Pressman and Wildavsky 1973). Because adoption and implementation intervene between policy analysis and policy consequences, the latter often fail to live up to the economic analyst's expectations.

A fourth limitation of cost-benefit analysis and other welfare economics techniques is their applicability only to the evaluation and comparison of a predetermined set of policy options. This set will normally be small in size due to the limited resources available to the analyst. The crucial question is, of course, who gets to determine the set of policy options to be addressed. In Smoketown, the economists themselves introduced the standards and charges option. More frequently, economists in government service are presented with options by their bureaucratic masters.

To recognize these limitations is not to deny the usefulness of the welfare economics approach as an injection of economic rationality into the policy-making process but merely to suggest modesty on the part of economists and an avoidance of undue reliance by others on the approach.

Is welfare economics policy analysis currently progressing or degenerating in its practical problem-solving capabilities? Superficial indicators—such as the number of microeconomic policy analysts employed (if not heeded) by the U.S. federal government—might suggest progress over the past decade. Cost-benefit analysis attained a zenith of acceptability in 1981 with the promulgation of Executive Order 12291 by President Reagan, which specified that henceforth a cost-benefit analysis be conducted for every major proposed federal regulation. Economizers have, though, met with false dawns in the past— notably in the introduction of PPBS in the 1960s.

If we look at the efforts of economists to overcome the

limitations of their approach, substantial progress is evident with regard to distributional equity. For example, Zeckhauser (1974) develops an ingenious efficiency-based approach to distribution—and redistribution. Zeckhauser believes all individuals should favor public programs that redistribute income within lifetimes (such as pensions or unemployment insurance). The lifetime utility of individuals is maximized by their receiving or being guaranteed a floor for their income during their old age or times of adversity, even though this is at the expense of income today. Zeckhauser sees redistribution as risk spreading through social insurance, which can be Pareto optimal (see also Dryzek and Goodin 1986). In the area of intangibles, the literature on shadow pricing becomes ever more extensive and refined.

Only with regard to the political aspects of policy adoption and implementation is no progress observable. Limitations here persist irrespective of new methods for apprehending distribution in efficiency terms or new tricks for quantifying and monetizing costs and benefits.

PERSPECTIVE

The welfare economics approach presents a very clear perspective on policy issues—and equally clear points on which that perspective may be questioned.

Consider first of all the time perspective associated with the approach. Techniques such as cost-benefit analysis can be either forward looking, in the consideration of a set of policy alternatives, or backward looking, with the intent of evaluating the performance of policies, programs, and regulations already in operation (such as the antipollution regulations discussed in our Smoketown example). However, the time perspective of the approach is slanted in two important ways. First of all, the policy environment is viewed as static. Each policy alternative is seen as taking effect in a world that is otherwise constant. So, for example, the future costs of antipollution regulations are normally overestimated, because future innovations in emission control technology are not taken into account.

Second, discounting systematically favors the present and near future and handicaps any long-term consequences of

policies.[6] Discounting the future at a positive rate has its
roots in the analogy of the profit-maximizing firm's investment decisions. Certainly, in the presence of interest rates,
the profit-maximizing entity, be it firm or state, must discount. While a case can indeed be made for discounting in
the public sector (see Baumol 1977), the practice remains
controversial. A minority of economists accepts the need for
a "social rate of discount" lower than the market interest rate.
A few even argue that discounting may be inappropriate for
large-scale collective decisions (Page 1977). But no mainstream microeconomist recommends dispensing with discounting entirely. One very practical reason for discounting is that
it maintains the precision of the approach in developing policy prescriptions. As future effects become more distant (and
hence less certain), they receive increasingly less weight and
are soon ignored altogether. The net result of discounting is
that future generations (or even the present generation a few
years hence) find their welfare valued negligibly in comparison to that of present populations, a profound ethical bias (see
Sikora and Barry 1978).

The audience assumed, and indeed sought, by the practitioners of welfare economics techniques consists of public officials with some well-defined area of responsibility. While this
audience may be conducive to policy applicability, conceiving
of audiences in terms of the existing bureaucratic division of
labor serves to shut the door to analysis delineated by the collective outcomes at stake, as opposed to the inherited allocations of missions of government agencies. Analysts can all too
easily end up expending their energies comparing alternatives
with similar consequences, while ignoring policy options that
do make some difference.[7] It should be noted, though, that the
people Elkin (1983) calls "broad economizers" (such as Friedman and Friedman 1979, 1984) are prepared to take institu-

---

6. Discounting is the practice of converting future streams of costs and
benefits to their "present value." This conversion is accomplished by applying
a discount rate—the mirror image of an interest rate. Thus at a discount rate of
10%, a benefit of $100 accruing in a year's time has a present value of $90;
$100 in two years' time has a present value of $81, and so forth.

7. See, for example, the dialogue between Cain and Watts (1972) and Coleman (1972) on education policy.

tions and their responsibilities as policy variables. It is only the technicians of the welfare economics approach who ignore these grander questions.

The above-noted bias against the future does not exhaust the normative leanings of welfare economics. To begin with, the Pareto principle, be it in its original or Kaldor-Hicks incarnation, requires acceptance of the distributive status quo as just. This acceptance can have some strange consequences—as when economists who study crime incorporate loss to criminals as a cost of more effective anticrime policy (see, for example, Posner 1972). Moreover, treatment of the status quo as just imparts a clear conservative coloration—a leaning shared by the economics profession more generally (see Kearl, Pope, Whiting, and Wimmer, 1979).

A further normative judgment emerges inasmuch as welfare economics treats policy and politics in mere instrumental terms. One could argue that the health of political life and the institutions through which this life is expressed matter far more than identification of cost-effective means for the satisfaction of consumer preferences.

It should be stressed that the welfare economics approach to policy analysis, and microeconomics more generally, do not possess any simple irrational bias to the interests of some ruling class or dominant group in society. It is quite possible for a piece of economic policy analysis to elicit howls of anguish from the captains of industry. To quote the reaction of a representative of the Ethyl Corporation to a 1984 EPA study recommending the abolition of leaded gasoline: "Some economists wrote most of the EPA report, using fancy terms. They calculated to the penny any costs of leaded fuel, but when it came to the benefits of leaded fuel, they don't have any numbers" (USA Today, n.d., 1984).

The welfare economics approach—and cost-benefit analysis in particular—deal with conflicting values by reducing all values to the simple metric of economic efficiency in monetary terms. Ultimately, all choices are seen as technical (as opposed to political), with an unproblematic consensus on goals. While lip service is occasionally paid to the need to incorporate values that cannot be so reduced, economists themselves have no good procedures for making the necessary trade-offs.

While the welfare economics approach has many shortcomings, the only ineluctable limit to its onward march is politics. The approach is uncomfortable with and does not fit too well within political reality, or with the values embedded in a democratic order. We now turn to an approach to the policy field that addresses the structure of policy-making institutions directly.

Chapter 3

Public Choice

PUBLIC CHOICE IN THE SMOKE VALLEY

*T*HE CAMELOT welfare economics policy analysis (discussed at the beginning of the last chapter) is bogged down in a political morass of multiple and unclear jurisdictions, weak authority structures, and bureaucratic infighting. Some concerned Smoke Valley civic leaders, eyeing this situation with distaste, suggest that what is needed is some kind of joint authority with jurisdiction over the air quality problems of the Smoketown region.

Currently, a number of separate geographical jurisdictions exists. The city of Smoketown proper embraces only some 30 percent of the valley's population (but a substantially greater proportion of its smokestack industry). Many of the (primarily residential) suburban areas are incorporated as separate cities, and there are also a number of smaller industrial centers in the Smoke Valley. In addition, exurbs spread into unincorporated areas. Aside from these local governments, the state government and, especially, the national government and its bureaucracy have considerable authority over pollution control in Smoke Valley. At all levels of government, air pollution decisions are frequently regarded as essentially technical matters, best dealt with by the executive and the bureaucracy (with occasional input from organized interests), but a number of citizens' groups are frustrated by a lack of access to public policy determination.

The various governments involved enter into negotiations about the appropriate structure for a joint authority. A proposal to create a Smoke Valley Air Quality Commission (SVAQC) meets with preliminary assent all round. This body would be composed of one member appointed by each of the mayors in the valley, two members appointed by the state governor, and two members appointed by the national government. The commission would have such powers as delegated to it by the participating governments, though at first its role would be strictly advisory. Further, a consultative board composed of representatives from industry, environmentalist organizations, and labor unions would be created to liaise between the SVAQC and important interests in the community.

The SVAQC proposal catches the eye of a group of public choice social scientists, whose membership is drawn from the political science, public administration, and economics faculty of Smoke Valley universities, and from Sources of the Future, the prestigious, privately financed "think tank." The public choice perspective points to potential shortcomings in the SVAQC proposal; hence at its monthly meeting the public choice group resolves to reason through the question of appropriate institutional designs for environmental management in Smoke Valley.

Our group reasons that the air quality issue in Smoke Valley is essentially a problem of social choice. That is, the matter is one of determining outcomes with consequences for the entire Smoke Valley population under conditions of conflicting preferences among these individuals. The question for policy analysis is therefore how these conflicting preferences may best be aggregated and resolved into collective outcomes.

The first social choice mechanism the group considers is the market. One Professor Faire argues (following Coase 1960) that optimal solutions to pollution problems may be achieved through reliance on bargaining between polluters and their victims, without government interference. Markets are additionally attractive because of their lack of administrative costs. However, the group as a whole recognizes that air quality is to a large extent a public good, which no unaided market can supply, and Faire is overruled. Hence some governmental structure is necessary: but what form should it take?

The first option analyzed by our group is the institutional status quo, which receives an unequivocal condemnation. First, the status quo vests substantial policy-making power in the hands of bureaucratic agencies (at all levels of government). As every public choice analyst knows, bureaucrats are motivated solely by a desire to advance their own material self-interest, rather than by any notion of the public interest. The consequences of this motivation include an unwarranted emphasis on spending programs (such as subsidies for pollution control equipment) and a proliferation of inspectors and monitors. Second, inasmuch as a great deal of policy is set at the national level, policy is insensitive to the trade-offs between conflicting values that a locality (such as Smoke Valley) would make if left to its own devices. For example: stringent national standards for the emission of oxides of nitrogen from automobile exhausts imply unnecessary expense in Smoke Valley, which does not suffer from the photochemical smog of cities in sunnier climes. Third, there is a disjointedness between levels of government, meaning that policies are often at odds with each other. For example: federal policies encouraging renewable energy conflict with Smoketown's expressed desire to reduce wood smoke pollution. Fourth, there are substantial spillover effects across the geographical boundaries of the cities in Smoke Valley. Pollution from the small industrial cities at the east end of the valley is blown toward Smoketown proper by the prevailing winds; hence there is little incentive for these small cities to do anything at all about air pollution control. Fifth, inconsistent policies are often pursued in different functional areas (often by different agencies). For example: a water pollution policy, which has undeniably cleaned up the Smoke River, has prompted some factories to incinerate their wastes instead of discharging them in liquid form, thus exacerbating air quality problems. Budgetary classification by functional area at national and state levels prompts local governments—abetted by their representatives in state and national legislatures—to maximize their "take" of expenditures in each area, irrespective of their preferred trade-off between different kinds of expenditure benefits. For these five reasons, the institutional status quo obstructs net-benefit-maximizing trade-offs based on the preferences of Smoke Valley residents.

Our group finds little promise of improvement in the SVAQC proposal. Its first fundamental defect is that the members of the commission are appointed rather than elected, which diminishes their responsiveness to citizen preferences.

Second, each city has equal voting power, irrespective of its population, thus responsiveness is eroded further. Third, the state and national members represent only bureaucratic interests. Fourth, the advisory board—inasmuch as it has any real influence—will legitimate rewards to special interests at the expense of both the public purse and the common good (in social welfare terms). Hence the likelihood of the SVAQC pursuing policies at all sensitive to citizen preferences is slim, even should it eventually possess substantial legislative and executive powers. Should it lack any clear powers, the commission could easily become just another bureaucratic interest feeding at the public fiscal trough and contributing to the disjointedness of antipollution policy.

Clearly, some alternative to the unsatisfactory status quo and the ineffectual SVAQC proposal is needed. The first such alternative our group addresses is the devolution of all policy-making power to local governments. This proposal reflects a central theme in the public choice literature based on the idea that people "vote with their feet" in deciding where to live. People with relatively homogeneous preferences in government services are assumed to cluster in neighborhoods. So people in one neighborhood might prefer green space, police protection, and air quality; those in another might prefer low taxes, easy access to city jobs, and lax air quality standards. In this light, an efficient institutional structure is one in which each neighborhood gets its preferred mix of services and taxes. Any such structure requires extreme decentralization.

Our public choice group would be prepared to endorse this decentralizing proposal for most functional policy areas, such as police protection, garbage disposal, and parks and open spaces. However, in the case of air pollution there would be massive cross-jurisdictional externalities. Hence some form of political structure for the entire Smoke Valley airshed is required: but what form should it take, if not the SVAQC?

The fundamental premise in public choice institutional design is that the self-interest of government officials should be harnessed to the common good. One way to accomplish this task is to elect these officials. Hence there should be a legislative body—the Smoke Valley Authority (SVA). To maximize responsiveness to the distribution of public opinion, the valley should be divided into equal-population districts, with one (or more) members elected from each. The SVA would exercise supreme authority for the airshed; there would be no state or national role. The authority would therefore be constrained only by constitutional limits and the preferences of voters, and—crucially—it would have to levy any and all of the taxes needed to pay for its policies. In this way, the SVA would reflect the welfare-maximizing combination of abatement and taxes for Smoke Valley.

At this juncture, the group is cautioned against the pitfalls of legislative government by one Professor Hamill, who argues that "responsiveness" can produce results at variance with social welfare. For example, legislators might deliberately create an inept bureaucracy, delegate powers to it, and take on the role of crusaders against it (just as in the U.S. Congress). Alternatively, legislators might profit by "bringing home the bacon" to their individual constituencies to the exclusion of addressing the interest in clean air of all valley residents.

The group foresees one further potential hitch in its SVA proposal. Residents of the small industrial cities at the east end of Smoke Valley have little concern for air pollution abatement—prevailing winds solve their problem. Not only would the East Valley be reluctant to join the SVA, it would be a permanent minority if it did join. Most decisions could be expected to go against its preferences (thus violating the Pareto criterion we introduced in chapter 2). The public choice group's solution to this "permanent minority" problem has two aspects. First, a voting rule requiring unanimity (or near unanimity) would give the East Valley the power to at least extract compensating benefits for agreeing to abatement of the pollution it sends to the rest of the valley. Second, the SVA's scope could be extended to cover water pollution, too. Fortunately, the Smoke River runs west to east, taking Smoketown's effluent into the East Valley. The potential for welfare-maximizing trade-offs between the air quality preferences of the main valley and the water quality desires of the East Valley is obvious. Further, including water pollution in the SVA bailiwick would promote coordination of policy across functional areas.

Having outlined a basic structure for the SVA, the group proceeds to devote itself to the details of systems for the election of SVA members and voting rules within the authority, bearing in mind Professor Hamill's warnings. The group reports its findings in a volume published by Smoketown University Press, a number of academic conference papers, and a series of articles in political science, economics, and public choice journals.

Behavior

THE PUBLIC CHOICE APPROACH

Public choice as a field of study straddles the disciplines of microeconomics and political science, though its tentacles reach into public administration, law, and sociology too. In essence, the field examines what happens when homo economicus takes a leave of absence from the marketplace in order to pursue his or her advantage through decision structures. Public choice therefore applies deductive reasoning based on individual rational maximizing behavior in order to determine collective consequences under different circumstances. Practitioners work on the circumstances of decisions in institutions, as opposed to the content of public policies. Public choice's purview ranges from the axiomatic study of rules for aggregating individual preferences into social orderings (for example, Arrow 1963; Sen 1970) to the evaluation of real-world political mechanisms.

We should note at the outset that, despite a common hard core, public choice is home to two discernible strands. The first is positive in character, seeking only to explain phenomena such as voting behavior and electoral strategy. The second is more normative and oriented toward practical problems (though it draws on work in the positive strand). We address this second strain, for this is where virtually all policy-oriented public choice work is found. Important themes in this literature include the optimal size of public agencies, the geographical and functional scope of institutions and agencies, voting rules, and incentives and disincentives for collective action to provide public goods.

[handwritten margin note: Think about everyone / Hard to know what / real. is good]

GIVENS

The hard core of public choice is very similar—if not quite identical—to that of welfare economics. Both recognize self-interested, rational, maximizing individuals. Unlike welfare economics, though, public choice admits of no benevolent, public-spirited, unitary government. As we saw in chapter 2, welfare economics sees the proper role of the state as effectively correcting for market failure. In contrast, public choice is all too conscious of the possibility of governmental failure. Government is interpreted as a set of mechanisms (voting systems, bureaucracies, legislatures, courts, etc.) through which individuals (be they EPA bureaucrats, Smoketown city councillors, ordinary voters, or labor union members) pursue their self-interest. Public choice apprehends only the formal structure of institutions.

Public choice seeks understanding of the behavior of groups by summing the self-interest proclivities of their members under particular systems of formal rules. There is nothing here to prevent individuals pursuing altruistic ends or their conception of the common good in a rational, instrumental way. But in practice, as we shall see below, public choice analysts prefer to work with self-interest narrowly defined. Any recognition of altruistic or public-spirited behavior dilutes the distinctiveness and power of the approach.

The approach's conception of the common good proceeds in terms of some aggregation of individual preferences, just like welfare economics. This derivation is usually based on actual preferences. But social welfare can also be aggregated from what Harsanyi (1955) calls "ethical" or "impersonal" preferences—the distribution a person would choose were there an equal probability of his or her occupying each of the possible positions in society (see also chapter 6).

While public choice's crude analogy is less easily pinned down than that of welfare economics, market analogies loom large. Indeed, many public choice practitioners conceive of the political system as an arena in which exchange can (or should) take place among individuals seeking personal gain. Public choice can of course handle mechanisms that do not resemble markets, such as bargaining, representative government, and hierarchy. Nonetheless, for reasons that will become apparent below, public choice practitioners are strongly disposed to market-type mechanisms.

We turn now to the capabilities attributed to the policy process, over which public choice is somewhat schizophrenic. On the one hand, a policy process capable of unitary, purposive action is ruled out. On the other, there must exist some process that can effect goal-directed institutional change. Accordingly, public choice requires that either (1) there exists an all-powerful, metapolicy maker, capable of changing decision structures, or (2) institutions are capable of incremental transformation, such that the analyst can have some input into their evolution.

Political and organizational constraints make the metapolicy maker with full control a rare animal. Moreover, the existence of a metapolicy maker motivated by the common good would be inconsistent with the behavioral premise of public choice. Alternative (2) is perhaps more realistic, though it consigns public choice policy analysts to the role of publicists in a debate that they themselves should expect to lose, given the forces of self-interest lined up against them. Friedman and Friedman (1984) argue that the best way to effect institutional change in the face of recalcitrant politicians and bureaucrats is through a ground swell of public opinion—though again there is a contradiction with the fundamental behavioral premise, for the Friedmans' method assumes widespread motivation toward the common good.

Public choice assumptions about the capabilities of the policy process are not, then, terribly realistic. The assumptions about individual behavior can be problematical, too. There is a sense in which the self-interest assumption is nonfalsifiable—hence vacuous—provided only that altruism and public spiritedness are allowed into the utility functions of individuals. In practice, vacuity is averted by a narrow specification of self-interest. Thus bureaucrats are assumed to be motivated by career advancement and the expansion of their budget rather than by the agency's mission or the public interest. Stated in this form, public choice assumptions can be and have been put to the empirical test. Not surprisingly, practitioners have found empirical support for their assumptions. It is equally unsurprising that critics of the field have found behavior more consistent with an ethic of public service than with budget maximization. Perhaps no final determination is possible one way or the other on this point, inasmuch as different agencies and situations are characterized by different mixes of self-serving and public-interest motivation. Any such variety would obviously detract from the power of public choice analysis.

CONTENTS

In principle, public choice provides a complete vocabulary and set of tools for the analysis and evaluation of all kinds of collective choice structures, including governmental institutions. Given its focus on institutional manipulation, public choice requires a knowledge of existing institutions, an inventory of preferred designs, criteria for the assessment of these designs, and methods for relating designs to criteria.

Consider first of all criteria for evaluation and design. Strictly speaking, there is no limit to the range of criteria one could apply. However, as we have already noted, the public choice world view recognizes only individuals with utility functions. Hence it is unsurprising that methodological individualism finds a counterpart in normative individualism. Evaluation criteria are based on some aggregation of the preferences of members of the public who consume government services. Individual perceptions should be trusted, because people are assumed to be rational, informed, and hence the best judges of their own interests.

Derivation of collective evaluation standards from individual utility functions is no simple matter. A huge literature in social choice theory addresses this question. Social welfare functions (aggregation rules) can be either *real valued* or *axiomatic*. Real-valued functions involve interpersonal comparisons of utility—as problematic in public choice as in welfare economics. The axiomatic alternative seeks to specify a social welfare function in terms of a number of ethical desiderata for the way it aggregates preferences. The seminal work here is that of Arrow (1963).

Arrow's impossibility theorem—the point of departure for

public choice as a field of study—was hardly an auspicious start, in that it demonstrated the impossibility of any collective choice rule satisfying a fairly innocuous set of desirable conditions or axioms. Once we extend the desiderata beyond Arrow's original set (unrestricted domain, weak Pareto, independence of irrelevant alternatives, nondictatorship), the problems multiply (see Sen 1970). The point about Arrow's four is that alone they are sufficient to disqualify any real-world aggregation mechanism. This result causes obvious problems for evaluation, as one must decide which condition or conditions to dispense with in the criteria set. Public choice offers little guidance as to what should be dropped: an external value judgment is necessary (see Mueller 1979: 199–201).

When push comes to shove, there is always the Pareto criterion to fall back on. In practice, public choice makes extensive use of the Pareto principle in its unmodified form, as opposed to the Kaldor-Hicks variant preferred in welfare economics. Buchanan and Tullock (1962) suggest that distributional judgments should be made through a social contract based on impersonal preferences (see above). Once these kinds of questions are settled at the constitutional stage, ordinary policy decisions should then be made subject to the Pareto efficiency criterion. It should be noted that the unmodified Pareto criterion is far more applicable to voting mechanisms than it is in welfare economics, for consensus and unanimity can be achieved through vote trading. This consideration leads public choice Paretians to advocate structures that facilitate the attainment of unanimity, or indeed to specify unanimity as a decision rule. Unanimity is, of course, most readily achieved in small groups such as committees (see Black 1958).

Irrespective of the kind of aggregation rule employed, individual preferences are the yardstick for the evaluation of institutions. Government agencies, then, are "means for allocating decision making capabilities in order to provide goods and services responsive to the preferences of individuals" (Ostrom and Ostrom 1971: 207). So in studies of alternative institutional arrangements for policing, crime rates are not an appropriate success indicator. Citizen satisfaction with police performance (as reported, for example, in sample surveys) is more relevant (E. Ostrom 1971, 1973).

What kinds of institutional structures are found in the public choice analyst's inventory? The market occupies a central place. Public choice has nothing to add to the welfare-maximizing verdict on markets developed by welfare economics. According to both welfare economics and public choice, government exists to supply public goods. Hence public choice as policy analysis focuses upon institutional designs for the supply of public and quasi-public goods (such as the air quality of Smoketown). A rational person acts through these structures, be it as a producer of public goods (for example, a bureaucrat or elected official), as a consumer (for example, a beneficiary of a public program), or as a funder (taxpayer).

It is noteworthy that public choice embraces proofs of both the undersupply of public goods by individuals acting on a voluntary basis (Olson 1965) and the oversupply of public goods (or at least their financing) once a government agency has been established and staffed with self-serving bureaucrats (Niskanen 1971). This latter kind of proof places public choice in the "limited government" tradition. The institutional design challenge becomes one of avoiding the extremes of public good undersupply and oversupply—that is, to ensure responsiveness to the preferences of citizen consumers rather than bureaucrats or politicians. Practitioners who emphasize the "bureaucratic leviathan" direct their attention to devices for limiting the scope of government, be it through mass rebellion or constitutional restrictions on government spending (Brennan and Buchanan 1977; Friedman and Friedman 1984).

One enduring theme in the public choice literature is that "small is responsive" in institutional design. Public choice contradicts more traditional public administration perspectives, which stress the economics of scale associated with governmental consolidation. Applied to governmental service delivery in urban areas, public choice reasons (following Tiebout 1956) that rational individuals "vote with their feet" in deciding where to live; hence neighborhoods differentiate into homogeneous preference clusters—and in the interests of a welfare-maximizing mix, services are best organized and financed at the neighborhood level. Only if there are substantial cross-neighborhood externalities (such as air pollution between communities in the Smoke Valley) should higher levels of governmental organization be considered.

Responsiveness is also enhanced to the extent that government is legislative rather than executive or bureaucratic (see Haefele 1973). Desiring reelection to further their own interests, representatives must be sensitive to citizen preferences. Bureaucrats are at greater liberty in their pursuit of career and budgetary success. Single-issue representative bodies—such as the SVA discussed at the outset of this chapter—may also represent citizen preferences more clearly than a general-purpose legislature. However, public choice arguments can be made on both sides of this issue, for Pareto-better vote trading is facilitated by a variety of different issues. Note that our Smoketown public choice analysis recommends combining jurisdiction over air and water pollution for just this reason.

Public choice analysts are, however, aware of potential defects in legislative mechanisms. Thus Fiorina (1981) and Friedman and Friedman (1984) berate the U.S. Congress for attending more to special favors for constituents than to representation of citizen preferences in legislation. The Friedmans prescribe a remedy of increased presidential power and reduced government; Fiorina contemplates electoral reform and the restructuring of the congressional committee system.

When it comes to relating institutional designs to criteria, the distinctive methodology of public choice is deduction from basic principles. This emphasis has often excluded systematic testing of predictions beyond casual empirical examples, such as horror stories of bureaucratic waste. Lack of more systematic empirical content has long plagued the approach. As Golembiewski (1977: 1491–92) points out, work in the approach often tends to go straight from assumptions through methods to prescription—the theory is treated as "end of the road" rather than as "hypothesis to be tested."

While some practitioners believe axiomatic models are sufficient in themselves as the basis for policy choice, increased empirical content is apparent in public choice as the years go by. Empirical tests have been undertaken of predictions concerning the overproduction of public goods by established bureaucracies and the relative effectiveness of service delivery in large and small urban jurisdictions. To date, though, the empirical evidence remains both scanty and mixed. A good example of empirical backing for a public choice prediction may be found in Ricketts' (1981) account of British housing policy in terms of its responsiveness to powerful political constituencies rather than to stated social goals (how else does one explain rent control, subsidized public housing, or tax relief for mortgages?). Equally compelling evidence against a central public choice prediction is the finding by Christenson and Sachs (1980) of a positive association between size of local governmental unit and public satisfaction with the quality of service rendered. This mixed empirical backing should make one wary of applying public choice prescriptions wholesale.

PRACTICAL USEFULNESS

Public choice clearly generates analyses directly applicable to public policy. Indeed, the approach can inspire a wholesale program of institutional reform in the direction of small, responsive, and decentralized government. However, there are several limitations on the adequacy of public choice in the policy field.

First of all, public choice remains generally uneasy with the distributional aspects of policy. For example, one reason for organizing policy at a high level of government—even when it could be undertaken at a lower, more responsive level—is to ensure equity among regions and among persons. The activities of the U.S. federal government in civil rights policy over the last three decades can be understood in this light. Public choice lacks any criterion for ordering distributional alternatives that is accepted to the degree of the Pareto or responsiveness criteria.[1]

Second, public choice treats public institutions as nothing more than instrumental means for preference aggregation. As a value, democracy is deemed synonymous with efficiency: an effective aggregation of preferences (Mitchell and Mitchell 1986). As an institution, democracy is evaluated in terms of its

---

1. Though note the attempt of Sen (1972) to specify such a criterion—a "weak equity axiom"—which requires interpersonal comparison of utilities.

facilitation of the expression of self-interest. Indeed, public choice theorists sometimes suggest that we dispense with democratic institutions in favor of demand-revealing processes (see Tullock 1979: 44; Mueller 1979: 68–89). But as Edelman (1971, 1977) demonstrates at length, the intrinsic qualities of a policy process matter a great deal to the people affected by its outcomes. A citizen is more than a consumer.

A third problem stems from the way public choice treats political leadership. Political leaders are thought of as self-interested maximizers, just like everybody else. Public choice would see any truly public-spirited individuals as obstacles to the efficient design of institutions; morality in politics becomes dysfunctional.

Finally, the approach has problems when the current distribution of individual preferences is known to be unstable, is itself the target of public policy, or is likely to be changed by the content of policy (whether intentionally or not). Contrary to public choice assumptions, individuals do sometimes adjust their preferences to social norms (Buckley, Burns, and Meeker 1974; Frohlich, Oppenheimer, Hunt, and Wagner, 1975). Moreover, as Tribe (1976) points out, today's values are in large measure a consequence of yesterday's policies. A good example is the mainstream American "corporate mentality" instilled in many Alaskan natives as a consequence of the 1971 Alaska Native Claims Settlement Act, which created corporations with natives as shareholders. One rationale for a policy of community participation has been to make the preferences of the poor more like those of the middle class.

Despite these limits, public choice is clearly progressing in its problem-solving capabilities, especially as regards policy applications—in part due to its youth. Its illumination of the causes of (and remedies for) governmental failure is of recent vintage. Some practitioners are even attacking the traditional weak points of public choice—such as distribution.

To date, though, public choice policy analysis has not been used to any degree in the policy process. Certainly, public choice has informed debates over bureaucratic reorganization and limiting the size of government. Arguably, various "new federalisms" (such as the one proposed by President Reagan in his 1982 State of the Union address) reflect the public choice contention that "small is responsive." As long ago as the early 1970s, then-Governor Reagan commissioned a report from a team of prominent public choice analysts on reforming the structure of local government in California (Hawkins 1973).

But public choice has yet to receive much in the way of direct application in public policy. One of the leading proponents of the public choice approach admits that by 1979 its major application had been in a voting system for a dormitory at the University of Rochester (Tullock 1979: 27–28). As Tullock (1979: 33) recognizes, "if, however, we look for specific actual changes in government policy which can be attributed to public choice activity, I think we would find that there are none." Of course, current lack of application of public choice does not mean the approach could not or should not be applied.

PERSPECTIVE

Public choice is essentially static and ahistorical. It can be both backward looking, in its analysis of existing structures, and forward looking, in its anticipation of institutional designs, though it can say little about alternative futures should the issues demanding institutional amelioration change. This kind of change might happen if, for example, locally generated pollution in Smoketown were to become less important than imported pollution.

The audience for the public choice approach includes all-powerful metapolicy makers (institutional architects) but is not limited to this category without members. Much existing public choice analysis is highly technical and mathematical and hence intelligible only to an audience of fellow cognoscenti. Nevertheless, it is clear that the 1970s and early 1980s have witnessed a growing potential audience of people pessimistic about the problem-solving capabilities of government and in favor of its retrenchment. Given the field's hostility to bureaucracy, the audience is unlikely to ever include bureaucratic insiders.

Turning to the normative stance of public choice, there are several reasons why most public choice work currently leans toward conservatism.

First, public choice theorists overwhelmingly prefer allocation by markets to that by governments. This preference is rooted in the logic of axiomatic social choice theory. Welfare economics tells us that perfect markets are efficient. On the other hand, impossibility theorems tell us that governments must fail in some aspect of their preference aggregation task. The possibility of strategic behavior (i.e., behavior in which individuals conceal their true preferences, such as willingness to pay) in collective choice structures means that self-interested maximizing behavior will lead to suboptimal results in a manner that is impossible in a perfect market (see Russell 1979: 8). Moreover, the assumption about bureaucratic behavior makes it unlikely that government agencies will serve the public interest. Public choice in the policy field stands welfare economics on its head; whereas welfare economics sees the role of government as correcting for market failure, public choice views market strategies as means to correct for governmental failure.

Second, any decision rule based on individual preferences means that consumer sovereignty reigns supreme. Other values are ignored.

Third, conservatism is further reinforced by any acceptance of the Paretian unanimity rule, which requires that potential losers from a course of action actually be fully compensated for their loss. A blanket compensation rule requires that any status quo be treated as legitimate. If a thief is apprehended, then he should be compensated for loss of earnings due to forced redress or imprisonment. If job security or earning power are reduced by measures undertaken to promote economic growth, then those adversely affected must be compensated. Practitioners of the public choice approach try to escape from the less attractive implications of the compensation rule by supplementing it with some additional ethical criteria. Buchanan, with regard to our first example, specifies that compensation should only be paid when the previous behavior was within the law (see Goldberg 1974:502). Some definition of rights is therefore necessary prior to the application of Paretian public choice to substantive policy problems. The conceptions of rights underlying much public choice work respect the legitimacy of the status quo: existing laws are assumed just.

Fourth, as we have already noted, public choice practitioners exhibit a preference for market mechanisms, opting for imperfect market strategies over imperfect governments. To support this predilection, they cast their nets wide to identify governmental regulatory interventions that produce consequences counter to their purported raison d'etre. Examples of such interventions include restrictions on cigarette advertising, which increase tobacco company profits (Doron 1979), and antipollution regulations, which secure the competitive advantage of regulated corporations (Buchanan and Tullock 1974).

Fifth, the idealized market of economics and public choice is a society of social isolates. Hence public choice is hostile to social and political organization. Organized interests and self-consciously social groups play havoc with social welfare (Olson 1982). Government invasion of the marketplace makes matters worse still by downweighting low-intensity preferences held by large numbers of people. Further, this invasion encourages the formation of special interest groups that will be as small and exclusive as circumstances permit (Riker 1962). Public choice would ridicule the notion of a public interest group. Interest groups are created only through private motives, seized upon by equally self-interested political entrepreneurs (Frohlich and Oppenheimer 1978: 66–89).

Public choice has three strategies for dealing with conflicting values. First, it can ignore particular values—especially when they do not fit into any individual-based utility calculus. Values about the intrinsic qualities of policy process fall into this category. Second, like welfare economics, public choice can attempt to subsume all values under efficiency-based notions of social welfare. The approach subsumes distributive values under this rubric—when it does not ignore them. And third, it can assign conflicting values to the utility functions of individuals in collective choice, to be aggregated through whatever institutional designs exist or are under analysis. Conflicting values concerning institutional designs themselves are, of course, more problematical. The problem is exacerbated by the impossibility theorems of public choice, which demonstrate that frequently there are a number of different values about process which cannot be logically reconciled.

Public choice in policy analysis is broad ranging in its scope, progressive in its problem-solving capabilities, and capable of coping with limited knowledge about policy consequences. Indeed, public choice is an ingenious way of evading knowledge constraints in policy analysis (see Bish 1975). So in our Smoketown example, the analyst need know nothing about sulfur dioxide pollution—or even that sulfur dioxide *is* a pollutant. The approach presents a plausible if controversial view of political reality and, if nothing else, contributes to a healthy scepticism about the capabilities of government. Yet public choice has a number of blind spots—especially in its neglect of distribution and political process—which ultimately disqualify it as sufficient in itself for the policy field.

Chapter 4

Social Structure

SOCIAL STRUCTURE IN THE SMOKE VALLEY

*T*HE PUBLIC choice group's recommendation that a Smoke Valley Authority be established appears in the local press. In a follow-up story the next day, negative reactions to the idea (as well as to the original SVAQC proposal) are reported from numerous leaders of local nongovernmental groups—WALO (Workers Against Layoffs), PUMP (Put Us Minorities in Power), and CARP (Citizens Allied for Representative Politics). These stories are read by the new chair of the Sociology Department at Smoke Valley University. He has been hired to move the department in a more applied direction in order to increase enrollments and generate greater external research funding. Earlier advances he made concerning a major role in an interdisciplinary public policy program with economists and public choice experts were rebuffed. Accordingly, at the next meeting of an informal group of department members with applied interests he suggests they treat the SVA and SVAQC proposals as opportunities to demonstrate their contribution to public policy and asks his colleagues to prepare a program to take advantage of this opportunity.

Several weeks later, the chair receives a proposal from the faculty working group and is struck once again by the diversity of his colleagues. The proposal contains suggestions reflecting the backgrounds of its authors.

Professor Gasman suggests that the real issues at stake involve inequalities in the distribution of environmental quality among Smoke Valley residents and in the determinants of this distribution. He proposes a sample survey, which would determine differences in experienced environmental quality and the extent to which these differences are a function of basic individual attributes such as income, education, race, and age.

Another colleague wants to model the residential choices made by Smoke Valley inhabitants to directly challenge the public choice group's view that locational decisions reflect the utility that people attach to air quality. The data to test this model would come from students enrolled in Sociology 1, who are required to participate in an experimental exercise.

Still another colleague, who has worked extensively on public health problems, suggests that controlling emissions from stationary pollution sources may miss other policies that would do far more to improve air quality and hence the health of Smoke Valley residents. He proposes to inventory the social practices that have a detrimental effect on air quality and thus health, including automobile use and smoking.

A husband-and-wife pair of political sociologists, Martini and Martini, provide several suggestions. They propose an analysis of who wins elections in the valley and who has backed those winners financially and politically. This analysis would be based on campaign records and interviews with elites. This information, together with data on the identity of the opinion leaders who influence area politics, should clarify the extent to which the qualities the public choice experts attach to their SVA proposal are likely to be realized in practice. The Martini's premise is that an informal power structure underlies the veneer of representative democratic forms. Because of what they have learned from studies of other areas, they suggest that a special authority such as the SVA will not be equally responsive to the preferences of every citizen and every neighborhood unless existing imbalances in political power are recognized and compensated for. Accordingly, they also pass on the suggestion of one of their graduate students that a plan be developed to secure community participation through the mobilization of support from WALO, PUMP, and CARP.

Finally, Professor Guttenacht argues that there is insufficient justification to believe that any regional authority will work to improve environmental quality. This recognition does not imply blocking the creation of the SVAQC or the SVA, but it does suggest the need to develop an evaluation strategy and incorporate it from the outset in the commission's or the authority's workings. Professor Gasman appends a note to this last proposal: any evaluation needs to pay special attention to the distribution of the benefits and costs of the workings of the authorized body.

One common theme underlying all these suggestions is that any policies pursued must take into account the existing social system in Smoke Valley: it is not a blank slate. The nature of that system makes residents unequal in their endowments and influence. Distributional questions therefore need to be addressed directly in terms of both the effects of policy and influence on policy. Further, all the proposals share an underlying conviction of the need to amass detailed information about the local situation before framing recommendations for policy content or process. General theories alone will not provide a sufficient basis for policy choice.

In other respects, the various suggestions differ markedly. Some emphasize the need to establish exactly what the policy problem is, rather than taking it as given. Others reject the model of calculating economic man in favor of purposeful social man. Still others want a more open-ended search for worthwhile policy interventions. And the community participation supporter assumes the desirability of steps to promote the influence of the grass roots as well as of social groups that cut across political jurisdictions.

After a frantic scramble to piece together grants to finance the empirical work, the required research is conducted, with substantial help from student research assignments. Eventually, the results are made available. It turns out that experienced evironmental quality in Smoke Valley is highest for the rich, college graduates, and whites between the ages of thirty-five and fifty-five. It is worst for those who have no more than a high school education, the very old, and the poor, especially the black poor. Those most in need of an improved environment will find it hardest to pay anything to attain it. Gasman seizes on this conjunction of circumstances to argue that the costs of policy should be placed on those whose environmental quality is already relatively good—that is, compensatory public policy should be pursued. The modeling exercise determines that air quality differences have no discernible effect on choice of residential location, due to ignorance of such factors and the greater weight assigned to other determinants. Thus "voting with one's feet" on air quality simply does not occur.

The public health specialist's results show that stationary source pollution has a much lower impact on experienced air quality than does the area's massive reliance on automobiles and the pervasiveness of cigarette smoking at work, home, and in recreation. The implication drawn is that public policy would best restrict automobile use and smoking, perhaps by incentives going beyond information campaigns on the effects of these habits. These problems lie well outside the domain of the proposed SVAQC, which is therefore an irrelevant response to them. Required instead is a different framework of institutional responsibility, which would integrate parts of the public and private sectors not normally classified as environmental. The analysis concludes by calling for a broad coalition of interest groups and community notables to persuade public officials to set up a cross-jurisdictional, cross-agency task force to address the environmental problem in all its facets.

The political sociologists find, not surprisingly, that Smoke Valley possesses an informal power structure in which the leaders of WALO, PUMP, and CARP play little or no role. Martini and Martini note remarkable stability in who selects candidates, who supports them, and who turns out to vote for them across a wide variety of Smoke Valley elections—from Smoketown city council to school board to sanitary district commissioners. Key participants in the power structure are remarkably successful in getting initiatives under way—be it in youth employment, community relations, or schemes to attract new business to the Silicon Smoke Industrial Park. The Martinis conclude that if the power structure wants better air quality it will get it. If it does not, new institutions will have little impact. Martini and Martini propose lobbying activities to convince the leaders of the power structure that improving environmental quality will contribute to the elite's established general objectives and conceptions of responsibility for the welfare of the valley. Meanwhile, the Martini's graduate student, a person not devoid of ambition for political office, has been in touch with WALO, PUMP, and CARP. He has managed to get their leaders interested in the SVAQC, pointing out the usefulness of an involvement when it comes to other matters dearer to their hearts. As a result, meetings are held by these groups to demand a major role in any authority, delegations meet with local government officials, and hecklers interrupt a meeting called by supporters of the SVAQC.

All of this social structural effort leads to publication, especially in applied sociology journals. Of more immediate practical interest are some developments in the valley. The backers of the SVAQC proposal modify it to allow for a substantial role for WALO, PUMP, and CARP activists on the commission's advisory board and commit themselves to "sunshine" procedures and community consultation. Professor Guttenacht receives a grant from the Hustle Thyme Foundation to evaluate the SVAQC "experiment." Yet the most prominent overall development is controversy. The SVAQC becomes a divisive issue, rather than one ignored by most Smoke Valley residents. Those committed to environmental quality split between supporters of a narrow program of stationary source control and those who would move on a broad front against all environmental abuses. Perhaps most troubling are the implications of the compensatory policy issue. A commitment to compensation was part of the maneuvering to defuse the ire of WALO, PUMP, and CARP. But this issue, like school busing, takes on a symbolic importance to the majority of the population who are neither civic leaders nor affiliated with WALO, PUMP, or CARP. The SVAQC's troubles are just beginning.

Meanwhile, back at Smoke Valley University, the no-longer-new head of the Sociology Department observes that his department's gain in national prestige among applied sociologists has not advanced his more local interest in public policy. If anything, his faculty colleagues in economics and public choice are more hostile than ever as a result of what they see as impractical and unwarranted interventions in the policy process, interventions that have diminished the chances for professional policy analysts to work out the environmental quality problems of Smoke Valley in an objective, technical atmosphere.

THE SOCIAL STRUCTURAL APPROACH

The social structure approach to policy analysis applies sociological reasoning to the content of public policies, with special reference to social consequences in terms of the distribution of goods (and "bads") among individuals and groups. In contrast to welfare economics, there is little concern with efficiency. The key ratios for the social structure approach are those of the assets of individuals and groups relative to each other, not of costs to benefits.

By analogy, the approach casts the policy analyst in a medical or curative role (Axelrod 1977). To alleviate social problems, the analyst acts as diagnostician, researcher of new treatments, and as an operative who selects and administers treatments (which can be either preventive or remedial).

The problems addressed may involve relatively intangible factors, such as integration, mobility, and morale, or more tangible ones, such as housing, employment, and medical care. The general intention is to achieve a world different from the status quo and projections from it.[1] Applications involve a "curious admixture of psychological assumptions, scientific concepts, value commitments, social aspirations, personal beliefs and administrative constraint" (Rein 1976: 103). Out of their fusion the analyst develops some notion of what course of action will alter social conditions as desired (Rein 1976: 130–33).

GIVENS

The hard core of the social structural approach might at first sight appear somewhat soft, given the eclecticism to which we have just referred. The core becomes harder once we distinguish two strands in the social structural approach.

The first strand focuses on the endowments and circumstances of *individuals,* who are thought of as possessing an "account" of psychological, social, and physical properties. This account is the target of public policy. Rooted in social

---

1. This is true whether the projections are statistical extrapolations or those of models devoid of purposeful public action (Brunner and Brewer 1971).

psychology, the individual endowments strand works from a model of man more complex than homo economicus. Social man has multidimensional motivations, preferences, and behavioral opportunities. Our sociological modelers of Smoketown residential choices are located in this first strand, as is our Professor Gasman's analysis of the determinants of experienced air quality. The second strand takes groups (actual or latent) as its focus. The Martinis' political sociology of the Smoketown power structure is an example of the group strand—with a vengeance, in the hands of their graduate student. Familiar dimensions for defining groups include sex, race, age, religion, region, social class, ethnicity, and profession. The strands differ, then, in that the first treats the individual members of groups as the primary targets of public policy, whereas the second takes the group as a unit. The two strands are ideal types; particular pieces of work can and do combine them.

The assumptions on which the social structural approach rests are realistic and plausible, especially in comparison to welfare economics and public choice. Hence it is not surprising that the approach has found an audience in policy circles, especially in social policy agencies. This receptivity (or at least lip service) has persisted in the face of changing social policy fashion, perhaps because of the wide range of views about the capabilities of the policy process that can be found among followers of the approach. Views range from great optimism about the capacity of policy instruments to achieve positive social change to the profound pessimism of Banfield (1970).

CONTENTS

The social structural approach is theoretically eclectic. The roots of the approach in social theory provide a number of different models to guide analysis. Functionalism explains individual and collective behavior through reference to its instrumental value in the harmony of social totality. Symbolic action theory interprets behavior in terms of its meaning to the individual in the context of dealings with others. Role theory assumes that people adopt the roles that promote their social acceptance. Socioeconomic determinism regards behavior as being determined by social and economic conditions. Interest theory contends action is based on a rational pursuit of real interests. Action theory sees rationality only in terms of subjective perceptions and attitudes.

Proliferation in theoretician's theory is reflected in the research theory that social structural investigators apply to specific empirical cases—even though the two kinds of theory typically differ in their content (see Menzies 1982). Note the diversity of social structural approaches applied in our Smoke Valley case. Theoretical proliferation is further compounded by the diversity of social problems of interest to practitioners. There is rather little in common between the operational theorizing of practitioners who work on criminal recidivism and those who study transportation policy choices. In the light of multiple theoretical possibilities, Coleman (1972) recommends that analysts in the individual strain consider a variety of models in any concrete situation. Thus theory merely informs the selection of variables (such as the determinants of experienced air quality in Smoketown).

Despite theoretical variety, practitioners of this approach hold the following questions in common. First, what is the prevailing distribution of resources among individuals or groups and what trends in this distribution are observable? Second, what factors are responsible for this distribution? Third, what has been, is, or will be the impact of specific policy measures on the distributions?

Theories in the individual endowments strand must encompass some conception of the behavior of target individuals. The analyst characteristically seeks to arrive at conclusions of the form $y = f(x)$: y is the vector of indicators of the endowments of individuals that the policy seeks to affect (such as experienced environmental quality), and x consists of the set of variables that drives these indicators. This set can include both policy (manipulable) and environmental variables. The analyst tries to discover the changes in the x variables that will change the y terms in the desired manner. Policy makers are seen as manipulating social conditions. In its extreme version, manipulation takes the form of behavioral technology, under which policy makers should induce individuals to behave in a manner conducive to the ends of policy. Cone and Hayes

(1980) explore the prospects for environmental policy in this image. In this context, it is noteworthy that Scott and Shore (1979: xiv) define social policy as "purposive coercive measures that are adopted by individuals and groups within government who are responsible for dealing with particular social conditions in our society to achieve certain aims."

Given this general framework, many kinds of methods for collecting data are acceptable. The theoretical openness of the approach is matched by its catholic taste in methods. Case studies, large-scale cross-sectional analyses, mass opinion surveys, and more or less controlled social experiments are all admissible. Analyses use statistical methods where possible, ideally, interval-level multivariate statistics. For example, if addressing the social problem of inadequate education of the children of the poor, the analyst could seek data on a host of possible determinants of educational achievement: expenditure on education, teacher competence, class size, social class and racial mix in the school, nutrition, community involvement, and parental education. The next step would then be to ascertain which of these have a discernible effect on educational achievement.

Theorizing in the group strand requires decisions as to which dimension of group definition is central. Thus Marxists define groups in relation to the means of production. More generally, the group strand assumes that distributional conflict pervades social and political life. The existence of public goods that in and of themselves do not raise distributional issues is not denied. But the supply of public goods (such as air quality in Smoke Valley) cannot be divorced from conflict over the burden of provision. Conflict can be avoided only by excluding some conceivable groups or social categories from consideration or standing. In sum, then, the group strand assumes that the analyst can identify key categories on the basis of actual or potential activity for and against some distribution (Tallman 1976).

Group definition can be controversial. While Marxists stress class divisions, non-Marxists might argue that religious, ethnic, or national memberships are more meaningful. After all, workers of different religion, ethnicity, or nationality have not been loath to go to war against one another. Marxists would reply that these people have yet to realize their true interests. Most people do in fact belong to several groups and accord fluctuating importance to these various memberships. Indeed, successful politicians are aware of the shifting emphases individuals place on their various memberships and deliberately manipulate the saliency of social categories.

The methods employed in the group strand vary from participant observation and elite interviews to formal deduction and aggregate data collection. The analyst treats the group or category as unitary, or in terms of an "average member." Distributional differences within target groups are not addressed.

Work under the social structural umbrella varies substantially in empirical content. However, the common distributional questions identified above do lend themselves to expression in terms of observable human behavior, social events, and tangible assets. Thus practitioners have been very active and creative in collecting data and developing measures and research strategies to secure empirical content.

Substantial as the empirical content of the social structural approach may be, though, it is noteworthy that this content is often divorced from sociological research theory and—especially—theoretician's theory. As Scott and Shore (1979: 21–22) point out, the methods of the approach (such as sample surveys) are applied in policy analysis much more frequently than its theories or concepts. Note the efforts of Professor Guttenacht in experimental evaluation of SVAQC activities. This atheoretical style surfaces most clearly in the British discipline of social administration, which combines descriptive statistics about disadvantaged individuals and groups with exhortation on behalf of these people, particular social values and the need for policies to alleviate distress (see Bulmer 1983). Social administration makes no attempt to construct and test theories of intervention; instead, the facts are supposed to speak for themselves.

PRACTICAL USEFULNESS

The social structure approach has been applied in areas as diverse as poverty, education, health, law enforcement, housing, criminal justice, and urban policy. The heyday of its use in American governmental circles was arguably in the 1960s, concurrent with expansion of antipoverty programs. Sociologists had prominent roles in a number of presidential commissions in that era, and benefited substantially from federal government largesse. More recent retrenchment of government social policy has meant retrenchment for the social structure approach too.

Intellectual fashions aside, social structural policy analysis has substantial attraction, especially in terms of its sensitivity to distributional consequences. Because the approach can treat polities as social structures, it can illuminate consequences in terms of who gets what—be it money, power, status, expertise, or environmental quality. It provides a more subtle and realistic picture of the world than public choice or welfare economics. Unlike information processing, it has little faith in betterment through improved information. Social policy ignores social structure insights at its peril; at best the result will be collective disappointment, at worst social disaster. Note, for example, the post–World War II U.S. experience with public housing and urban redevelopment.

Unfortunately, there is a large gap between what this approach offers in principle and its contribution in practice. The observations of Reiss (1975: 218) on work on delinquency are more broadly pertinent: the "science-building activities of understanding . . . causes . . . probably are less relevant to matters of social policy than . . . how one may change behavior, situations, organizations and systems. Theories of social intervention and social control that produce change are generally poorly developed."

Consider, for example, one of the more well-received (if controversial) pieces of social structural policy analysis of recent years—that of Titmuss (1971) on alternative systems for the medical supply of human blood. Titmuss combines sociological analysis of human motivation with technical evidence and empirical data about blood and its uses. His major conclusion is that a market-type system of the kind prevailing in the United States is markedly inferior (in terms of safety, efficiency, and effectiveness) to the voluntary "gift relationship" of blood donation in the United Kingdom. This conclusion runs directly counter to that of economists who have studied the same issue. The policy implication for the United Kingdom is clear: do nothing. But no policy prescription for the United States is possible. Titmuss himself recognizes that the presence of a market eliminates the altruistic motive for giving, for it makes blood a commodity like any other. Abolition of the market by fiat cannot be expected to change motivations overnight in the manner necessary to ensure an adequate supply of blood.

Scott and Shore (1979) explain the social structural approach's frequent lack of policy applicability through reference to the motivation of sociologists: they are preoccupied with advancing disciplinary knowledge, not effective public policy, even in purportedly policy-directed studies. But this explanation does not convince: sociology should be no more prone than other social scientific disciplines to this problem. Even if this explanation is correct, it says nothing about the potential of the approach.

Two deeper reasons underlie the general lack of applicability of the social structural approach. The first is that demographic variables often play a larger role than variables easily open to manipulation by public policy. To return to our Smoketown example, Professor Gasman finds age, race, and income the primary determinants of experienced environmental quality. Discipline-oriented social structural analysts may judge analytical success by the percentage of variance explained in the dependent variable, rather than by the effective policy levers identified. Second, even when manipulable factors loom large, they often lie outside the jurisdiction of the institutions responsible for the issue area at hand. (Our Smoketown public health sociologist stresses policy to affect automobile and cigarette use—clearly outside SVAQC's jurisdiction.) The analyst may then face the Hobson's choice of recommending policy actions that promise only trivial impact or recommending ones that are impossible for his audience (see Levine and Williams 1971). Third, the approach rarely relates social outcomes to specific changes in budgetary resource allocation.

These problems are highlighted in a dialogue about education policy between two welfare economists, Cain and Watts (1972), and a sociologist, Coleman (1972). The former suggest the use of regression coefficients to capture the effect of budgetary allocations on dependent variables. These coefficients would yield precise, actionable recommendations for expenditure allocation. Coleman demurs on the grounds that the relatively tractable observed policy variables are often merely reflections of less manipulable policy variables or environmental characteristics that are slow to change.

Another set of practical limitations centers on measurement problems related to indicators of social outcomes (dependent variables), which are often controversial. In principle, economic indicators have the same problem; practically, they benefit from broader consensus. Envious (or cautious) social structural analysts are tempted by less controversial, economically inspired indicators; the result is that their analyses become virtually indistinguishable from cost-effectiveness analysis. For example, studies of education policy employ outcome indicators such as diplomas granted or minority student enrollment, rather than the quality or pertinence of the education received.

Even if all these problems can be handled, analysts remain bedeviled by weak understanding of complex social systems. Consider, for example, the stipulation of a multivariate statistical model. First, the form of the model must be specified in advance. If the analyst assumes that determinants are substitutable for one another, then an additive formulation is appropriate:

$$y = a + bx_1 + cx_2 \ldots$$

If he or she assumes little substitutability, a multiplicative formulation is required:

$$y = ax_1' x_2' \ldots$$

Second, because of the pervasive interconnections in complex social systems, it may be extremely difficult to pass judgment on the effectiveness of any single independent variable in isolation from all others. The controversial Coleman report (Coleman 1966) supporting school integration dealt with this difficulty (as manifest in statistical multicollinearity) by reporting results in terms of the percentage of variance explained by groups of independent variables, rather than regression coefficients for individual variables. This carried the price of vague and unfocused policy implications.

Success with these technical obstacles does not overcome the central problems referred to earlier. Absence of consensus on the proper standing of various social groups (for example, conservatives may deny the validity of categorization by race or ethnicity) leads to conflicting interpretations of observable results.

Analytical and ideological preconceptions can have substantial bearing on the interpretation of social structural empirical studies. For example, findings that the Head Start child development program had little impact on its target population led some observers to judge the program ineffective. Others held that the findings established that such programs could work with enough effort. After all, the evaluation did find local instances of success (see Williams and Evans 1969).

To take another example: studies of the effects of income maintenance policy on marital dissolution and remarriage (see Hannan, Tuma, and Groeneveld 1977) have found that such policies often promote the rate of marital breakup for blacks, whites, and Chicanos. For Chicana women, but not for black or white women, income maintenance also reduces the likelihood of remarriage. The policy import of these findings depends on the value placed on marriage relative to the alleviation of poverty and the weight accorded to policy impact on each racial group.

Where are we left, then, in terms of the practical usefulness of the social structure approach? First, it can clarify the real consequences of public policy in terms meaningful to citizens as well as experts. Further, it can counterbalance tendencies to automatically define relevant outcomes according to the existing institutional division of labor (missions) in the policy process. For example, it is important to assess the impacts on poverty of family planning, education, racial equality, and employment opportunities in combination rather than each in isolation. The approach is less successful in identifying with any precision the content, duration, and magnitude of appropriate policies.

Accordingly, the major impacts of social structural analyses have been in affecting climates of opinion and in suggesting broad levers for change. Notable examples are G. Myrdal's (1944) work on race in America, Harrington's (1962) on poverty, and the sociological evidence pertaining to the effects of segregation on the psychological and intellectual development of black children used by the U.S. Supreme Court in the landmark 1954 school desegregation case. The part played by social structural analysis in policy debates means that many of the better-known pieces have an advocacy style: for example, those of Jencks (1972) on education and Piven and Cloward (1982) on welfare policy. Sociologists (in the group strand) often find themselves advocating the interest of some group in society in an adversary stance toward policy makers.

The approach shows few signs of progress in its social problem-solving capabilities. Despite the enormous attention paid by sociologists to methodology, dated works such as those of A. Myrdal (1941) and G. Myrdal (1944) or methodologically primitive pieces such as Harrington (1962) or Titmuss (1971) contribute to policy debate as effectively as anything more recent or sophisticated. Sociologists themselves perceive little progress in their endeavors; moreover, in an age of retrenchment, policy makers seem more inclined to heed economists.

PERSPECTIVE

In its time perspective, social structural policy analysis can be forward looking and dynamic. Examples here include forecasts of changing demands on the public sector, as a result of demographic shifts, and time series analysis of the determinants of social indicators. Nevertheless, much of the work done to date (especially in the individual endowments strand) has been static and retrospective. This emphasis reflects a concentration on hypotheses suitable for testing with readily available data.

The audience for social structural policy analysis is potentially large and diverse. It includes all those who have an interest in social outcomes and distributions of goods and "bads," be they SVAQC commissioners or leaders of PUMP, WALO, and CARP.

Normative leanings vary by specific application; none is

intrinsic to the approach. Starting points about group definition or plausible causes of human behavior can take on a self-fulfilling character. Think, for example, of Margaret Thatcher's application of social policy based on assumptions about Victorian values in British society. People are assumed to be competitive and self-reliant, rather than cooperative and community oriented; after policy has been applied, they have no choice but to be the former. Policy analysis models are more than analytic tools; they come to be believed as diagnoses of the ills of society, thus taking on a life of their own. As March (1972: 414) points out, "independent of its truth value, a model has justice value." So, for example, models of deviance stigmatize (and may even convince) the supposed deviants. Other models might regard the interests of "deviants" (such as homosexuals) as legitimate and worthy of expression in public policy.

The prevalent assumption of ubiquitous value conflict was noted earlier, though social structural analysts disagree on how to handle it, because they cannot agree on its severity. To illustrate, Alford (1975: 28–29) reports that cities with a high proportion of black or poor people receive relatively large amounts of poverty program funds if they have a large number of local voluntary organizations or headquarters of national organizations. One explanation would emphasize muted competition: a high degree of community integration enables the demand for funds to be pursued effectively through "interorganizational activity." In contrast, an explanation stressing conflict over fundamental values would see a large proportion of the population in poverty raising the potential for violence. When cities have "national elites or local institutions which have successfully legitimated the rule of local elites," the threat tends to be recognized and responded to, at least by having money thrown at it. Irrespective of the severity of value conflict, handling it is less a matter for policy analysis and more one for politics—be it friendly negotiation or aggressive assertion of the claims of a social movement.

Chapter 5

Information Processing

INFORMATION PROCESSING IN SMOKE VALLEY

*W*HEN WE left Smoke Valley at the beginning of the previous chapter, the Smoke Valley Air Quality Commission (SVAQC) had been established, but in a cloud of controversy. One of the first actions the commission now takes is to offer staff appointments to two individuals associated with Smoketown University. Gloria Meander, who had been teaching political science courses in organizational behavior and the policy process, is hired as executive director. George Hamburger, who recently received an MBA with specializations in information systems management and corporate planning, is appointed director for planning and information systems. Both move quickly to capitalize on their close ties with the university. Meander establishes several internships, which will provide her with special assistants in exchange for dissertation opportunities. Hamburger sets up a technical support contract with his former professors.

Hamburger is confident of his immediate priorities and proceeds to draw on the support contract for three purposes. First, he wants a set of procedures that will enable the members of the SVAQC to arrive at a shared and ranked set of goals. He regards success here as vital for his subsequent planning responsibilities. Second, he requests that a management information system be developed to support SVAQC decision making. This system's elements should include a determination of the desired information on environmental quality, which will be collected and updated on a regular basis, a tracking system to monitor the extent to which commission decisions about pollution charges or permits are put into practice, and the projections the commission will need to make sound choices. Hamburger makes it clear that system design should include specifications for computers and staff expertise. Third, he asks his old professors to develop a comprehensive plan to guide the first ten years of the SVAQC. The plan should include a clear set of air quality targets for specified years, programs to secure these results, and resource allocations to the programs. He sends Meander a memorandum informing her of the work he has initiated, pointing out how his approach simply applies strategies now favored in the best business schools, high-prestige firms, and innovative public organizations.

Meander reads Hamburger's memo after returning from the first regular meeting of the commission and after a series of telephone conversations with individuals who have held jobs similar to hers in other special regional authorities. She reacts to the memo with the utmost skepticism and puts it in the outbasket for her secretary to file, which he duly does. Over the weekend, she makes a list of her tasks for the next week. The list includes

1. Lunch with each of the commission members, to establish rapport and find out "where they are coming from."
2. Arrange to visit similar organizations elsewhere in order to learn from their problems and successes, particularly as they pertain to the role of executive director.
3. Assign some of her interns to determine what external influences beyond SVAQC control will have an impact on its functions and performance (for example, economic climate, elections, and commission members' health and intensity of involvement).
4. Assign some other interns to study the standard operating procedures of other organizations that SVAQC will have to rely upon to implement its decisions.

She also makes a note to herself to do two other things once immediate priorities are taken care of. One is to determine which (if any) of the interns is suited to the role of her "eyes and ears" with commissioners, with Hamburger's people, with important groups in the community, and with key implementation bureaus and officials. The other is to locate and cultivate the local journalists who will be covering the commission.

Clearly, Meander and Hamburger have very different conceptions of how the SVAQC can really work and how they can play effective roles. Meander assumes that many factors lie well outside her control and hence must be approached through bargaining and negotiation. There is little possibility of once-and-for-all decisions and commitments. Hamburger, in contrast, assumes that comprehensive rationality is both desirable and feasible; hence it should be pursued in technically sound fashion. He realizes that bargaining and negotiation may indeed take place, but he does not intend being party to them. He is convinced that the processes he envisions can generate clear and stable conclusions, such that the SVAQC can pursue its mission in a coherent and orderly way. The external factors that can affect the SVAQC process and performance should be recognized for what they are: knowable and predictable. Hamburger is too sophisticated to believe these factors can be forecast with precision, but he does believe that instability can be anticipated well enough that information and planning systems can be designed to cope with contingencies as they arise (rather than starting from scratch every time).

In subsequent months, Meander and Hamburger proceed their separate ways. After much grumbling, the commissioners agree to participate in the goal-clarification exercise developed by Hamburger's helpers. Although in the end some members do not show up and others arrive late and leave early, Hamburger and his consultants believe they have enough information to construct a cardinal utility schedule for the SVAQC and to develop a ten-year plan based on it. While they are doing that, other members of their team complete the design of a management information system, recommending computer purchases and the hiring of an information specialist to support the commission.

Meander has also been busy, albeit in different ways. She learns that one commissioner is particularly looked up to by several of the others, that each shares an outlook with various organizations in the valley (ranging from PUMP to the major paper mill and its legal firm), that another commissioner believes government should champion the interests of the "little man," and that several would like a convention weekend with Meander. She also finds out that pollution emissions on-site supervisors (PEONS) have reason to believe they should "blink" when confronted with violations by major employers in the valley, and that the unit supposed to set emission fees has no idea how to do so, being staffed by former members of the Smoketown residential appraiser's office.

As the first anniversary of the SVAQC approaches, a commission meeting is scheduled to consider Hamburger's ten-year plan and information systems proposal. Meander views the meeting as the time to establish her preeminent staff position and to get some decisions taken to defuse criticisms that the SVAQC has yet to do anything other than hold meetings and send its members to conventions. Hamburger distributes copies of the plan and proposal before the meeting to Meander and the commissioners. The pieces fit together tightly into a comprehensive and reinforcing set of decisions based on the utility schedule attributed to the commission and a set of computer-generated predictions about external factors. In his cover letter, Hamburger emphasizes that the plan must be treated as a whole and that separate information systems have been optimized to support the plan.

Alas, poor Hamburger. Two days before the crucial meeting it becomes clear that his documents have been selectively leaked to the local media. Follow-up coverage features charges that the SVAQC is trying to impose its will on Smoke Valley in a way that overlooks prior commitments to consult with the various interests in the valley. Adoption of the plan would render the commission a meaningless body, hence the political process for the selection of its successive members would be equally meaningless. A prominent commissioner is quoted to the effect that "nobody elected Hamburger," and that "we will not stand for his attempt to preempt our role as representatives of the people of Smoke Valley." Meander distances herself from the Hamburger documents, telling reporters that her role is simply to make sure the commissioners have the chance to consider options generated by the SVAQC staff.

Hamburger is publicly attacked at the commission meeting, and only the goals section of his plan is adopted (without its numerical-importance weights). The rest is passed on to subcommittees for further study. As for the management information system proposal, the commission does decide to buy a computer and hire a caretaker for it but defers decision on implementing procedures for the triggering of specific actions once threshold levels of key environmental quality indicators are crossed. Shortly thereafter, Hamburger resigns and becomes vice-president for environmental information systems for a major consulting firm, Calvin R. Giant.

In the weeks and days before the crucial meeting, Meander has been meeting regularly with commissioners—especially the most influential among them—to persuade them to take several limited yet specific decisions at the meeting. She makes it clear that each step will have effects independent of the others, and that each will both defuse some emerging criticism of the SVAQC and appeal to a particular vocal interest in the valley. At these private meetings she gives the commissioners several decision memoranda, one for each area of action. The areas are: improving the administrative efficiency of the SVAQC implementation arm; involving citizens in priority setting; demonstrating SVAQC's determination to crack down on polluters; and exhibiting SVAQC's desire to work harmoniously with the business community. Each decision memorandum suggests three possible steps. One is extremely bold and controversial, another amounts to virtually nothing, and a third strikes some middle ground. Her formulation of these possibilities is based on information from her network of interns about the thinking of each commissioner and the people to whom he or she listens. After some elaborate juggling, her interns negotiate a situation where each member of the council will propose a specific step (the middle one in every case), and all the members will agree to support all the proposals. Thus all the proposals are passed at the meeting. Meander is charged with beefing up the expertise of the regulation and charge-setting bureaucracy and with arranging regular citizens' meetings. She is authorized to initiate legal action against a highly visible polluter (one with few employees and about to relocate away from the valley). Further, on behalf of the commission, she orders plaques to be awarded to environmentally minded leaders of the Smoke Valley Chamber of Commerce. All these actions are reported in the local media as initiatives from the commission, and Meander is not mentioned. Shortly thereafter, she is given a five-year contract at a substantial increase in salary and is instructed to hire a new director for planning and information systems, who will report to her. She picks one of her former interns who has shown negotiating skill, loyalty to Meander, and the ability to lose gracefully to her at the end of an exciting match of tennis.

THE INFORMATION-PROCESSING APPROACH

The information-processing approach reaches into many specialized subdisciplines in the social and natural sciences, including cognitive psychology, decision science, information science, artificial intelligence, organizational behavior, small group behavior, communication, and bureaucratic politics and decision making.

The approach is home to a great variety of practical policy analysis pursuits. These pursuits share an interest in how individuals and organizations (alone or in combination) arrive at judgments, make choices, deal with information, and solve problems. Practitioners seek desirable and feasible methods for judgment, choice, information gathering, and problem solving in a world whose constraints and opportunities flow from the real nature of persons, institutions, and technology. The focus is on process, which is seen as the primary determinant of content.

Work under the information-processing umbrella ranges from study of the generic capabilities and characteristics of individuals (Slovic, Fischoff, and Lichtenstein, 1977), to influence and interaction in cabinet-level committees in national government (Axelrod 1976), to decision rules applied by government officials such as mayors and department heads (Crecine 1969), to case studies of particular events such as the Skybolt missile crisis (for example, Neustadt 1970). Important themes in the literature include the extent to which individuals shape and interpret information, function in terms of a preestablished set of conceptions, and generally stop well short of optimal, maximizing decisions. Recurrent themes above the individual level of analysis include the importance of organizational routines, and the "loose coupling" of judgments, choices, and implementation of decisions within and across organizations. Debate is frequently joined between those who, like our George Hamburger, hold rational modes of analysis to be both desirable and feasible and those who, like our Gloria Meander, believe incrementalism must and should prevail.

GIVENS

At the hard core of the information-processing approach is a complex conception of man far removed from the simple rational maximizer of welfare economics and public choice. Individuals are seen as making decisions based on some internal, simplified model of an external situation. Such models are generally based on what individuals already know and remember. The cognitive "stock" held by individuals determines what information they will search for in a novel situation, what heed they will pay to it, and the options for action they will recognize, examine, and pick. Individuals develop a set of scripts embodying both a menu of alternative representations of a novel situation and an appropriate response once a selection from this menu has been made. So, for example, "hawks" and "doves" on the appropriate posture of the United States toward the Soviet Union subscribe to scripts one can label 1939 and 1914, respectively. The 1939 script suggests that evil should be confronted with military might; the 1914 script that excessive preparations for war can lead to a conflict whose costs no side desires.

The information-processing approach views government as a collection of numerous (and partially independent) structures with their own agendas. Unlike public choice, though, these structures are not interpreted as mechanisms for aggregating the preferences of rational utility maximizers. Instead, they are viewed as persistent social systems with particular styles and habits. Organizational units develop different (and conflicting) objectives and perspectives as a result of functional divisions of labor, involvement with particular technologies, history and experience, and the cultural socialization of new members. One can therefore expect a coalition of units with "partially conflicting interests . . . rather than a coherent body with perfectly shared values" (Crecine 1982: 35).

The different schools of thought within the information-processing approach do seem to agree on a small number of basic assumptions. First, information is necessarily incomplete and imperfect, lending uncertainty to decisions. Second, information is costly. The challenge becomes to find the "least-cost, best-return decision net of computational costs" (Simon 1978: 495). Third, the information-processing capacity of individuals and organizations is finite, though often capable of improvement. These assumptions suggest that the outcome of public policy will never be completely on target. As a set, they generate an additional given: the need for adaptation to fresh information and feedback as the future unfolds. Finally, there is a common conviction that policy analysis faces high orders of complexity, large numbers of interaction effects, and phenomena of "extreme indeterminacy and instability" (Wiener 1948: 185).

One aspect of its diversity is that the information-processing approach features not just one but four crude analogies in its hard core. These are the human brain and nervous system (Ashby 1963), the computer (Newell and Simon 1972), the organized anarchy of the garbage can (Cohen, March, and Olsen 1972), and the servomechanism.

Historical precedence goes to the servomechanism analogy, which underpins the field of cybernetics. The cybernetic tradition sees urgent need for improved communication, authoritative decision (command), and effective implementation (control). Wiener (1954: 11) defines cybernetics as the study of "problems centered about communication, control, and statistical mechanics, whether in the machine or in living tissue." So "the social system is like the individual, that . . . is bound together by a system of communication. . . . It has a dynamic in which circular processes of a feedback nature play an important part" (Wiener 1954: 24). Those who have applied cybernetics to public policy make an extension from machines and organisms to social organizations. The essential conception is that of an "array of self-controlling machines that react to their environment, as well as to the results of their own behavior;

that store, process and apply information; and that have, in some cases, a limited capacity to learn" (Deutsch 1963: 80).

Whatever its present imperfections, the policy process is treated by cybernetics as a potentially self-adjusting system. Like a thermostat, the policy process can make decisions and trigger their execution in the adjustment of "temperature." Of course, the thermostat will only perform well if four conditions are met. First, it must be provided with some criterion to steer toward (desired temperature). Second, it must be provided with decision rules about what actions are appropriate given the prevailing temperature (rules of the sort George Hamburger wanted to build into the operations of the SVAQC). Third, it must receive timely, relevant, and clear information about the prevailing temperature. Finally, its actions are really instructions to machines that implement them (furnace or air conditioner). The thermostat must have appropriate linkages and signal strength to make these machines do its bidding.

Unfortunately, public policy servomechanism analogs sufficient to meet these demanding requirements are not easily identified. Hence the computer analogy comes into play as an ideal for the individual and organizational behavior that will meet these requirements for information, applicable decision rules, and reliable implementation. The desirable properties are a set of procedures for the storage and updating of large amounts of information, recognition of patterns, rigorous application of decision rules, and exploration of the sensitivity of future states of affairs to different policy actions and environmental developments.

The computer analogy can lead in two directions. The first treats persons and organizations as imperfect computers. The second would turn decision functions over to computers and "intelligent software" to the greatest possible extent. Doing so completely would require embedding in a computer-based model the values and decision rules of politicians, political philosophies, and policy analysts. Pending that brave new world, one settles for periodic man-machine interaction to couple the intuitive, implicit, and private skills of policy practitioners and analysts with the information exploitation capacities of computers.

Those who draw more heavily on the human brain analogy

arrive at very different ideas. They dwell on the myriad of possibilities and ambiguities in the way human beings really do make decisions. March (1978) provides a useful summary of the "rationalities" that actually do operate in human behavior. These forms include the willful simplification of "limited rationality," the accidents of simultaneity affecting "contextual rationality" (Bobrow 1969), the strategic interaction informing "game rationality," and the focus on intrinsic qualities of process in "process rationality."

All four of these rationalities involve goal-directed calculation. However, observers can find other general forms of sensible action taken by individuals who are not themselves conscious of its real justification. Thus adaptive rationality consists of servomechanism-like behavior, selected rationality emphasizes the contribution of behavior patterns to organizational survival, and posterior rationality involves adjustment of goals after the fact in order to justify actions taken.

In common with welfare economics and public choice, the servomechanism and computer analogies prescribe choices on the basis of tastes that are relevant, stable, consistent, precise, and independent of the choice they control. To those who subscribe to the brain analogy, a more appropriate vocabulary about preferences emphasizes strategizing, exploratory probes, inconsistency and ambivalence, avoidance, denial or suppression, instability, and vagueness.

Diversity in analogy is further reflected in differing assumptions about the capabilities of the policy process. The alternative models of man and rationalities can back both optimistic and pessimistic views of the possibility of using good methods to make good decisions, which are then implemented effectively. Both optimists and pessimists can find real-world evidence to support their views. It therefore makes sense to attend to the characteristics of individual cases, rather than pursue sweeping summary judgment on this score.[1] In particular, it should be recognized that public policy problems vary substantially in their degree of closed and stable structure, recurrence in similar form, ambiguity, and value conflict. Highly structured, stable, unambiguous prob-

---

1. This discussion draws heavily on Crecine (1982).

lems with consensus on values lend themselves to the "modern technologies of reason" (March 1978: 588) such as operations research, information systems, large data bases, simulations, problem networks, and decision analysis. Problems lacking these attributes—such as environmental quality in Smoke Valley—render these technologies helpless, as our George Hamburger discovered to his sorrow.

Further, the settings of problem solving differ; participants vary in their homogeneity and exposure to common information. They can interact in tightly coupled, hierarchical structures or in more informal, loosely coupled mechanisms. If participants are diverse, exposed to dissimilar information, and interacting in a loosely coupled manner—a common situation in public policy—then pessimists are justified in their contention that "technologies of reason" will lead to disaster. In such cases, even officials who, like George Hamburger, try to act as rational utility maximizers can expect to be buffeted by forces beyond their control.

If we entertain the full range of schools encompassed by the information-processing umbrella, then we possess a far more realistic (though diversified) basis for policy analysis than can be generated by the givens of welfare economics and public choice. Accordingly, information-processing analysis starts in a strong position to provide forecasts that are plausible and relevant and techniques that are usable in the real world of public policy. This position is further strengthened by recognition of ways in which policy can go wrong due to imperfections of information, communication, decision, and control, and to the complexity of external environments. Of course, the demands the approach makes on calculation, inquiry, and judgment may themselves hinder and distort policy making. We return to this important question later.

CONTENTS

The diversity in analogies, rationalities, problems, and contexts is mirrored in the range of theories and methods sheltering under the information-processing umbrella. To give a flavor of this variety, we focus on three pertinent dimensions for the clarification of policy and decision. The first is concerned with whether policy making is (and should be) incremental or instrumentally rational. The second addresses the question of whether policy making occurs in a highly structured, tightly coupled manner, or in a loosely coupled, organized anarchy. The third concerns the tension between the rationalistic ideal of decision analysis and the reality found by empirical (behavioral) decision theory.

Incremental and Rationalistic Policy Making

The two most prominent advocates of, respectively, rationalistic and incremental policy making are Simon and Lindblom, who are in substantial agreement at the descriptive and explanatory level. Lindblom's "disjointed incrementalism" and Simon's "bounded rationality" accept the basic assumptions introduced above. Strong differences characterize their prescriptive models. While Simon pursues the rationalistic ideal type, Lindblom is content with incrementalism. For Lindblom (1965) the "intelligence of democracy" is that, like the free market, it produces good outcomes from the interplay of self-interests.

Lindblom and Simon agree that the policy process fails to work as a valid simplifier of information. Unlike a market, it does not concentrate information into price signals.[2] The policy process involves complex bargains and coalition side payments. There is no ready equivalent to money as a means of exchange (simple vote trading will not do). Information inputs to individuals in politics are complex, voluminous, and lacking any common metric. The individual can choose to ignore much of this information, or try to absorb it all and experience information overload, or devise complex routines for information processing. Lindblom and Simon (and those occupying middle ground between their positions) differ about the degree to which policy-making capabilities can and should be extended in a rationalistic direction. The precise implications of their different approaches are discussed under "practical usefulness" below.

---

2. Of course, market prices themselves have substantial ambiguity as indicators. Discriminatory pricing, monopoly, and other forms of market failure can distort the signals.

Tight and Loose Coupling

Decision making in a tightly coupled organization is described by Cyert and March (1963; see also Inbar 1979). The process of decision is built upon organizational goals, the expectations an organization imposes on its members, and established routines. Activity is driven by the need to resolve internal conflict, avoid uncertainty, solve problems, and learn. Tightly coupled organization may be found in institutions dealing with clear and recurrent problems and facing unambiguous expectations of their roles. Such organizations tend to develop a stable division of labor among subunits, accepted procedures for handling conflict among subunits, fixed information requirements, and highly programmed procedures for performing customary tasks. One may expect simplification of complex problems, the treating of issues one at a time, a generally conservative and incremental style of search and decision, and a high degree of predictability. Good examples here would be the U.S. Postal Service, the Social Security Administration, and the Internal Revenue Service. These organizations are really not very exciting, but they do keep the wheels of government turning by undertaking much of what used to be called administration.

The loosely coupled style of decision in an organized anarchy, described by Cohen, March, and Olsen (1972) and March and Olsen (1976), is very different from the orderly world just discussed. One enters a realm of ambiguous goals, unclear ways of proceeding, and transient participants. Decision and policy emerge from interactions among persistent problems, favored solutions (which tend to be retained and advocated even as problems change), participants who pick and choose among an array of occasions for involvement, and choice opportunities (times when the process is called upon to take a stand). Such organizations are termed loosely coupled precisely because of a lack of coherence among these four elements of decision. Unlike the tightly coupled model, the four streams combine in a variety of unpredictable ways. Any particular mode of integration is largely fortuitous and fleeting (see, for example, Kanter's 1975 analysis of Department of Defense budgeting and personnel decisions). Hence what appears to be a recurrent problem may at different times attract varied participants, who tend to move in packs between choice opportunities.

Loosely coupled organizations tend to address problems on the basis of their urgency. That problems are addressed does not imply that they are solved. Instead, problems are more usually "taken off the boil" through actors either jumping to a problem that provides a more receptive venue for ideas (flight) or taking minor steps that give the illusion of activity (oversight).

Both loosely coupled and tightly coupled models are more compatible with incrementalism than with rationalistic thinking. Some further implications of the two models for policy analysis are, however, strikingly different. The predictability of tight coupling lends itself to forecasting, systematic policy intervention, and structural design. A loosely coupled world is more of a crap shoot, defying modeling and prediction. "Modern technologies of reason" fare somewhat better in the tightly coupled case, where they may at least capture the behavior of the organization—if not improve it very much. Both models cast doubt upon the possibility of bold and effective policy intervention.

Decision Analysis and Behavioral Decision Theory

Our third dimension of the information-processing approach focuses on the decision capabilities and possibilities of individuals and only secondarily on those of organizations. At one end of this dimension is found decision analysis, highly optimistic about rational human judgment. At the other end is behavioral decision theory, highly sceptical about that rationality. Both allow that information is inevitably imperfect, but they diverge on the reasons for imperfection and the possibilities for coping with it.

Decision analysis is an applied outgrowth of the utility theory associated with von Neumann and Morgenstern (1947). Uncertainty is recognized but treated in terms of precise probability judgments. Further, decision makers are assumed to possess a fixed and discoverable utility function. In contrast to the traditional wisdom of economics (which recognizes only ordinal utility; apples may be preferred to oranges, but one cannot put a number on that preference), utility is treated as cardinal, amenable to interval-scale measurement. Decision analysis is a technique for assisting individuals with the choices they already make by providing explicit utilities, probability judgments, and calculation procedures. Decision-analytic man resembles economic man in rational utility maximization but differs (in a public policy context) in that utility is not purely selfish but based on some conception of the public interest. Hence decision analysis is largely inapplicable in a loosely coupled setting. The practical procedures of decision analysis are outlined in the section on practical usefulness, below.

Behavioral decision theory sees man the decision maker as having more limited capabilities. He ignores much pertinent information, treats the information he does use in odd ways, grossly oversimplifies problems and action alternatives, attends to only a few aspects of utility, and is highly selective in the lessons he learns from experience. He also gives undue weight to concrete examples in assessing probabilities of future outcomes. His most potent memories are vivid images of a few events. His information-processing capacity is highly limited; hence increased information may impair his decisions. He selects actions on the basis of analogy rather than expected utility maximization.

Behavioral decision theory proves compatible with both loosely coupled and tightly coupled conceptions of organizational choice. If its findings are accurate, then—clearly—decision analysis, and for that matter any rationalistic decision procedure, rests on a foundation of sand.

Methodological Diversity

The variety of information-processing pursuits finds further reflection in methodological commitments; indeed, just about every method known to the social and behavioral sciences is used by some practitioner. Methods range from large-scale computer modeling and information systems design to more impressionistic and informal participant observation of the kind favored by our Gloria Meander. The diversity is such that it would not be particularly helpful to list even the more prevalent methodologies.

Empirical Applications

Given that many social science methods do lend themselves to analysis with empirical content, and most of these methods may be found somewhere in the information-processing approach, substantial empirical application should come as no surprise.

Much of this empirical work is rationalistic in tone. Thus decision analysts have made recommendations on everything from airport siting (Keeney 1973) to negotiating positions for participants in international bargaining (Ulvila and Snider 1980). Deutsch (1953) has engaged in descriptive study of message transmission and communication links within and across communities. Abundant prescriptive studies of organizational design emphasize lines of communication, information channeling and filtering, and authority under varying degrees of centralization. Work on information-based activities has addressed data gathering, information processing, attention-focusing mechanisms, storage and memory systems, and retrieval processes (Tompkins 1979). Numerous procedural suggestions have been made to counter distorting organizational behavior and human predispositions. A vast literature emphasizes evaluation to provide systematic after-the-fact feedback (Berlin and Weiss 1977). A smaller but growing literature uses computer-based models to provide anticipatory feedback (Forrester 1971), or "feedforward."

There is substantial empirical work under the incremental banner, too. Incrementalists tend to seek a rich understanding of real-world organizational processes and the hectic interplay of the policy process. Incrementalist investigators have generated explanations of, and prescriptions for, both repetitive processes such as budgeting and singular events like international crises.

PRACTICAL USEFULNESS

Given the sharp differences between optimistic and pessimistic factions of information-processing practitioners over what is feasible and desirable in public policy, it is hardly surprising that the two camps differ profoundly in their work's relevance and applicability to the policy process. The two camps agree on but one point: the work of the other lacks policy relevance and applicability. Our own judgment is that both camps produce relevant and applicable work. The products differ markedly because the optimists seek to identify an ideal policy process and means for its attainment. The point of departure for pessimists is how processes really do function, which severely constrains potential reforms.

Pessimistic Applications

The pessimists are clearly limited in the prescriptions they can generate for the policy process and for individuals within it. The process is so complex, uses information so partially, and learns so little from experience that perhaps one can hope only for relatively orderly "partisan mutual adjustment" (Lindblom 1965), rather than the chaos of the garbage can.

Pessimistic analysts have far greater capacity (and proclivity) to warn against the introduction of rationalistic procedures like program budgeting, computer models, and decision analysis. Further warnings concern the validity of information produced by organizations. Instead of taking FBI crime statistics or Pentagon estimates of Soviet military strength at face value, pessimists must point out how such information is likely to be shaped by the organization's interests, often as "social vindicators" (Biderman 1966) of an agency's activities. A third kind of warning targets widely shared illusions—such as interpretations of official U.S. arms-negotiating positions in terms of considered judgment of national interest, rather than the vagaries of a loosely coupled interagency system. Finally, behavioral decision theorists highlight individual tendencies that may hurt the overall quality of choice. For example, individuals often confuse the difficulty or ease of the first step in a course of action with that of the course of action as a whole.

These warnings are clearly policy relevant. They bear directly on resource allocation decisions, on evaluations of program performance, and on how much deference should be accorded political elites and governing institutions. Yet the pessimists can offer more than warnings.

Their suggestions for useful, practical policy analysis seem to be as follows. First, the policy analyst should address only policy alternatives that have some chance of acceptance: those only marginally different, at least in their visible aspects, from the status quo. Second, the analyst should understand his or her role in partisan mutual adjustment (Gloria Meander's attitude toward Smoke Valley politics is exemplary here). The resulting policy analysis could meet ready acceptance by stakeholders, for the analyst and his or her points would be familiar and tied to existing agendas and practices.

Unfortunately, analysis of this sort has little intrinsic virtue. The pessimists, especially those stressing loose coupling and behavioral decision theory, dwell on the imperfections of the policy process. Yet they still tell us that the world will go on pretty much as it always has, grim though that may be. Moreover, one can expect little progress in the problem-solving power of the pessimistic approach. For if all cases are inherently and predominantly political, the analyst must always devote most of his or her energies to mastering the peculiarities of the case at hand. In sum, incremental analyses can help us understand events in particular instances. They fail to provide any substantial leverage on policy process or content. The Gloria Meanders of this life are destined to leave the world pretty much as they found it.

Optimistic Applications

Optimistic information-processing practitioners provide prescriptions for the policy process rather than just warnings about its flaws. Applications range from indicative economic planning as practiced in France and Japan to the development of information systems for decision makers (such as military threat assessments and intelligence estimates; see Hunter 1984).

Optimists occasionally make extensive claims about the capabilities of their particular approach. Thus Mihram (1977:27) argues that government should be treated as the cybernetic system essential to the survival of society—"the downfall of reason is viewed as imminent unless the established historical necessity for tele-cybernetics is heeded." Such grandiose claims are unwarranted by the very sporadic success rate to date. One suspects little improvement is likely in the future, as should become clear in the following discussion.

Let us begin with cybernetics. A major limitation arises because, as the field's founder put it, "For a good statistic of society, we need long runs under essentially stable conditions" (Wiener 1954: 25). Wiener's own scepticism on this score led him to doubt that cybernetics could have an "appreciable therapeutic effect on the present diseases of society" (Wiener 1954: 24). If these conditions are met, there may be little need for policy analysis. When they are not, attempts at policy intervention must fall short, in cybernetic terms.

The successes of cybernetic-based control theory (Bailey and Holt 1971) in the development of decision systems for the management of complex production processes involve stable— or at least predictably unstable—environments. So too do treatments of tightly coupled structures such as public sector budgeting processes. But in most social affairs, contextual shocks and badly behaved feedback cycles challenge cybernetic process prescriptions. An obvious public policy example is U.S. macroeconomic stabilization policy in recent years, which has often exhibited the brusque overcorrection called "hunting." Cybernated macroeconomic stabilization could fare little better under such environmental conditions.

To ameliorate contextual instability, Steinbruner (1974: 58–61) suggests dividing the organization or policy process in question into subsystems, such that each decision-making unit operates in an environment where most decisions are programmed or routine. Unfortunately, progressive routinization provides a weak defense against entropy (disorder), which cyberneticists regard as their prime enemy. The assumptions that justified the initial decomposition of organizations and tasks become reified, and their obsolescence may easily go unrecognized. These shortcomings have certainly characterized some instances of centralized national economic planning and defense planning.

Decision analysis, too, requires a stable, repetitive, and familiar context of decision. This point will become clearer as we review what practical decision analysis involves.

Decision analysis is, ideally, a "Socratic discovery" process (Keeney and Raiffa 1976: 9) in which the analyst attempts to elicit the preferences and probability assessments of the decision maker through understandable questioning. The analyst commences by structuring the decision problem, identifying choices, possible consequences, and the information required. A decision tree can then be drawn, containing decision nodes and chance nodes. Each path leading from a chance node must be assigned some probability; the end-point of each path running through the decision tree must be assigned some utility. Calculation of the best strategy is then a simple matter.

Decision analysis requires that the problem at hand be self-contained and highly structured. When problems are complex, unstructured, and the shared responsibility of many actors, the decision tree proliferates into a bushy mess. Bushy messes can be dealt with by iterative pruning—bringing the time horizon forward, eliminating noncontending options that perform badly even when probabilities are biased in their favor, and eliminating options on a largely intuitive basis as part of a "pre-analysis" (Raiffa 1968: 242–43).

In reality, public policies are rarely (if ever) made by single individuals. Decision analysis copes by treating multiple actors as a group. The analyst must hammer out a group utility function before proceeding as normal (see Edwards, Guttentag, and Snapper 1975). George Hamburger followed this procedure with the SVAQC commissioners. With profoundly conflicting values or large numbers of actors, this strategy is helpless.

By making its prescriptions the products of the views of the institutionally responsible actors, decision analysis can expect to find these recommendations accepted. Application is easiest in the case of decisions within an ideologically homogeneous bureaucracy. By pressing decision makers to be explicit about their problems, decision analysts promote transitivity and consistency. And by creating explicit chains of reasoning, they contribute to communication within the policy process.

These practical assets are accompanied by some notable limitations. The clarity provided may be unwarranted. The probabilities may be in substantial error; the utilities, pernicious or highly unstable. Indeed, behavioral research intended to improve decision analysis has uncovered a number of human tendencies to err in these respects (Tversky and Kahneman 1975).

The more optimistic, rationalistic variants of information

processing have on numerous occasions identified ways to make a policy process behave in a better (or at least different) manner. This kind of capability is progressing with the help of advances in information science and technology. But rationalistic applications are always highly vulnerable to decay. The vigor with which an approach is pursued may decline in the real world of bureaucracy and politics, where capture by groups favoring more incremental approaches is always a live possibility. Brewer and Shubik (1979) have chronicled capture of this sort in the context of computer simulations in the U.S. Department of Defense. Even decision analysis may slip into the hands of bureaucratic defenders of the status quo.

A major limit to the practical usefulness of rationalist approaches stems from the lack of sympathy they can expect from most policy process participants, who quite reasonably fear being displaced by impersonal method. Accordingly, participants tend to hedge on accepting rationalistic procedures in the very cases where the prescriptions are the least incremental, such as the SVAQC's ten-year plan. In such cases, potential usefulness works against acceptance in the policy process.

PERSPECTIVE

As far as time perspective is concerned, the more rationalistic variants of information processing—especially cybernetics and decision theory—clearly address the future. Incrementalists, in contrast, focus on the here and now. These differences in time perspective should not be exaggerated, though. Rationalist treatment of distant futures assumes substantial stability in the environment of decision. Cyberneticists are comfortable with—and often attracted to—a future that consists of a wholly different state of affairs and decision procedures, such as George Hamburger's plan for the SVAQC. But when it comes to process within that altered state, stable decomposition and routinization of tasks motivate static conceptions of policy process reforms that will be stable over time. Note that George Hamburger specified that his ten-year plan could only be adopted in its entirety.

Two types of audience are sought by information-processing practitioners. First, the appropriate audience within the policy process includes individuals and groups concerned with process questions, be it as information procedures, information consumers, policy formulators, or policy implementors. Outside the policy process, the audience is limited to people concerned with good policy process (such as the League of Women Voters). Information-processing work makes cognitive rather than emotional appeals to these outsiders, and as such may find a limited hearing.

Consider finally the normative stances of information processing and its treatment of conflicting values. The normative position of the incremental school clearly favors the status quo and the values it reflects. Value conflict can be resolved through the standard political mechanisms—partisan mutual adjustment, vagueness, and ambiguity. Incrementalists see any rejection of value pluralism as opening the door to tyranny.

While rationalistic approaches are less committed in principle to the values of the status quo, they are prone to drift toward a position similar to that of incrementalism. Rationalistic approaches can prescribe radical restructuring of decision systems, but any need for stable decomposition can obstruct subsequent change in patterns of search, judgment, choice, and implementation. Adaptation to new circumstances is left to incremental learning. Even decision analysis will depart from incrementalism only if those who apply its tools have perspectives different from policy process incumbents. Otherwise, decision analysis in practice is tightly bound to the status quo that yields its probability and utility (value) judgments.

Rationalistic approaches try to avoid incrementalism's temporizing about value conflict. To cyberneticists, organized anarchy of the kind incrementalists are prepared to accept is a threat to collective welfare. Like the rest of the universe, policy processes tend to chaos. However, there are islands of a "limited and temporary tendency for organization to increase" (Wiener 1954: 15). In these islands, progress can occur and cybernetics can battle against disorder or entropy. Control and communication, and therefore cybernetic policy analysis, fight entropy. In this light, the value commitment of cybernetics to the design of systems better able to oppose entropy is profound.

In contrast to incrementalism, rationalistic approaches do

require that normative priorities be set and value conflicts resolved. To return to the thermostat analogy of cybernetics, someone must provide the target temperature. But rationalists have trouble in setting such goals. Some suggest that it should be evaded by straining to "eliminate value calculations" and assuming some "simple and conservative . . . motive force" (Steinbruner 1974: 64–65). This strategy can leave us with analyses essentially similar to those of incrementalists. Decision analysis might seem to go to the opposite extreme by recognizing the existence of multiple and conflicting objectives. Yet decision analysis regards these values in simplistic fashion by treating them as items to be placed in the stable utility function of some individual or group, rather than as the focus of persistent bargaining and modification.

Ultimately, all rationalistic approaches must delegate the choice and weighting of values to some identifiable group external to the analysis. This is obviously true of decision analysis. It is less obviously true for cybernetics, but even here someone has to be the arbiter of performance criteria and hence feedback content. The rationalist schools are silent on who should undertake this crucial task. Hence there is no internal barrier against their techniques being used to increase the effectiveness of the policy process in carrying out abhorrent purposes, such as political repression, genocide, or nuclear destruction. As Weiner (1948:38) recognized long ago, there are major risks involved in entrusting tools of improved information and control to the "world of Belsen and Hiroshima."

Chapter 6

Political Philosophy

POLITICAL PHILOSOPHY IN SMOKE VALLEY

SHORTLY AFTER the establishment of the SVAQC, a less-publicized institutional innovation occurs in the valley. Smoketown University is the site chosen for a new Institute for Philosophy and Policy. The incoming director of this interdisciplinary institute, Justin Reitz, decides that an appropriate first project would involve a prominent local policy issue. Such a focus could help establish the institute's "applied" credentials, not to mention gaining local financial support. The air pollution issue is prominent, controversial, and apparently amenable to philosophical discourse. Professor Reitz sets about recruiting participants for a weekly seminar on air pollution from his own (small) staff, the departments of philosophy and political science at local universities, and Smoke Valley University Law School.

Reitz regards this project as an open-ended venture. He expects no final report or consensus on policy conclusions. However, he does believe that philosophical analysis can inform policy determination, and so extends invitations to Gloria Meander, George Hamburger, and the SVAQC commissioners. Meander sends a message of support and promises to attend the first meeting (while secretly expecting nothing useful from any such exercise in academic speculation). Hamburger declines the invitation on the grounds that the goals of the antipollution policy are already settled, so the choice of means is a technical rather than philosophical matter. The commissioners send their thanks and regrets that busy schedules do not permit their attendance.

At the seminar's first session, Reitz receives unanimous congratulation for the establishment of the institute. Meander gives a ten-minute presentation on the state of policy making on the air pollution issue. She makes an early exit as the participants begin to debate the purposes and format of the seminar. After several hours' discussion, it is agreed that the group will meet every two weeks and that each session will feature a presentation by one or more speakers.

The first such presentation is made by Reitz himself, who surveys and scrutinizes the policy analyses to date that have addressed the Smoketown air pollution problem. He is unsurprised to find these analyses either evade moral judgment or surreptitiously enter questionable normative judgments. Reitz berates the Uteil Report for its reliance on the crude preference utilitarianism of welfare economics: the idea that public policy should seek to maximize consumer preferences as revealed in market-related transactions. This point hardly needs laboring, for all the philosophers in the audience are aware of the discrediting of preference utilitarianism over the past few decades. The various public choice analyses commit similar utilitarian sins, and hence merit similar condemnation. The only saving grace of public choice is its sporadic recognition of the principles of justice that may be derived from individualistic utilitarian premises, though Reitz notes that this dimension is not in fact reflected in any of the school's policy analyses. Smoketown sociologists receive grudging approval for their introduction of distributive questions, but clearly they have no way of determining whether one distribution is better than another. Hamburger is criticized for his total inattention to the moral standing of the success criteria his team is developing, and Gloria Meander is gently disparaged for her commitment to the political status quo and concomitant neglect of the ends of policy. Above all, it seems that none of these analysts has paid any attention to the intrinsic rightness or wrongness of actual and proposed policies. All focus only on policy consequences and as such are inconsistent with the way many philosophers are beginning to think about public policy.

Reitz's presentation is well received by his colleagues, who agree it opens a rich agenda for applied philosophical discussion. The next presenter furthers this agenda in the context of the welfare economists' argument for a system of standards and charges. Professor Essen allows that such a system offers a cost-effective mechanism for pollution reduction but argues that if pollution is intrinsically immoral, then society should strive to stigmatize polluters. A charges regime implies pollution is ethically acceptable, provided the polluter pays for his actions. Essen would prefer a system that forces polluters to acknowledge the immorality of their acts and that obligates them to maximal reasonable abatement effort—irrespective of the consequences of such a system for pollution levels. He notes further that this kind of policy is consistent with the moral intuitions of environmentalists, citing Kelman's (1981) account of why environmentalists are lukewarm to charges systems. A member of the audience points out that Essen has yet to demonstrate the intrinsic immorality of pollution. Essen replies that if the results of a large number of people engaging in an action are bad, then no one should undertake that action; moreover, everyone is obligated to prevent that action by others. He supports this contention through drawing analogies with several real and hypothetical cases unrelated to air pollution, ranging from the responsibility of concentration camp guards in Nazi Germany to the behavior we expect of individuals in a cinema audience. Another participant notes that one might also condemn pollution through reference to the basic ethical principle that we all have a special duty to those who are vulnerable to our actions.

The next session of the seminar takes the form of a debate between a critic and a supporter of Professor Essen. The critic argues that public institutions and policies can be justified only through reference to the protection and promotion of the basic human rights of unique and separate individuals. One of the foremost such rights is that to unrestricted use of private property. No matter the benefit to society, interference with this right is unjustifiable, for one's gain cannot compensate another's pain. Pollution control violates private property—for example, by forbidding a homeowner to light his wood-burning stove—and hence has no rightful place in public policy.

Professor Essen's supporter argues that the critic errs in failing to recognize that human health is a right too, basic in the sense that its establishment is a necessary precondition to the enjoyment of many other rights and pursuits. Pollution threatens human health, therefore pollution should be restricted; though by how much, the supporter cannot say. Nor can she determine the degree to which the right to health should be traded off against property rights, nor can she derive any precise policy measures.

Two weeks later the discussion is joined by Ivy Sagebrush, who contends that previous sessions have focused too narrowly on the rights of individuals in the present. First, Sagebrush argues that natural systems such as the ecology of the Smoke Valley region have rights too and hence merit public policy to protect them against pollution damage. While philosophers have traditionally been willing to assign rights only to individual people, Sagebrush notes the historical expansion of the population deemed worthy of moral and legal rights. At various points serfs, women, blacks, and children have been the beneficiaries; so why not animals, plants, and ecosystems, too? The implication is that controls beyond those necessary to protect human health may be required. Sagebrush's second point is that policy should attend to the rights of future generations as well as the present one. An elaborate justification of this stance fails to yield too much in the way of policy implications, beyond the principle that this generation should leave the earth—and perhaps Smoke Valley—no more (irreversibly) polluted than it found it.

The penultimate seminar in the series is conducted by one Felicity Goodenough, who questions the focus of previous discussions on the intrinsic rightness and wrongness of acts to the exclusion of the consequences of actions. Goodenough suggests this emphasis would be laughable to most participants in the policy process. While she agrees that the expected utility maximization principle adopted by welfare economics and public choice is dubious, she avers that much more can be said about consequences. For example, public policy could be designed to maximize sustainable net benefits, or to keep open potentially attractive options, or to maximize the minimum expected benefit from alternative policies. When pressed, she argues that these principles all have implications for environmental policy, some of which are more easily traced than others. So the "maximin" strategy rules out risky, untested policies, but the sustainability principle has few implications for Smoke Valley air pollution policy (though it does have clear implications for long-lived pollutants or global climatic change). Pragmatically, Goodenough points out that her focus on consequences might be one way of overcoming the inconclusiveness of arguments based on rights. Conflicting rights produce moral paralysis; consideration of consequences could act as a tie breaker.

The seminar series draws to a close with a round table discussion on political institutions for pollution control. Debate is joined between those who argue that policy content as it affects human rights, utilities, and the integrity of natural systems is all that matters and those who also stress the value of participatory, democratic policy making in both securing legitimacy for policy outcomes and stimulating the moral development of citizen participants. The philosophers who emphasize participatory values are highly critical of both the bureaucratic SVAQC and the elected Smoke Valley Authority proposed by the public choice group.

Justin Reitz is thoroughly pleased with his creation. While the seminar produces no normative consensus, still less precise policy proposals, it has demonstrated the moral dimension of policy, which is the institute's raison d'etre. He believes that further endeavors along such lines could contribute to the ethical consciousness of society and hence ultimately might produce better public policy. He asks the seminar contributors to polish their presentations for inclusion in a book he will edit. The book is eventually published by Smoketown University Press and proves a good advertisement for the institute.

POLITICAL PHILOSOPHY AND PUBLIC POLICY

Political philosophy is both a subfield of political science and an interdisciplinary endeavor reaching into philosophy and law, with offshoots in economics and sociology. Our focus here is on the interdisciplinary dimension, which is where most policy-related work may be located. By way of establishing boundaries around a somewhat amorphous field, our discussion excludes the preference utilitarianism of welfare economics, the contractarian side of public choice, and the epistemological aspect of political theory—all of which are covered elsewhere in this book. We also pay no attention to the pretwentieth century work of the classical political theorists, on the grounds that if contemporary political philosophers are doing their jobs properly then they should be reflecting the best that the classics have to offer. The field thus bounded can address moral aspects of both the process and content of policy. Though pronounced dead in the 1950s (Laslett 1956), political philosophy has since experienced a remarkable rebirth and has extended its concern to matters of public policy. Expressing this renewed confidence and policy emphasis, Brandon (1984) suggests that public policy analysis is nothing other than "the continuation of moral philosophy by other means."

Practitioners of this tradition are mostly grouped into two camps. Utilitarians such as our Felicity Goodenough focus on the consequences of actions such as public policies and on arrangements such as policy-making institutions. Kantians, like the majority of our Smoketown philosophers, address the intrinsic moral standing of actions and arrangements. As with information processing, this internal diversity complicates summary assessment of the approach.

Practical policy applications to date have tended to focus rather narrowly on traditional issues of moral responsibility such as abortion, euthanasia, racial discrimination, and war, which are obviously amenable to ethical analysis. But a more recent broadening of focus is apparent. Ventures into nuclear power, environmental preservation, the welfare state, food policy, and foreign policy on human rights are indicative of the possibilities. Some areas—for example, urban policy, budgetary resource allocation, and macroeconomic stabilization—still seem to remain off limits.

GIVENS

In keeping with its classical liberal roots, political philosophy accords the individual a central place in its hard core. Individuals, and individuals alone, merit moral consideration (directed toward their interests, their dignity, or their rights) and are called upon to account for their actions and omissions. Thus man is seen as a (potentially) moral being, who also has various needs—about which there is little consensus. Even attempts to extend moral consideration beyond human beings can remain individualistic. Thus Stone (1972) argues that we should care about the natural environment by according rights (in the spirit of individual human rights) to chunks of it, such as mountains and trees.[1]

In analyses of policy content, government is treated in the image of the individual, as a moral judge presumably capable of hearing and understanding different ethical arguments on an issue. Analyses of policy process take a more subtle approach to the structure of government, treating it as a fit target for adjustment to suit various human ends (such as participation, political education, or rights protection).[2]

Moral individualism is set aside only in attempts to articulate a holistic environmental ethic, to which Smoketown's Ivy Sagebrush subscribes. This kind of ethic treats man and nature as parts of a valuable integral whole. Ecosystems and their related human systems are accorded moral worth. An environmental ethic is limited in its issue-area coverage to questions of policy for natural resources, energy, and the environment. Policies inspired by this ethic would attend to values at the system level and be sensitive to the hazards of piecemeal intervention.

Political philosophers make no explicit assumptions about the capabilities of the policy process. But in addressing questions of policy content they imply (or implore) a government acting as a moral judge. Failing such unitary action, individual public officials must be willing and able to exercise moral judgment within the policy process. At a minimum, participants must be open to philosophical pleas. Philosophers who

---

1. Stone's argument was accepted by U.S. Supreme Court Justice William O. Douglas. For a more sceptical view, see Ackerman, Rose-Ackerman, Sawyer, and Henderson 1974: 139–40.

2. Though political philosophy shares the moral individualism of welfare economics and public choice, it does not share their methodological individualism. The latter applies only to explanations of individual and collective behavior. Political philosophy does not develop explanations of empirical phenomena—except in terms of agents' applications of moral principle.

address the proper institutions and processes of governance assume much more: the possibility of metapolicy.

How plausible is this set of assumptions? This question has no conclusive answer, for it is tantamount to the eternal question concerning the essence of human nature. The human condition is both moral and venal, principled and opportunistic. Political philosophy attends only to the virtuous aspect of character, ignoring less savory possibilities of the sort that might interest economists and information processors.

CONTENTS

Theoretical themes in political philosophy are usefully grouped into utilitarian and Kantian categories, as we have already noted. The utilitarian heritage reaches back to the late eighteenth century and Jeremy Bentham's suggestion that public affairs be conducted in pursuit of "the greatest good for the greatest number." Classical utilitarianism's felicific calculus of pleasure and pain finds contemporary reflection in welfare economics, which attends to revealed preferences rather than felt pleasures and pains. Few philosophers still take the hedonism of unreconstructed utilitarianism seriously, mainly due to the difficulty of interpersonal comparison of utility. Given that virtually all public policies produce some winners and some losers, this inability to compare pychological states across individuals paralyzes the utilitarian calculus. Circumvention of this difficulty through conversion of utility into money satisfies only economists, and not philosophers.

However, utilitarianism does possess some more respectable variants, which require only that some aspects of utility be comparable across persons. So "negative utilitarianism" argues that pains are largely common and comparable across individuals, even if pleasures are not. Thus public policy should minimize suffering rather than promote happiness (see Acton 1963). Practically, this tack leads to remedial policy for agreed-upon ills such as poverty, disease, and violent crime, and away from pursuit of grand designs.

Similarly, Georgescu-Roegen (1954) argues that there is a common hierarchy of needs in individual utility functions, such as food, shelter, and clothing. Once these are satisfied further desires are released. Such a hierarchy would justify redistributive public policy, such as taxation and transfer payment, or in-kind benefits.

Harsanyi (1955) prefers to work with the "ethical" or "impersonal" preferences of individuals: the values about society individuals would hold if they were ignorant of their social position. Empirically, it is hard to identify such preferences, but the analyst can appeal to them in justifying policies and institutions. Harsanyi's argument suggests an egalitarian distribution, and hence redistributive policy, without specifying exactly how much redistribution should occur.

Finally, individual preferences may be censored before being admitted to the utilitarian calculus. So preferences that conflict with the principle of human dignity, which is arguably central to the liberal individualism underlying utilitarianism, can be excluded (Goodin 1982: 73–94). Thus preferences for racial or sexist discrimination and exploitation might be disallowed. Dworkin (1977) suggests governmental action such as reverse discrimination to protect minorities against the invidious "external preferences" of majorities.

These modifications of utilitarianism notwithstanding, most contemporary political philosophers prefer to work in the Kantian tradition, which judges actions by their intrinsic qualities. In practice, this tradition boils down to commending protection, promotion, respect for, and facilitation of action upon the moral rights of individuals. Thus, as Hart (1979) puts it, moral philosophy is today suspended "between utility and rights." There is little consensus on the nature of these rights. Hart suggests there are two basic kinds of moral rights, based respectively on the separateness of unique individuals and the "equality of concern and respect" that is everyone's due.

The best-known analysis based on separateness is that of Nozick (1974), to whom the thorough incommensurability of individuals suggests that nothing should be taken from anyone, regardless of the benefits of so doing. The implication is libertarian: individuals have absolute rights to their persons and property, and the only legitimate functions of government are preservation of order and protection of rights. Public policy should exist only to dismantle the excessive apparatus of government. Professor Essen's critic would concur.

A slightly different set of basic rights can generate radically different conclusions and far greater obligations toward other individuals. For example, if basic human rights cover a minimum of food, shelter, and education, as well as property, one could argue for a full-fledged welfare state (Grey 1976).

The most famous analysis rooted in "equality of concern and respect" is that of Rawls (1971). Rawls' first principle of justice is that "each person is to have an equal right to the most extensive total system of basic liberties compatible with a similar system of liberty for all" (Rawls 1971: 302). These rights are a product of consent of rational individuals behind a "veil of ignorance" hiding knowledge of their actual standing in society. Rawls argues in similar manner for a second principle: any social inequalities are to be "to the greatest expected benefit of the least advantaged" and subject to "conditions of fair opportunity." The policy implications of this second principle are murky. They seem egalitarian and redistributive: the least advantaged are always the first concern. On the other hand, the second principle could justify "trickle-down," free-market capitalism. Rawls himself reaches no concrete judgments here.

In the context of our Smoke Valley example, the second principle could be adduced in arguments both for and against pollution control. One might justify control on the grounds that it is the least advantaged (in terms of income) who suffer most from pollution by virtue of their residence in inner-city areas close to polluting industry. On the other hand, low-income workers (though not necessarily the lowest-income welfare recipients) would be hurt most by any production cutbacks, reduced earnings, or plant closings resulting from effective pollution abatement. In practice, one might try to overcome this ambiguity by making sure that the relatively rich finance pollution control (though it is unclear how this could be accomplished).

At first glance, political philosophy might seem to lack methodological commitments beyond an affinity for argument. But this predilection itself points to several methodological principles. The most widely shared is criticism: philosophers spend much of their time picking one another's arguments apart. Criticism is, of course, possible both within and between our other frames, too, but work in these frames can proceed without criticism. Political philosophy is special in that its practitioners see progress in terms of the erection of better arguments on the foundations of worse ones; thus criticism is essential to progress. Like our Professor Reitz, philosophers can also dissect the moral premises of public policy and the more technical policy analysis.

On the constructive side of argument, philosophers can reason by deduction, induction, or analogy. Particular pieces of analysis can combine these methods in varying proportion.

Deductive moral argument is simply the application of general principles to specific cases. Thus our supporter of Professor Essen argues that if human health is a basic moral right, then pollution is immoral. General principles might include treat like cases alike; protect those vulnerable to your actions; maximize utility; and the golden rule, treat others as you would wish them to treat you.

An inductive moral methodology is sketched by Rawls (1951). Rawls begins by defining a "competent moral judge," an individual of intelligence, knowledge, reason, sympathy with the interests of others, and impartiality. One should then examine the conclusions such a judge reaches in an actual case. The judgments of similar competent persons in essentially identical cases (in different times and places) constitute a data set from which general moral principles can be inferred. Any principle thus generated can be verified by presenting it to the judges in question for further consideration. In practice, Rawls himself uses the intuitions of hypothetical rather than real people as his data points, especially in his later construction of a theory of justice.

Induction can, however, proceed through reference to the intuitions of real people faced with real dilemmas. One of the best examples of moral reasoning in this genre is Walzer's (1977) exploration of the ethics of armed conflict. Walzer undertakes a monumental historical survey in search of universal moral principles for the conduct of war. He finds such universal standards do indeed exist, as historical figures and ordinary soldiers alike attempt to account for their actions. Even violation of these principles is informative, for it requires special justification. Hypocrisy too can be instructive: the elaborate procedures adopted by the Nazis to disguise and deny the Holocaust shows that they knew the immorality of their actions. Walzer's inductive analysis yields several universals: do not harm civilians intentionally, treat prisoners with respect, invade a country only when you are threatened by it (or another party has already invaded), and so forth.

Moral reasoning by analogy begins with a complex real-world case for which guidance is sought. One then turns to a hypothetical case supposedly similar in key respects, determines what should be done in this hypothetical case, and argues for an analogous action in the real-world case. For example, abortion has been likened to removing a parasite and killing a human being, and its prohibition to letting a group of music lovers kidnap a person to force him to give blood to a musician near death (Thompson 1971). The proper action in the hypothetical case is obvious and uncontroversial (otherwise there would be no point in introducing it). The trouble is that the real-world case may not resemble the hypothetical one in enough key aspects to enable persuasive policy implications to be drawn (see Goodin 1982: 8–12).

Empirical content was for long absent in political philosophy's applications to public policy. But this absence was always a matter of choice rather than necessity; philosophers tended to select cases on the basis of how well they supported an argument, rather than on their social importance. Political philosophy's applied turn in recent years has been accompanied by increasing empirical content in the form of examples, illustrations, and applications, if not systematic data collection. Inconvenient empirical evidence can be simply ignored in any piece of analysis—though such evidence will often be picked up by a critic. Empirical content remains minimal in some of the more fanciful arguments by analogy, appearing only in the introduction of an issue and in the implications drawn.

PRACTICAL USEFULNESS

Political philosophers can make arguments that are both relevant to and applicable in public policy. Applicability can range from broad principles for action to specific policy instructions. Broad principles such as our Professor Essen's injunction against air pollution are most common. A more involved and interesting real-world example is Walzer's (1983) defense of "complex equality" in society. Walzer contends that distributive justice should be pursued only within spheres (the education sphere, the workplace, the marketplace, the community); pursuit across spheres leads to repression and tyranny, and hence cannot be justified. Public policy should respect the autonomy of different spheres.

Detailed prescriptions for policy are comparatively rare and are generally found only in the classic conscience issues. So a philosophical argument can determine that abortion is wrong or that euthanasia is acceptable. Assuming that fine moral lines can be drawn (e.g., should we make exceptions to a prohibition of abortion in cases of rape and incest?) and that policy makers find the case persuasive, such arguments are sufficient in themselves to determine public policy. The decisiveness of the ethical mode of argument on such issues does much to explain their continued popularity among moral philosophers.

The comparative rarity of such conscience issues in public policy highlights the limited applicability of political philosophy. Most obviously, philosophers are not good at filling in any technical details required in a policy. For example, just how shall we control pollution? Through what mechanism should the policy be implemented?

A further limit exists inasmuch as philosophical arguments are insensitive to political reality. Policy-making processes are populated by the self-interested and the bureaucratically programmed as well as the high minded. Moreover, these individuals work under funding constraints and under the constraints of commitments made in past and concurrent choices on related issues. Political philosophers prefer clean cases in isolated boxes. This preference can lead them to attack contrived problems and ignore messy real-world ones: complex issues linkages in the real world can muddy moral conclusions. For example, one could imagine a SVAQC guided by moral prohibitions against pollution. Equally, a Smoke Valley Industrial Reconstruction Commission might be informed by the principle that basic needs for valley residents must be secured. Satisfaction of these needs might be promoted through job provision—but if more jobs means more pollution, what is the philosopher to make of it?

This kind of linkage can bring moral principles into conflict, but such conflict can also occur within the bounds of a single clean case. The arguments over the rights and wrongs of abortion over the years suggest no closure is likely on this issue.

Despite these limitations, political philosophy has clearly been progressing in its problem-solving capabilities in recent years. In part, this progress is a function of the shot in the arm to a seemingly moribund field provided by Rawls (1971). Rawls' own analysis has since been extended and applied (not to mention criticized) in a variety of ways. For example, Rawls himself paid no special attention to the intertemporal dimension of justice. But if we extend the veil of ignorance to cover an individual's knowledge of the generation in which he will be born, then principles of intertemporal justice can be generated. One such principle might be that each generation should leave its successors an endowment of nonrenewable resources equal to the one it started with (Routley and Routley 1978).

Perhaps more important than the Rawlsian revival is the simple fact that philosophers have decided that public policy is worthy of their attention. As relative newcomers to policy analysis, it is hardly surprising their contribution is progressing. This increased supply of philosophical policy analysis has yet to be matched by a corresponding explosion in demand. But the avenues of influence may be indirect; for example, Nozick's (1974) arguments for a minimal state have been taken up and popularized by the U.S. Libertarian Party.

PERSPECTIVE

In its time perspective, political philosophy can look to both past and future. Retrospective analysis can praise or condemn actions and omissions (such as the bombing of Hiroshima). Prospective analysis can prescribe actions (for example, abandonment of nuclear technology). Arguments tend to have a static, once-and-for-all air. This static quality might not be too worrying if feedback from an unfolding future concerns only empirical rather than moral matters. Yet if the moral intuitions of political actors are data points for philosophical analysis, as in inductive moral methodology, then the omission may be more serious. One could overcome this difficulty by repeating philosophical analyses at intervals. So the elements of an environmental ethic might appear different before, during, and after an energy crisis.

The audience for political philosophy consists of anyone prepared to spare more than a thought to the moral dimension of policy. Given the depth and nuance of particular pieces of analysis, and the likelihood of counterargument, serious attention is time consuming. Policy practitioners often have short attention spans. Hence much of the time the audience will be restricted to fellow philosophers.

Political philosophy does have an additional point of entry into policy debate through its affinity with legal argument. The language of the legal system, like the language of many moral philosophers, is one of rights. Legal rights often differ from moral rights, but connections can be drawn. So law schools contain legal-political philosophers, and law journals publish articles in this tradition. A polity such as the United States, where lawyers and the courts play a major role in policy determination, is therefore more likely to be sympathetic to political philosophy than systems where the law plays a lesser role.

The approach has no uniform normative stance beyond a widely shared, vague commitment to liberal tradition. One finds substantial variety even among practitioners paying homage to liberalism. All pieces of political philosophy have a clear normative position, but unlike our other approaches, this position is explicit and argued toward, rather than implicit and assumed.

Conflicting values are multiplied rather than reduced by political philosophy, which can make us aware of latent or unsuspected normative dimensions of an issue. However, the approach does not leave us with a hopeless plurality of ethical positions. Such positions can be compared in the context of specific issues—perhaps through full elaboration of the consequences of each principle (see, e.g., Dryzek 1983a: 124–33). Comparisons might even be made in the abstract. For example,

Dworkin (1977) suggests certain rights should "trump" majoritarian (utilitarian) arguments on the grounds that rights have no meaning at all if a majority can legitimately impose its will on a minority. Shue (1980) contends that certain subsistence rights are "basic," and hence more important than other rights to which they are preconditions. Unfortunately, such priority arguments find no shortage of philosophers ready and able to muster rebuttals. Of all our approaches, political philosophy has the deepest internal divisions. Uniquely among practitioners of all these frames, most political philosophers would actually applaud continued division. Philosophical discourse would be impoverished without critics and targets.

CONCLUSION

Political philosophy is valuable in forcing systematic and sophisticated scrutiny of the normative dimensions of public policy. Many policy issues reduce to disputes at the philosophical level. Thus the approach can correct the blind spots of some of the frames addressed in previous chapters. But public policy consists of technical questions in the choice of means, under constraints of political feasibility, not just moral judgment. Hence political philosophy is insufficient by itself as an approach to policy analysis. Philosophers with policy interests might be the first to accept this conclusion.

Part Three

Knowledge Orientations

Chapter 7

From Technical Frames to Theories of Knowledge

Our dissections of frames of reference and recurrent visits to Smoke Valley have made it abundantly clear that the policy field covers a diverse collection of enterprises. That variety calls for procedures for making choices among approaches through comparing their capabilities—or, at a minimum, a rationale for shunning comparison and for coping with the medley of enterprises in some other manner. Hence we need to determine if and when any of the approaches discussed in part 2 merit widespread application. If, as we will suggest, a variety of tools survives this weeding-out process, it becomes that much more important to develop principles to assist the policy analyst to pick the right tool for a particular job.

There is no shortage of sweeping judgment in the literature designed to convince the reader to accept or reject a particular approach. Welfare economics, public choice, and cybernetics all have adherents who believe their favored approach is the only legitimate form of policy analysis. On the other side of the coin, welfare economics, public choice, and both incremental and synoptic information processing have critics who think the approach in question should have been buried long ago.

Some once-and-for-all judgments do indeed follow from our comparisons. Such judgments are perhaps most easily (if not most defensibly) made in terms of the policy analyst's likely career rewards. Fledgling policy analysts who wish to advance in a clearly structured intellectual community would do well to adhere to approaches with a highly technical flavor—welfare economics, public choice, and optimistic information processing. Those who would like to be lifted on a rising tide of technical acclaim would be well advised to select from within that set approaches with progressing problem-solving capabilities—public choice and optimistic information processing. Practitioners of progressive approaches are more likely than followers of more stagnant frames to have social science honors heaped upon them. If analysts have ambitions as political operators, they may find pessimistic information processing useful.

While we do not commend career ambition as the primary determinant of one's choice of approach, our own judgments about the relative merits of the various technical approaches and subapproaches are less than fully conclusive. This lack of any clear and general ordering of approaches is in large measure a necessary consequence of our application of multiple criteria (the set developed in chapter 1). Thus welfare economics performs well on the policy applicability criterion, but its problem-solving adequacy and progressiveness are questionable, and its assumptions (including those it makes about the capabilities of the policy process) are shaky. Public choice is applicable and progressive, but only moderately adequate, highly demanding in its requirements for a metapolicy process, and somewhat unrealistic in its assumptions. Social structure is marginally adequate and hardly progressive or applicable (at least in most of its variants), but its assumptions can be realistic, and its group strand does not make excessive demands upon the capabilities of the policy process. Optimistic information processing is applicable, sometimes realistic in its assumptions, occasionally adequate, and even (in one sense) progressive, but it generally demands too much of the capabilities of the policy process. Pessimistic information processing scores high on realism but not on applicability, adequacy, or progressiveness.

Clearly, different criteria produce different rankings among our technical approaches. The picture is clouded further inasmuch as many of our judgments have an "it all depends" air. For example, we noted in chapter 5 that the progressiveness of optimistic information processing represents clear advances only in information management technology, not in actual or potential social problem solving. Public choice we find "applicable" only to certain kinds of policy issues.

Worse still for those who seek simple truths and clear rankings, some of the approaches we have discussed (especially information processing and social structure) are so divided and amorphous that unqualified, simple summary judgments are not readily made. Cybernetics is not assessed quite the same as decision analysis, and Marxist social structural analysis warrants a somewhat different assessment than its more reformist cousins.

One way to make sense of the frames of reference in the policy field is through critical scrutiny in terms of theories about the generation and social uses of knowledge. As we saw in chapter 1, such theories can contain clear notions of what knowledge-based interventions in social problems should involve. Hence they may give us a way of making strong comparative judgments about the relative desirability of our various frames of reference. In the following chapters we discuss the major contemporary schools of philosophy of science, with special reference to what they make of the multiple frames of policy analysis. But before we can accept their judgments, we must also determine the extent to which each school offers a persuasive and defensible conception of the field's enterprise. Hence each chapter contains a critique of an epistemological school of thought, as well as a description of the school and an account of its attitude towards the frames of reference introduced up to now.

Chapter 8

Positivism

POSITIVIST POLICY ANALYSIS

*T*HE "HARD" sciences have had many social scientists in their thrall for some time now. Advocates of imitation by the social sciences of the theory-practice relationship alleged to characterize natural science include many social scientists influential in the teaching and practice of policy analysis. The hard sciences, it is argued, are successful because they are, well, scientific. Social science should follow suit through inquiry that proceeds from assumptions through deductive theory to the construction and empirical test of hypotheses, establishing verified causal explanations and general laws. The epistemological school of thought holding this view of science is termed *positivism*.

The appeal of the positivist argument is rooted in three factors. First, the ability of natural science to explain complex natural phenomena continues to impress. Second, applied natural science and engineering have yielded many practical benefits. Third, natural scientists and engineers have often been called upon to provide expert input to policy decisions. For example, nuclear engineers inform the development of nuclear safety regulations, medical scientists contribute to health care policy, and meteorologists receive a respectful hearing on acid rain. Many policy analysts would like to be treated with equal respect.

Positivist policy analysts believe we could emulate the results and respect of science and technology by relating basic research to policy applications in the way they think basic natural science relates to applied science and engineering. So just as scientists and engineers intervene in the natural world based on an understanding of the causal laws governing that world, policy analysts should intervene in the social world based on an understanding of the causal laws of society. The first step in positivist policy analysis is to establish these laws as they pertain to valued social outcomes.

We should stress that the positivist counsel for policy analysis is one of emulating natural science, not adopting it as a means for shaping public policy. The idea that natural science can be decisive in determining public policy is seductive. This idea has even managed to dominate a policy issue area from time to time—for example, in the first two decades of nuclear energy. But the more recent history of nuclear power highlights the importance of economic cost, perceived risk, social values, bureaucratic politics, and human behavior more generally, in even seemingly technical issue areas. Natural science is silent on such questions; as one of the leading proponents of a new technocratic age recognizes, many of the most fundamental policy questions about science and technology are ultimately "transcientific" in character (Weinberg 1972). Appealing to the experts is no help, because the experts disagree—even on scientific questions, let alone transcientific ones (see Douglas and Wildavsky 1982: 49–66; Margolis 1973). Natural science speaks with many voices on the benefits and dangers of biotechnology, the feasibility and cost of "star wars" defense technology, and health risks from pollution. Indeed, the inadequacies of hard science lead some natural scientists to turn to social science for answers to troubling problems. Hardin's (1968) account of "the tragedy of the commons" is a classic example of a perplexed natural scientist seeking social science answers to problems with no technical solutions.

Natural science will not, then, suffice in itself as an orientation to policy analysis. We will pay it no further attention, except as a model for emulation by policy analysis. Our exclusion does not gainsay the legitimate contributions of natural science to public policy—for example, concerning the safety and benefits of a proposed food additive or the technical efficacy of a proposed means for disposing of nuclear wastes.[1] We

---

1. A good collection on the uses and abuses of natural science in public policy processes is found in Crandall and Lave (1981).

simply note that, unlike the theories of knowledge discussed in the remainder of part 3 of this study, natural science cannot constitute a comprehensive orientation to the policy field.

In keeping with our focus on the social science of policy analysis, we shall not address the question of whether positivism really is a good account of successful natural science practice. In fact, positivism has received substantial punishment at the hands of contemporary philosophers and historians of science. This punishment is no concern of ours; we address positivism only as a program for policy analysis.

Beyond their shared advocacy of policy based on causal laws, positivists can disagree somewhat on how to proceed. For example, positivist political scientists (sometimes called behavioralists) often suggest that research topics should be selected for their scientific tractability, or amenability to statistical analysis and mathematical modeling. Thus political scientists devote time and energy to study of the determinants of voting behavior out of all proportion to its social or policy importance. Any practical benefits would then be purely fortuitous.[2]

An alternative positivist position gives greater weight to social problems in determining the agenda of inquiry. In political science, this strain is known as postbehavioralism. Thus scientific methods should be used in the context of the need to explain and resolve social problems, be they severe and recurrent strains in social systems amenable to the generation of cumulative knowledge or items on the political agenda of the day.[3]

Policy analysis as hard science would adopt the second of these two versions of positivism. The role of the policy analyst is to establish a body of (cumulative) empirically verified theory about the social situation in question, which can then be drawn upon to inform policy actions. Positivist policy

2. Practical benefits of the natural sciences are often fortuitous, too; Laudan (1977: 218–19) argues that most discoveries in the natural sciences have absolutely no practical import.

3. Eulau (1977) suggests that Lasswell (1951) is the foremost exponent of this "interventionist synthesis." For very different interpretations of the Lasswellian approach to policy sciences and its implications, see chapter 11 and also Brewer and deLeon (1983) and Brunner (1984: 3–5).

analysis looks to the past for empirical verification of causal propositions and to a future of policy actions informed by such propositions. Thus policy analysis in this image has both prospective and retrospective aspects.

Interventions should, then, be based on a knowledge of causality. Logically, a successful policy intervention demands two verified causal theories. First one needs to know the causal determinants $(x_1 \ldots x_n)$ of a set of valued outcomes $(y_1 \ldots y_n)$. For example, if one is dealing with poverty and social welfare, the y variable might refer to family income, nutritional level, and quality of living conditions. The x variables might include educational achievement level, employment, ethnicity, age, and attitudes. A knowledge of the $(x_1 \ldots x_n)$ determinants of $(y_1 \ldots y_n)$ is not sufficient to direct policy choice, though. One also needs a causal theory of intervention—a theory of the effects on $(x_1 \ldots x_n)$ of a set of manipulable policy variables $(p_1 \ldots p_n)$. Policy variables in the poverty and social welfare example might include compensatory education programs, labor retraining schemes, or welfare payment systems. The two causal theories in combination can then tell the policy maker how the p variables should be adjusted to achieve any desired change in the y conditions.

Along these lines, a great deal of policy analysis seeks knowledge of the effects of p variables on y variables after the policy has been carried out. These "impact evaluation" studies seek causal explanation following significant policy action, rather than prior to action (see, e.g., Nachmias 1980). So, for example, Doron (1979) finds that government restrictions on tobacco advertising have done nothing to reduce smoking, while they have secured the competitive position of the major tobacco companies. Similarly, Peltzman (1975) finds that automobile safety regulations have not affected traffic death rates. Such studies have policy implications—both Doron and Peltzman counsel deregulation. But these studies do not verify any theory of intervention in the way positivism requires (i.e., prior to the intervention itself). They are more consistent with the approach to public policy outlined in the next chapter, inasmuch as they have tested a theory of intervention after the fact.

In the light of these specifications for policy analysis, what would positivists have to say about the plurality of frames we identified and discussed in part 2?

THE SCIENTIFIC STANDING OF FRAMES

To begin with, the very multiplicity of frames extant in the policy field (and social sciences more generally) might make some positivists uneasy, especially those whose ideal is an integrated, unified body of theory and causal propositions. Even those with lesser ambitions would be troubled by the suggestion that each social problem has no unique theory applicable to it—only multiple theories that can be applied. Such reservations notwithstanding, clearly some of our frames approximate positivist specifications more than others.

Public choice is perhaps closest. Public choice reasons deductively from simple premises about human behavior. Empirical testing of the results of deduction is possible through examination of the consequences of different kinds of institutional arrangements. Practical policy advice could be based on the resulting body of tested propositions about the qualities of institutional forms.

Welfare economics too would meet with positivist approval inasmuch as it is rooted in microeconomics, the most elaborate body of deductive theory in the social sciences. As with public choice, the extent to which this theory has been verified empirically remains an open question. Certainly, welfare economics policy analysis develops applications to policy practice as if its theory were verified. The one aspect of welfare economics that might make positivists uneasy is the overconfident application of forward-looking techniques such as cost-benefit analysis, whose shadow-pricing tools require substantial speculation about future happenings. Such techniques assume unwarranted certainty about the future. Their conclusions are rooted in accepted method rather than established cause.

Some practitioners of the individual endowments strand of social structure are positivist in intent, but much of the work in this strand tends to lack parsimony. Numerous theoretical models are drawn upon, and no apparent accumulation of theory occurs. Consider, for example, the extensive social structural studies of the determinants of individual educational achievement. The better-known studies include those of Coleman (1966), Jencks (1972), and the *Stockholm Report* (International Association for the Evaluation of Educational Achievement 1973). The preferred method of these studies tests statistically the effects of some determinants $(x_1 \ldots x_n)$ on educational achievement $(y_1 \ldots y_n)$. The x variables typically include family background, teacher quality, and school resources. Educational achievement is usually measured by standardized test scores. Coleman (1966) found that school resource or quality of instruction factors generally have little impact on the educational performance of children. Background variables are much more important. One school-related variable that does appear to have significant impact is the character of the child's peers. This finding was used, especially by the courts, as intellectual backing for a policy of busing children to achieve a mixing of peers—racial integration—which in turn would supposedly enhance equality of educational opportunity. Certainly, no theory was unambiguously verified by Coleman; the selection of possible determinants was ad hoc, and critics of the report were unhappy with the performance indicators and statistical methodology employed. Subsequent studies produced different (and disparate) results. Moreover, the theory of intervention that justified busing was never tested—or, indeed, given any serious intellectual attention by policy makers and policy analysts prior to the enactment of that policy. Coleman (1975) himself recognized after the fact that policies of forced busing may have been mistaken.

If the individual endowments strand is uneasily positivist, the group strand of social structure strays still further from hard science precepts, mainly because of the arbitrariness and controversy involved in group definition.

Of the various schools sheltering under the information-processing umbrella, only the studies of individual behavior that pursue deductive theory and systematic hypothesis testing might be approved by positivists. More generally, positivists would be troubled by the degree of dispute about fundamentals, which continues to plague information processing. Pessimistic practitioners might be condemned for being more attuned to the complexity and nuance of the real world (not to mention the limits of policy analytic understanding) than to deductive theory and systematic empirical test. The optimists are suspect inasmuch as they share the welfare economics tendency to reason from elegant method rather than from established cause, a weakness exacerbated rather than ameliorated by the use of advanced computer software.

Positivists have little time for political philosophy. Now, positivist policy analysis must be directed toward social values, which constitute the dependent variables in causal empirical analysis. But it is not the task of the policy analyst to address the value judgments required for evaluation and recommendation. Positivism consigns value judgments, and hence the normative reasoning of political philosophy, to an extrascientific limbo. Positivists would regard the extreme internal divisions of political philosophy as further justification of their banishment of value judgment from the realm of rational inquiry.

For their part, political philosophers would have little time for positivists. Kantian moral philosophers, particularly, would criticize positivism's treatment of policy (p) and determining variables (x) as simply means to y ends. The p or x possibilities may be intrinsically attractive in moral terms—or intrinsically repugnant. To take an extreme example, one might control crime effectively through a policy of executing the members of any convicted criminal's immediate family (see Walzer 1977: 272). Or, to take a less contrived example, a policy might promote abortion as a means for controlling congenital health problems.

In sum: positivism would not approve of too much that is currently practiced in the name of policy field frames of reference. But, as we shall see, there is little reason for policy analysts to approve of positivism.

A CRITIQUE OF POSITIVISM

As the dominant metascientific belief in contemporary American social science, positivism has substantial (if often unreflective) support in the policy field. Our critique addresses its troublesome nature, its desirability, and the very possibility of its theory-practice nexus. It does not address methods (such as multivariate statistics) often used by positivists but not unique to them.

Tribulations

To what extent can general laws on which to base policy practice be identified? Let us consider one of the more apparently successful examples of the generation and application of such laws: Keynesian economics. Keynesian economics grew from a challenge to the orthodoxy of academic economics into a set of widely accepted principles for the conduct of macroeconomic stabilization policy. It provides a set of lawlike statements about the causal connections between economic aggregates (interest rates, employment, taxation and expenditure levels, aggregate demand and supply).

Keynesian economics provides somewhat ambiguous lessons about the utility of general macrolevel theories in public policy. Considerable atheoretical pragmatism persisted in macroeconomic stabilization policy throughout the Keynesian era. Keynesian policy instruments have always proven extremely blunt—anything approaching fine tuning of the economy seems impossible. Critics such as Hayek and Friedman continued to denounce the apparent success of Keynesian economics as an illusion. Stagflation in the 1970s demonstrated that Keynes did not capture any general laws. In this context, it is noteworthy that Keynes himself warned against the hazards of applying the theories of defunct economists (Keynes 1936).

To take another example, consider the case of anticrime policy. A plethora of empirical studies has addressed the causes of violent crime. These studies are summarized and synthesized by Wilson (1983), who believes their cumulative thrust is that the best way to reduce violent crime is by making punishment more certain. Yet these studies are just fragmentary bits of evidence. Certainly, no causal laws about violent crime have been established. Wilson himself suggests the best we can therefore do is to "intelligently make policies designed to reduce crime without first understanding the causes of crime" (Wilson 1983: 7).

The complexity and dynamism of the real world can make absolute, as opposed to contingent, truths elusive. Some policy analysts plead complexity as sufficient reason to retreat from positivism. So Greenberg, Miller, Mohr, and Vladek (1977: 1532) conclude,

Facets of public policy are more difficult to study systematically than most other phenomena investigated empirically by political scientists. Our attempt to test hypotheses with some rigor demonstrated that public policy becomes troublesome as a research focus because of inherent complexity—specifically because of the temporal nature of the process, the multiplicity of participants and policy provisions, and the contingent nature of theoretical effects. . . . Examples of policy making taken from the case study literature . . . show concretely how such complexity makes it essentially impossible to test apparently significant hypotheses.

However, there is no logical reason for the intrinsic complexity of public policy to be greater than that of the subject matter of ordinary social science—or even natural science. An ecosystem is just as complex as a policy system. Complexity of itself is insufficient reason to reject the positivist search for causal laws. One day, perhaps, we will be able to act with confidence.

Unattractiveness

Positivist policy analysis recognizes social values only in terms of a goal set $(y_1 \ldots y_n)$. At first sight, this posture might seem reasonable enough, but consider the ramifications.

To begin with, ends can be controversial. Most interesting policy issues are characterized by conflicting values. In economic policy, some suggest that unemployment should be the prime target; others are more concerned about inflation. In environmental policy, some care about healthy ecosystems; others are more concerned about healthy economic systems. Which values, then, should enter the y set, and what should be their relative priority? Positivists believe that such questions have no rational answer; one set of values is as good as any other. No help is sought or expected from moral philosophers on this matter.

Yet some y values are needed for analysis to proceed. The positivist policy analyst normally gets them by ascertaining and adopting the values of the powers that be—legislators, executives, or administrators (see, for example, Nachmias 1979: 13–15). Policy analysis of this sort is inevitably and uncritically "in the service of the king."

Clearly involved here is a form of the traditional politics-administration dichotomy. Political reality, however, does not respect any such split. Administration is inherently political. Policy analysis blind to this reality is at best irrelevant, at worst an attempt to supplant political interaction with a rationalistic "administration of things" by a "king" (client) and his advisors (policy analysts).

Taken to the extreme, a positivist conception of policy making conjures up visions of a technocratic rationalization of political life based on scientific "laws" that thoroughly displace more traditional politics (see Fay 1975). Criticism would come to appear as subversion, tempting repression. Consider the contemporary situation in the Soviet Union, where policy practice, as Ball (1984: 257–58) argues, rests intellectually on a positivist version of Marxism (which can be traced to Engels). However, as even contemporary Soviet society shows, complete technocratic rationalization is unlikely. This dire state of affairs can never be fully realized, because positivist policy analysis is a logical impossibility.

Impossibility

The positivist program for policy analysis contains three internal contradictions, each sufficient to paralyze its practical realization.

The first contradiction may be termed that of *agency*. Positivism sees the social world in terms of deterministic notions of cause and efffect. That is, individual and social behaviors are caused by forces external to the individual (or group), rather than chosen by the individual. If one allows for intentional aspects of behavior, then one must embrace a very different kind of social science, one that accounts for social phenomena in terms of the intentional actions of individuals in particular and unique situations as they are understood by those individuals. So even if positivism did offer a good account of successful natural science, it could still fail as a program for social science.

Positivists would have policy makers (assisted by policy

analysts) presiding over systems of cause and effect, intervening where appropriate to achieve desired effects. As such, policy makers and analysts are granted an exemption from behavioral laws. Thus policy makers are goal-directed, intentional agents, whereas policy recipients or targets are behavioral automata.

A good illustration of this distinction may be found in Jacobson's (1980) excellent study of the impact of campaign finance on the competitiveness of elections in the United States. Jacobson develops some lawlike generalizations about the effects of spending levels on the chances of incumbents and challengers. These laws are about systems that the policy makers themselves help constitute (they are all incumbents). Thus members of Congress are simultaneously data points for causal analysis and intentional agents making policy; but neither role is treated as affecting the other.

How can one justify this duality? One certainly cannot defend it through reference to the canons of positivist social science. Marx recognized this point over a century ago in his critique of Comte's *scheisspositivismus* (shit positivism; see Ball 1984: 241). If one grants immunity from behavioral laws to policy makers and analysts, why should it not be granted to ordinary people?

A second paradox in the positivist program is *verification:* theories of intervention cannot be verified. Recall that a successful positivist policy intervention must be based on two empirically verified causal theories: a theory of the determinants of a valued outcome, and a theory of intervention. Before one acts, one must be reasonably sure that the theory of intervention is true. And how may that truth be ascertained? Presumably, an empirical test is required—that is, one should observe the effects of policy alternatives $(p_1 \ldots p_n)$ in operation. Hence one cannot verify a theory of intervention prior to actually carrying out the policy. The notion of "verify theory of intervention, then act" is incoherent. The hazards of acting as if a theory of intervention were correct are illustrated by a long list of failed policies.

This question of nonverifiable theories of intervention can be illuminated by an apparent exception to our contention. Jacobson's (1980) campaign finance study contains an empirical test of a theory of the $(x_i \to y_i)$ variety. The y goal is competitiveness of elections. The x variables refer to the campaign funds of incumbents and challengers, respectively. Jacobson finds that challengers' chances vary positively with their level of funding but that incumbents' funding has no effect on their chances of reelection. In establishing a causal relationship of this sort, Jacobson does not stand out from run-of-the-mill positivist analyses. Jacobson is exceptional because he also determines the effect of some p variables on his x variables. The policy variables he addresses are funding ceilings and public funding. Ceilings improve the chances of incumbents and hence reduce competitiveness, because they harm only challengers. In contrast, public funding enhances competitiveness by helping challengers while having no effect on incumbents.

How do we explain this apparent exception to our nonverifiability claim? The answer is that in Jacobson's case the connection between p and x is a matter of logic, not theory. If a law says only $100 thousand can be spent per campaign, then only $100 thousand will be spent (assuming widespread compliance and an absence of loopholes): p_i simply imposes a cutoff point on x_i; no theory about the connection of p and x exists to be tested.

Such cases are rare; Jacobson's analysis is an exception that proves the rule. Many well-received pieces of policy analysis in a positivist image are content with establishing only $(x_i \to y_i)$ links. For example, Lave and Seskin (1977) trace the effects of pollution levels on mortality rates (and eventually dollar benefits of abatement). But the link between policy measures and pollution levels is not addressed.

A further difficulty arises when one combines the questions raised about agency and theory of intervention. If policies are indeed the goal-directed choices of agents, then the elements of any policy set $(p_1 \ldots p_n)$ are likely to be extremely unstable. Such volatile actions make poor material for independent variables in any "scientific" theory of intervention. Eulau and Prewitt (1973: 465) attempt to overcome the problem of instability in the $(p_1 \ldots p_n)$ set by defining it away: "Policy is defined as a 'standing decision' characterized by behavioral consistency and repetitiveness on the part of both those who make it and those who abide by it." In defining policy as habit,

Eulau and Prewitt are identifying a category with few (if any) members.

Our third and final logical contradiction in the positivist program is *self-negation:* causal knowledge can be self-negating. For example, if sufferers from respiratory diseases find out that high pollution levels cause high mortality rates, they may move to low-pollution locations. If they die from the diseases anyway, their behavior will confound empirical relationships between pollution levels and mortality rates (see Lave and Seskin 1977: 22).

Further negation can result from interaction effects between variables in the policy set $(p_1 \ldots p_n)$ and the nature of the causal links between environmental variables (some members of the x set referred to above) and the goal set $(y_1 \ldots y_n)$. As Elkin (1974: 419–20) points out, policies can, in effect, nullify the causal laws $(x_i \ldots y_i)$ that prompted the application of those policies in the first instance. This result ensues because knowledge about the policy and its intended effects is disseminated along with the policy itself. Knowledge, of course, can change behavior. Think, too, of the Hawthorne effect in social experimentation—subjects in experiments change their behavior simply because they know they are participating in an experiment. And note the way the animal spirits of investors (to use Keynes' term) respond to changes—and signaled changes—in government economic policy.

Causal laws about society can also be undermined, inasmuch as a policy decision affects not just the way people behave but also what those people shall become (see Tribe 1973). The point here may be made most plainly using the example of public policies toward the manipulation of human genetic material. However, inasmuch as human beings are subject to the forces of technology, this point is of more general applicability. For in remaking the world around us—in part through the application of public policy—we also remake ourselves. People living in the shadow of nuclear power and nuclear bombs are not the same as people living in an isolated peasant community. All human actions—including public policies—are, as Tribe notes, at once instrumental and constitutive. And as we reconstitute ourselves and others, then the "behavioral laws" about us clearly change.

CONCLUSION

Our condemnation of positivism does not gainsay the contributions of causal analysis—be it natural science or social science—to policy debate. Nor does it rule out the methodological tools favored by positivists. It is the pursuit of verified causal laws of society as the basis for public policy for which our harsh words are intended. However, a rational rejection of the positivist approach must await the articulation of some superior alternative. The burial of positivism—and any dancing on its grave—must, then, be postponed for the moment.

Chapter 9

Piecemeal Social Engineering

*T*HE POSITIVIST VIEW of engineering—be it of highways or day-care programs—is that the activity simply applies the causal laws already discovered by science. However, in the real world, engineering often proceeds without full prior theoretical understanding of the system operated upon; that is, through systematic trial and test. We now turn to a conception of the policy field that treats public policies themselves as tentative hypotheses, to be tested through experiment. Unlike positivism, which seeks to establish verified causal links between p_i, x_i, and y_i variables before undertaking policy action, this approach tries to discover tentative causal links in the process of policy action.

Such an approach to public policy found one of its earliest and most forceful proponents in Popper, who coined the term *piecemeal social engineering* in the 1930s. Popper's major initial intent was to articulate a practical (and democratic) critical rationalist alternative to the utopian dreams of the people he derides as "holistic planners"—especially those of fascist or Soviet Marxist bent. To Popper, piecemeal social engineering is the policy practice appropriate to decentralized political systems, whereas holistic, large-scale change is the hallmark of authoritarian centralized systems. Popper's advocacy of piecemeal social engineering proceeded hand in hand with his articulation of a "falsificationist" account of natural science to contrast with the verificationist views of positivism.

Popper's program has since been taken up by those more concerned with the methodology of policy inquiry than with epic political or philosophical struggles, although the piecemeal social-engineering/social-experimentation approach is shared by many who are unaware of its debt to Popper. Arguably, this approach is the dominant one within the policy evaluation fraternity. We will consider the roots of the approach in the falsificationist view of the logic of scientific inquiry and then identify the strands in the policy field consistent with this view. A critique of piecemeal social engineering concludes this chapter.

THE POPPERIAN ORIGINS

To Popper, the positivists' primary error is their belief in the possibility of verified scientific truth and of policy based upon it. Popper (1959) claims scientific theories can only be falsified. Successive attempts to refute a theory do, if they fail, increase our confidence in it; but no number of failed refutations can ever confirm a theory. History shows that the fate of every theory is falsification and replacement by a better theory. But it is rational to tentatively accept and then to act upon the best available theory—that is, the one that has best withstood serious and strenuous falsification attempts. Actions such as public policy interventions provide occasions for both further learning and potential refutation of the theory.

Practice is the crucible in which the flaws of social science are revealed. As Popper (1972) puts it, "The social sciences are developed very largely through the criticism of proposals for social improvements, or, more precisely, through attempts to find out whether or not some particular economic or political action is likely to produce an expected, or desired, result."

To Popper the essence of all rational human activity (whether or not we call it science) is problem solving. Problem solving should always proceed thus:

$$p_1 \rightarrow ts \rightarrow ee \rightarrow p_2 \rightarrow \ldots$$

where; p_1 is an initial problem;
ts is a trial solution to that problem;
ee is error elimination (generally through empirical test); and
p_2 is the set of problems remaining after error elimination.

In public policy, the initial problem (p_1) is a social concern (for example, the poverty trap). The trial solution (ts) is an experimental public policy (for example, a negative income tax scheme). Error elimination (ee) is a field test of the policy. Remaining problems (p_2) are any residues of the initial concern together with unwanted side effects caused by application of the policy (for example, a financial incentive structure that promotes the breakup of poor families).[1]

For a scientific experiment or a policy experiment to yield meaningful results, conditions must be kept constant in the experimental environment—extraneous variables must be controlled. Hence, for Popperians, rational policy interventions must always be limited and piecemeal. If one attempts to change many variables at once, then it is impossible to disentangle the numerous relations of cause and effect.

Policy Field Exponents

The idea that social experimentation is the proper basis for rational public policy has many adherents among policy analysts. Rivlin (1971: 108) states the point firmly: "The argument for systematic experimentation is straightforward: information necessary to improve the effectiveness of social services is impossible to obtain any other way." The approach has been applied in policy areas such as social welfare, education, health, labor and human resources, and law enforcement.

The tenets of social experimentation in public policy are firmly Popperian:

1. If at all possible, undertake (on the basis of a tentative theory) a policy experiment using a treatment group and a demographically identical control group. Random assignment of individuals between the two groups is the best means for ensuring this identity.

---

1. In purely contemplative scientific activity, p_1 is an anomaly—something puzzling that demands explanation (for example, why do species exhibit a greater stability over time than Darwinian evolutionary theory predicts?), ts is a theory (for example, the evolutionary theory of punctuated equilibrium), ee is an attempted refutation of the theory (for example, through examination of the fossil record), and p_2 is any puzzle remaining (for example, just what is the mechanism through which speciation occurs?).

2. If control-group experimentation is impossible (for example, in the case of public goods), employ quasi-experimental methods. Treat historical variety in public policy as a natural experiment. Such second-best methods include monitoring of time series of a social performance indicator (for example, monthly pollution levels) before and after a policy intervention, monitoring control time series of the indicator (for example, for different cities), and searching for discontinuities in these sets of observations.

3. If the experiment produces clear positive results, repeat on a larger scale.

4. If the experiment produces no clear results, or negative results, try again with a different or refined tentative theory.

Cognizant of weaknesses in social science understanding, Popper himself stresses the importance of a critical spirit to be shared by policy makers, social scientists, and—crucially—anyone else who wants to participate in policy debate. This free interplay of proposals and criticisms constitutes, for Popper, the defining feature of the liberal "open society" (see especially Popper 1963). The unintended consequences of policy will often be substantial, given imperfect understanding of the social world. Hence criticism must be admissible from the people who know about the effects of public policy at first hand: the target population. Knowledge—and hence criticism—cannot be centralized in the open society. This situation is in stark contrast to positivism, where the expert reigns supreme.

Some adherents of the experimental approach in public policy would accept the extreme degree of free criticism characterizing the open-society ideal. For example, Goldfarb (1975) praises the role played by journalistic muckrakers in stimulating bureaucratic learning about past disasters in urban renewal policy. Campbell (1969) has little to say about criticism from the general public, but he does stress the desirability of a critical spirit in administration. He distinguishes between trapped and reform administrators. Reform administrators are prepared to experiment and to accept the possibility of nega-

tive results. Trapped administrators are afraid that poor performance of a policy or program will have personal repercus-
sions. Campbell accepts that any one experiment is likely to
produce inconclusive results, and hence that, in social as in
natural science, an experiment is of itself no more than an
argument (Campbell 1982: 330–31). He calls for a "dialectic of
experimental arguments" based on multiple policy experiments carried out by a variety of investigators.

However, the majority of those who practice an experimental approach to policy analysis have little time for the critical
ideals of the open society. Instead, they are more interested in
establishing the client-analyst relationships that yield the resources that field experiments require. Let us overlook this
departure from open-society ideals, and consider what piecemeal social engineers would make of the frames of reference
enumerated and discussed in part 2.

FRAMES AS SOURCES OF ENGINEERING HYPOTHESES

Popperians are hostile to frame-bounded thinking and
would see only heuristic utility in policy analysis frames of
reference. Nevertheless, piecemeal social engineering is more
at ease with a variety of frames than is positivism. The sources
of hypotheses are regarded as unimportant in comparison to
the possibility of their empirical test. Indeed, the major question piecemeal social engineers should pose to a frame concerns its ability to inspire policies that can be implemented on
a piecemeal reversible basis, enabling clear inference about
policy success or failure.

In this light, the first casualty is public choice, which involves all-or-nothing changes in institutional structure through
confident application of a body of deductive theory. Public
choice and piecemeal social engineering share only a recognition of limited knowledge about the content of policy, though
even here public choice would admit of no learning spirit or
"reform administrators."

Welfare economics fares little better than public choice,
given its practitioners' general lack of modesty about their
frame and the methods through which they derive policy prescriptions. But welfare economics does not rule out limited

experiment. Thus our Smoketown economists could systematically vary pollution charge levels and observe the results.

Instability and controversy in group definition should make piecemeal social engineers wary of the group social structure approach. Moreover, any treatment of groups as unitary wholes precludes piecemeal operation on their attributes. The individual endowments strand of social structure has greater kinship with piecemeal social engineering. Falsificationists regard the origins of hypotheses as irrelevant, and hence would be untroubled by the theoretical eclecticism of this strand. And individual endowments' empirical work is highly conducive to direct application of experimental designs. Many of the more prominent advocates of piecemeal social engineering in the policy field themselves undertake analysis in this strand. The only unease Popperians might experience here is with the negative conclusions about the efficacy of modest reform that are sometimes reached—for example, concerning the inability of policy manipulable variables to influence educational achievement in an unequal society (Jencks 1972). Such conclusions leave total inaction or revolutionary change as the only effective alternatives (see Gouldner 1970).

Despite their variety, all the pursuits under the information-processing banner seek to facilitate intelligent action in a world of imperfect understanding, and as such are compatible with piecemeal social engineering. Even in the rationalistic variants of the approach, such as Simon's (1960) "new science of management decision," bounded rationality limits the extent of feasible change. The world can only be operated upon piecemeal, after it has been broken up into comprehensible and stable subsystems (Simon 1969). Less rationalistic variants, such as incrementalism and cybernetics, prescribe a sequence of test-learning-test activities, which is the essence of piecemeal social engineering.

Piecemeal social engineers would be sympathetic to political philosophy and, unlike positivists, regard it as a potentially rational enterprise. Value systems and political institutions have histories, which can be understood in evolutionary terms as the products of proposals and criticisms by rational individuals. Any such value system is one possible source of criteria for evaluating policy interventions. But the evolution of policy would be treated by Popperians as largely independent of the evolution of ethical systems, hence the real substance of policy analysis would be mostly separate from political philosophy.

In sum: piecemeal social engineering would suggest discarding welfare economics, public choice, and group social structure. Equally important, this orientation provides a context for the intelligent use of hypotheses derived from frames. Unfortunately, that context is not itself beyond criticism. To explore the capabilities (and shortcomings) of the piecemeal social-engineering conception of the policy field, we will now compare it with positivism.

PIECEMEAL SOCIAL ENGINEERING AND POSITIVISM CONTRASTED

Perhaps the most significant difference between piecemeal social engineering and the positivist approach lies in the degree of confidence each has in its theories. Positivists are unafraid to recommend large-scale policy actions on the basis of their theories *once those theories have been confirmed.* A positivist would recommend complete inaction if a theory has yet to be confirmed (or refuted). In contrast to the positivist's extremes of action and inaction, piecemeal engineers would always commend some cautious, moderate action.

Here, it would seem, social experimentation offers a clear improvement over positivism. A number of questionable large-scale policy interventions have been carried out in recent decades backed by professionals who acted as if their theories were true. Think, for example, of large-scale urban "renewal" in the United States and the United Kingdom; anti-poverty programs with perverse incentive effects; the Anglo-French Concorde project; and various other great planning disasters. The theories on which such policies were based may have eventually been accepted as false, but only after years of huge financial cost or massive human suffering.

Prolonged anguish of this kind can be averted by an experimental orientation toward public policy. To return to the education policy example discussed in the previous chapter: a piecemeal social engineer would hardly have commended a policy of forced busing as a strategy to ameliorate inequality of educational opportunity on the basis of the (rather slender) correlation found by Coleman between peer group attitudes and individual achievement. Instead, Coleman's correlation might have stimulated a conjecture that busing *could* produce positive effects. If the proposed policy withstood prior criticism successfully, forced busing would have been tried on a limited and experimental basis. Each experiment would have been designed with care; selected localities would have been representative of the larger society, and the performance of minority and majority students both before and after the implementation of the busing program would have been ascertained. After a suitable amount of time had elapsed, information gathered from the experiments would have formed the basis of decisions to terminate, revise, or expand the busing program.

Coleman himself acted in exemplary Popperian spirit by admitting that forced busing proved to be a mistake. But the policy process to which his report was an early contribution was less cautious and less open to adjustment. The federal courts, especially, acted as if the theory were true and locked busing policy into court orders.

This education policy example illustrates a second way in which piecemeal social engineering can improve upon positivism. It was noted in the previous chapter that positivistic theories of intervention are immune to empirical test, inasmuch as the notion of "verify theory, then act" is incoherent. The piecemeal engineer has no such problem. The theory to be tested is a theory of intervention, and the piecemeal method of testing the theory is through actual application of the policy.

A third key difference between a Popperian approach and positivism arises because positivists believe that verified theories accumulate in a stock of scientific knowledge. Clearly, the people with the best understanding of this stock are the relevant experts. Hence policy analysis and policy making should be left to expert technocratic administration of the scientific laws of society, protected from public interference. In contrast, the open society gives no special legitimacy to technocrats. Criticisms and proposals are allowed from policy makers, analysts, and citizens alike. Hence it is crucial that administrators and analysts be subject to democratic oversight. In the open society, liberal democratic principles are not adhered to for their own sake but for the sake of effective social problem solving.

The experience of one of the more closed-society policy-making apparatuses of the industrial world—the British civil service—adds force to open-society precepts. Frequently, knowledge of error in British central government is suppressed through devices such as the Official Secrets Act; when error does surface, it takes the form of exposé and scandal. The past three decades of British history have witnessed massive errors in weapons procurement, the adoption of nuclear power by stealth, soulless "new cities" planned for "overspill" from the older industrial cities, and urban demolition and redevelopment based on questionable theories about the "useful life" of housing stock (see James 1980).

SIMILARITIES WITH POSITIVISM

While there are some striking differences between piece-meal social engineering and positivism in the policy field, there are also some major similarities. Most fundamentally, both perspectives believe causal laws of society can be discovered that are invariant across time (see, for example, Popper 1972). For those who adopt a piecemeal experimental approach to public policy, invariance is necessary because policy experiments must be limited in their scope—confined to single issue areas or single institutions, and involving only small changes. The process of conjecture and test is a tortuous one. While the issue of how long to wait before judgment can be passed on a social experiment is a difficult one for the piecemeal social engineer (see Goodin and Waldner 1979: 5–6), it is clear from real-world policy experiments that this period is generally measured in years rather than months. Critics of the insidious implications of Keynesian economic management (such as Hayek and Friedman) seem to imply that the relevant period is one of decades. Hence any corroboration of theories through social experiments is painfully slow; such gradual corroboration only makes sense in the context of stability in the effects of a policy intervention.

The foregoing suggests that piecemeal social engineering is vulnerable to two of the criticisms leveled at positivism in chapter 8. First of all, the approach is helpless in the face of rapid social change; the feedback from experiments will simply fail to arrive fast enough. Second, the possibility that interventions based on causal laws may in fact undermine the conditions those laws describe and explain (see chapter 8) is not recognized.

The latter point is especially devastating in a Popperian open society, where a process of unrestricted criticism—including participation by any target population—should accompany any policy experiment. Yet this participation cannot, according to the doctrine of causal invariance, alter the way these people behave. If any change in behavior does result, we enter the realm of the experimenter effect dreaded by psychologists (see Badia, Haber, and Runyon 1970) and the infamous Hawthorne effect.

An insistence on causal knowledge means that, like positivism, limited social engineering treats any policy as merely instrumental to some goal. Hence, as in the case of positivism, the possibility that policies may be intrinsically right or wrong (irrespective of their consequences) is ignored, and the ends or goals of policy are treated as simple and uncontroversial. In the real world of conflicting values, Popper himself argues that public policies should be confined to areas where there is normative consensus. He believes that such cases will generally be those where obvious wrongs exist and cry out to be righted. Thus public policy is for the modest rectification of clearly undesirable social conditions, as opposed to the steering of society toward grandiose blueprints. Given that most interesting policy issues are characterized by unclear and conflicting values and criteria, the Popperian approach may be highly limited in applicability (see also Phillips 1976: 409–10).

One final criticism applicable to both positivism and piecemeal social engineering arises from their insistence on causal invariance, which leads them into the contradiction of agency we discussed in chapter 8. According to one strand in the Popperian world view, all rational individual behavior—not just policy making—proceeds in terms of problem solving through conjecture and test. Why, then, should not society be interpreted in terms of such choices, rather than in terms of causal laws about some (but only some) people?[2]

SOME FURTHER CRITICISMS

The very idea of piecemeal social engineering requires that issue areas and social problems be decomposed into their component parts, each thenceforth to be attacked and (one hopes) resolved in isolation. Think, for example, of the problems related to the construction of a sewer system; one might reasonably divide the problem into categories pertaining to domestic sewage, industrial wastes, storm runoff, and so forth. An overall solution to the problem could be built up (quite literally) from solutions in each category. Simon (1969) argues that most social problems are at least "near decomposable," and hence amenable to treatment in such terms. Unfortunately, one of the distinguishing features of contemporary industrial society is its substantial and growing complexity. Complex systems cannot easily be broken down into their component parts, because interactions between any conceivable subjects are too rich (see La Porte 1975; Alexander 1965). Under complex conditions, successive piecemeal interventions only fortuitously produce convergence on any less problematic state. Self-perpetuating chaos is more likely, as each intervention will have spillover effects into other subsets.

Examples of misplaced or unwarranted decomposition are numerous. Consider the chaos bedeviling the U.S. energy policy during the 1970s as a result of policies designed—inconsistently and in isolation—to attack both "high prices" and "shortages." Environmental policy is subject to the first law of ecology: "everything is connected to everything else" (Commoner 1972: 29–35). In health care policy, apparently progressive innovations such as health maintenance organizations often run into trouble rooted in the larger system of health care within which they are embedded.

A related problem posed by complexity to piecemeal experiments is difficulty in controlling for all the relevant vari-

---

2. Popper himself has proposed such an approach to social science in the form of "situational analysis" (see Farr 1985).

ables with potential effect on the goal of interest. Consider, for example, the famous (or infamous) New Jersey negative income tax experiment, conducted in the early 1970s. A number of changes in conditions occurred during the course of the experiment, most notably revisions in state programs for welfare recipients. While the experimenter might bemoan such "contaminating factors," they often simply reflect the inherent complexity of contemporary society. Both Campbell (1969) and Rivlin (1971: 114) suggest that experiments be repeated several times, with an averaging out of contaminations and convergent validity in mind. But how many times should an experiment be repeated? It may be the case that one particular factor is by chance constant across several repetitions of an experiment. Clearly necessary here is a theory of contamination (see Goodin and Waldner 1979: 16–17), which cannot itself be established by piecemeal experimental means.

Setting aside these difficulties associated with complexity, there is another problem inherent in any piecemeal experimental approach. A policy or program may require a threshold level of resources—or critical mass—before it can generate any positive results. Piecemeal experimental steps along the way will give absolutely no indication of that eventual success. So premature evaluation might unfairly devastate a fledgling program and deny it the time and resources to reach fruition. Schulman (1975) makes this point in the context of the U.S. space program. The success of the Apollo program depended on a continued massive mobilization of resources and enthusiasm—anything else, and the program would have collapsed. A related point here is that policy success may be a function of the enthusiasm and support (rather than criticism) that administrators can muster (see Palumbo and Nachmias 1983: 74–75).

CONCLUSION

Despite the ambiguities and defects detailed in this chapter, the piecemeal social-engineering approach to policy analysis and policy practice scores some clear advances over the positivist model. Specifically, the approach suffers only one logical contradiction (that of agency) rather than three; and critical trial and error in a world of tentative knowledge improves upon positivism's swings between extremes of action and inaction. Yet the approach is applicable only under a fairly narrow range of circumstances. Most fundamentally, there must be a well-structured, reasonably static, and highly decomposable policy problem at hand, with consensus on the criteria to be applied to it. Such circumstances are increasingly rare in today's world. Some of the more prominent earlier exponents of systematic piecemeal experimentation in public policy are beginning to recognize the methodological rethinking this rarity necessitates (see Patton 1984).

Chapter 10

From Rationality to Relativism

PARADIGMS AND PERSPECTIVES

WHILE POSITIVISTS concede that policy analysis frames of reference are potential repositories of verified theory, and piecemeal social engineers allow that frames can be sources of testable hypotheses, both groups remain somewhat uneasy with the very idea of multiple frames—for they both prescribe policy determination in eminently rational terms. Theory, evidence, and (perhaps) criticism can and should decisively identify the proper policy for any given context. However, frames at their strongest condition perceptions of the world in which policy operates. Hypotheses are tested according to the precepts of the frame that generated them, rather than by any frame-neutral procedure. Each frame comes complete with a lens for the interpretation of evidence. Hence a variety of strongly held frames can frustrate the rationalistic ambitions of positivism and piecemeal social engineering, alike.

The real world of public policy features dynamic, intertwined policy problems and multiple, conflicting values. The more complex a case, the greater the number of plausible interpretations of it, and the harder it becomes to adjudicate among them. Thus the real world of policy is conducive to multiple frames and is correspondingly inhospitable to a rationalism that transcends frames.

In this chapter we deal with several related conceptions of the policy field, which explicitly acknowledge an irreducible plurality of frames of reference. These orientations differ somewhat in the uses they would make of frames such as those we examined in part 2. One orientation would use them eclecti-

149

cally as sources of insight for policy advice. A second sees frames as grist for the mill of forensic policy arguments. A third is more negative, claiming that hopeless plurality and incommensurability rule out anything more than heuristic stimulation of political actors, and perhaps implies we dump the idea of a distinctive policy field.

These three frame-sensitive conceptions of policy analysis owe much to the account of science developed by Kuhn (1962), who contends that the practice of scientific inquiry requires a paradigm—a way of seeing common to and enforced by practitioners. This framework is taken as given and is largely immune to criticism. All "mature" sciences (read natural sciences) are, according to Kuhn, characterized by a single paradigm under normal circumstances. Clearly, the situation in the social sciences is somewhat different. Each discipline generally possesses a variety of paradigms. Policy analysis cuts across and draws upon a variety of social science disciplines (and other fields such as engineering, philosophy, history, and law); hence paradigms proliferate.

On one interpretation of Kuhn, there is no good way to make comparisons across paradigms. This thesis of total incommensurability pulls the multiparadigm policy field into relativism. Any kind of knowledge can only be contingent upon—that is, relative to—the perspective or framework of an individual or group. The implications of a relativist conception of the field are examined later in this chapter. We first pursue the implications of Kuhn's own avowed view, that paradigms are only partially incommensurable. This conception of the policy field—like Kuhn himself—straddles rationality and relativism.

ECLECTIC POLICY ANALYSIS

Policy problems have no respect for the boundaries of paradigms or frames of reference. Hence one might argue that all pieces of policy analysis must be multiparadigm. But a paradigm is, if anything, a way of seeing; how can one truly see from more than one direction at a time?

One answer is provided by Rein, who advocates a multiparadigm, eclectic orientation. Rein (1976: 259) notes "that there are competing paradigms of policy interpretation and that there is no fundamental way to resolve the disagreements among these perspectives." Broad-ranging paradigms or frames of this sort would include the approaches we discussed in part 2. Narrower, issue-specific frames abound—and include, for example, a rehabilitation perspective on criminal justice, a Communist conspiracy interpretation of Central American politics, and a frustration-aggression approach to antisocial collective behavior.

Despite his recognition of multiple frames, Rein (1983:101) believes "we have to resist drifting into hopeless pluralism." The primary mechanism of resistance is through an approach to policy analysis he calls storytelling. The policy analyst as storyteller is eclectic, drawing pertinent insights from different frames while remaining aloof from subscription to any one of them. Storytelling mixes positive and normative statements in its sage-like dispensation of wisdom to the mighty. Thus any piece of policy analysis is a plausible or interesting story, drawing morals from past events, extending metaphors, and making suggestions or secreting implications for action.

Imagine an analyst weaving a story about antipoverty policy. He or she might draw insights from microeconomics—for example, concerning the incentive effects of different welfare systems, especially on those caught in the poverty trap— without subscribing to the microeconomic paradigm in its entirety. Lessons could also be drawn from sociopsychological work that stresses the pathological effects on welfare recipients of forced dependency on the whims of service-delivery bureaucrats—without any attempt to undertake a full-fledged sociopsychological analysis. The analyst could enliven the story by likening a plethora of categorical programs to a many-headed hydra. Incentives might be stressed further through reference to historical cases where incentive structures were apparently effective—for example, in capitalist societies prior to the rise of the welfare state. A suggestion that the welfare system be streamlined into a negative income tax might easily emerge from such a story.

Unlike positivism or piecemeal social engineering, eclectic policy analysis would delight in the variety of frames we discussed in part 2. Its only unease might be with frames whose practitioners seek supremacy over their rivals and imposition of their own particular orthodoxy on analysis and policy making. Welfare economics, public choice, and some variants of optimistic information processing might be guilty here. Storytellers would be especially happy with social structure practitioners, who acknowledge their need to apply a variety of models to inform selection of variables in analysis. Thus what looks like a weakness from a more rationalistic vantage point can be turned to social structure's advantage from an eclectic perspective.

Unfortunately, it is impossible to determine whether a story is good or bad, true or false, corroborated or falsified. At best, storytelling can yield some heuristic stimulation; at worst, it is simply more noise in the system. The audience for equally stimulating stories about the same event may feel enriched by all of them, but in no better position to select policy alternatives.

FORENSIC POLICY ANALYSIS

Rein's storyteller pays little attention to the formal construction of his narrative. A more widely held position for the policy field recommends that analysis cope with an irreducible multiplicity of frames by devoting its energies to the logical structure of arguments for or against a particular frame, or (more usually) for or against a specific policy. The forensic image here is that of a lawyer building a case for a client (or against an opponent). To make a case, empirical evidence, interpretations, and appeals to normative principles are adduced selectively. While a policy analysis case can rarely be proven conclusively true or false, some cases are clearly more persuasive than others. Forensic policy analysis therefore occupies the middle ground between rationality and relativism staked out by Kuhn in "partial incommensurability" guise.

A forensic conception of policy analysis, which takes frames as the units of argument, is developed by Paris and Reynolds (1983), who look at the world of politics, policy making, and policy inquiry and see only ideology. An ideology is understood here as an encompassing world view with metaphysical, empirical, and normative components (Paris and Reynolds 1983: 205).

An irrational ideology is pure dogma in that its metaphysical core allows for no falsifying instances. Many religions fall into this category; critics of Marxism and psychoanalysis (such as Popper) would place these two frameworks in the irrational camp, too.

A rational ideology, in contrast, seeks coherence, congruence and cogency (Paris and Reynolds 1983: 207). Coherence refers to the internal consistency and full articulation of the value judgments and action principles of an ideology. Congruence is the degree to which an ideology's empirical component is consistent with empirical evidence. Cogency is the capacity to provide good reasons for proposed actions or policies. These three desiderata can be met only imperfectly; no rational ideology can be adjudged "correct." In this context, it is noteworthy that Campbell (1982: 331) admits that scientific experimentation is itself an ideology—but one that can be backed by good reasons (initially, the reasons Bacon and Galileo advanced for rejecting medieval scholasticism). Other contemporary rational ideologies might include incrementalism, an evil empire view of Kremlin rationality, psychoanalytical accounts of the pathological culture of bureaucracy, and a cornucopian view of the unlimited resource potential of the earth.

Paris and Reynolds (1983: 251) believe "the proper goal of policy inquiry and analysis is the construction of rational ideology." They consider the only function of empirical policy inquiry is to test ideology, not policies (as in piecemeal social engineering) or theories (as in positivism). Their ideal is a "polity of rational ideologies," a pluralistic system purged of dogma.

Rationality in ideology can be further promoted by a Rein-style confrontation of different ideologies or frames. A good example here is the Friedmans' (1984: 117–23) critique of the frame underlying proposals for the establishment of an industrial policy in the United States. Their critique proceeds from a neoclassical microeconomic frame, which of course attributes an essentially self-interested motivation to all social actors. In the light of the Friedman frame, an industrial policy would amount to little more than an organized conspiracy against the smooth operation of the free market by government bureaucrats, big business, and big labor. The frame of those backing an industrial policy presumably has a very different, benign view of the motivations and cooperative leadership capabilities of people in government, corporations, and labor unions.

What part would the frames discussed in part 2 play in a polity of rational ideologies? At a minimum, we would distinguish rational from irrational frames. Clearly, none of our frames is pure dogma. But they do vary in their degree of articulation, capacity to generate prescriptions, internal consistency, and resistance to counterargument and empirical test. None of the frames is perfect across these criteria. However, any imperfection here is no argument for downweighting or discarding a frame, but suggests merely that more effort should be devoted to its articulation and testing.

The adjective rational implies that some ideologies are to be preferred to others. The desideratum of congruence implies the possibility of empirically grounded comparison. Indeed, Paris and Reynolds (1983: 210, 212) state that there is typically a "common body of basic data" against which ideologies can be tested. On the other hand, no ideology can be dismissed as false, and no "standings table" of degrees of rationality can be constructed. For ideologies also resist explicit comparison— they are selective in the empirical evidence they allow, and vary in their criteria for selection. So ideologies must be of varying degrees of rationality; but degree of rationality is hard to ascertain. This position on the fence between rationality and relativism is precarious. But Paris and Reynolds are less in error than incomplete; the missing link is between frames and policies.

To make this connection, one might allow that precise standards for the comparison of frames are problematical but still try to establish rules for policy arguments that draw upon frames (lacking any standards, Rein's storytelling is no help here). Rules of the latter sort are analogous to the restrictions a legal system imposes on the admissibility of evidence and argument. The possibility that a policy argument may fail to meet some standard and hence merit rejection now surfaces. Forensic approaches along such lines generally involve a systematic checklist of the points a complete policy argument must contain.

Thus Dunn (1981: 41–43) believes a policy argument should lead up to a claim (action proposal) in which the analyst has a degree of confidence expressed in a qualifier. To justify the claim, the analyst must apply a warrant to transform information. Backing for the warrant consists of further assumptions and arguments, but both warrant and backing are ,open to rebuttal.

For example, let us take a claim that government should act to limit fluorocarbon pollution. This claim could be based on information that fluorocarbon emissions have been increasing in recent decades and that the ozone layer in the stratosphere (which protects life from ultraviolet radiation) has been depleted in the same period. The warrant in this case could combine scientific speculation on macrolevel chemical reactions in the atmosphere with premises about the proper role of government in controlling pollution. Backing for that warrant would come in the form of laboratory chemistry experiments (or belief in the authority of chemists) and welfare economics theories of externalities and the role of the state in a market economy. Rebuttal could come from competing scientific views—emphasizing, perhaps, the natural homeostatic qualities of the atmosphere, or alternative sources of ozone destruction, such as high-altitude supersonic flights—or from competing interpretations of the state, such as libertarianism or Marxism.

A policy argument can be deemed good or bad depending on whether it possesses all the required elements. More important, there is a point of entry for counterarguments (rebuttals), implying that a rational choice between argument and counterargument is conceivable.

Unfortunately, if warrants and rebuttals come from different frames, then no rational acceptance or rejection of a claim is possible. To return to the fluorocarbon example: a warrant for pollution control could be based on laboratory chemistry and an interventionist theory of the state, whereas its rebuttal could come from competing frames of systems ecology and a minimalist conception of government. The trouble here is that rebuttal can be directed only at the warrant in its entirety. Relativism would be ameliorated if each argument could be systematically dissected and hence probed at a large number of different points, along lines proposed by Brown (1976) and Hambrick (1974).

To Brown, the hallmark of objective—that is, nonarbitrary—policy analysis is that every step is justified through reference to explicit normative arguments. Reasoned value judgments are necessary in problem definition (a policy problem only exists in relation to a set of values), criteria specification, the determination of what range of means is acceptable (some effective options—for example, compulsory sterilization for population control—might be ruled out on absolute moral grounds), and the weighting that policy choice (or recommendation) must entail when different options perform most successfully on different criteria.

Brown's contribution to forensic policy analysis is a checklist of necessary value judgments, which the critics of any particular piece of policy analysis can take issue with if they so desire. Hence, instead of a titanic clash of frames, arguments can be compared in terms of the language of ethics on a piece-by-piece basis. One could perhaps supplement Brown's procedures with the formal tests proposed by MacRae (1976). MacRae suggests that performance criteria can be probed through reference to standards of clarity, consistency (freedom from ambiguity), and generality (applicability to other policy areas).

Brown's approach fails to address the empirical and metaphysical differences that can arise in policy debate. In stressing the latter, Hambrick (1974) develops a set of questions that could be combined with Brown's to form a comprehensive checklist. Thus a policy argument leads up to a policy proposition, stating that action p_i will lead to goal y_i. Behind this policy proposition must be a "grounding proposition" defining key concepts: a normative proposition (which effectively takes care of Brown's complete checklist) of goals or value-based constraints on admissible means; a causal proposition of the form $x_i \rightarrow y_i$; and an instrumental proposition of the form $p_i \rightarrow x_i$. Also required are an external impact proposition, referring to any positive or negative spillover effects; a time-place proposition, which defines the existing conditions of the key variables (thus establishing the need for a policy intervention);

a constraints proposition, concerning the feasibility of p_i; and a comparative proposition to establish that p_i is better than any alternative p.

Checklist in hand, a critic can probe the adequacy of any policy argument; a defender or advocate of a policy can attempt to muster an adequate case. Forensic policy analysis can therefore ameliorate relativism. But relativism can still surface in debates or disputes over each of the propositional types. For example, education policy analysts subscribing to different frames might disagree about a grounding proposition such as the meaning of educational achievement. An economist might view achievement in human capital terms with reference to future income, whereas a humanistic psychologist might define achievement in terms of overall well-being and adjustment to one's environment.

Forensic policy analysis would adopt a generally catholic outlook toward the frames discussed in part 2 and, like eclectic policy analysis, experience unease only with those claiming technical correctness. In practice, we find many practitioners putting frames to forensic use. For example, Schultze (1968: 96) believes the proper role for the welfare economics policy analyst is that of "partisan efficiency advocate." Thus in our Smoketown example, the case for a system of standards and charges cannot be demonstrated with hard data; it can only be argued from an economic perspective. Public choice, too, proves highly forensic, especially when its more messianic practitioners advance confident proposals for institutional reform with little empirical backing. A similar style characterizes the arguments of optimistic information processors about the bright future offered by "smart" computers. There are numerous examples of forensic social structural analysis, as should be clear from our references to advocacy-oriented works in chapter 4. Nevertheless, it should be stressed that analyses that are de facto forensic rarely if ever consciously attend to the logical structure of their arguments along the lines specified by Dunn, Brown, and Hambrick. The only exceptions to this rule are provided by political philosophers, who are more fastidious than most about such matters and who, of course, delight in constructing arguments and rebuttals.

RELATIVISTIC POLICY ANALYSIS

Forensic policy analysis requires intelligibility across frames, which in turn demands that paradigms be at least partially commensurable. We now examine the implications of strict incommensurability—relativism—for the policy field. The tenets of relativism are as follows.

First, within science no once-and-for-all judgments can be made as to the comparative merits of competing frames, paradigms, or theories. Feyerabend (1975) argues forcefully that all the rational standards for comparison proposed by other philosophers would, if applied, stifle scientific inquiry; and, moreover, that those standards are systematically violated in even the best examples of scientific practice (such as those of Copernicus or Newton). Feyerabend's approach to science can be summed up by his slogan "anything goes."

The role science itself should play in the larger society is equally at issue. Feyerabend is highly critical of the homage we pay to science, whose superiority over other frameworks holds only through reference to the canons of science itself. If one judges instead by practical benefits, then traditions or frameworks such as religion, myth, witchcraft, astrology, faith healing, intuition, folk wisdom, common sense, and political ideology can perform as well as science—or better. The implication for political organization is that a free society allows equal standing to all such traditions.

This anything goes attitude finds some clear echoes in the contemporary policy field. Consider first of all the thesis of strict incommensurability. Robinson (1982) argues that each side in the contemporary debate over long-term energy policy engages in a "ritualized performance" that can never narrow the gap between supporters of "soft" and "hard" energy frames. The most prominent soft path advocate is Lovins (see especially Lovins 1977), who is generally credited with provoking the debate. The soft path stresses renewable energy, decentralized supply systems, appropriate technology, and conservation; the hard path emphasizes nuclear power, centralization, high technology, and high energy use. Robinson argues that the two sides have irreconcilable views as to the nature of the long-term energy problem and the admissible kinds of empirical evidence and arguments. Paradoxically, both sides claim to adhere to the same basic value set—political liberalism and a free market. Each side does, though, denounce the values of the other: soft path advocates see technocratic authoritarians on the hard side, whereas hard path defenders cast their opponents as anarchistic hippies. The explosion of empirical studies on the energy issue since 1977 has succeeded only in widening differences between the two sides.

The general point here is that if differences are fully determined by frame, then policy analysis can only be relativistic. The ambitions of the field would have to be scaled down substantially; one suspects that heuristic stimulation of partisans might have to be the order of the day.

Avowed relativism in the policy field is, in fact, quite rare. More common is the second major plank in Feyerabend's methodological anarchism: that science is a tradition just like any other, with no legitimate claim to special standing. Critics such as Tribe (1972) argue that policy analysis in toto is just another ideology. Some defenders of the field assert little more—even if it can provide a useful counterweight to special interests in the policy process (McAdams 1984). Some policy analysts would take a small step on the road to Feyerabend's free society by granting that policy analysis can allow extrarational understanding—knowing how without knowing why (Dror 1976), and "tacit knowledge and personal experience" (Dror 1971b: 15–16).

Further along the road to a free society may be found Lindblom and Cohen (1979). Their purpose—which Feyerabend would undoubtedly approve—is to denigrate the role of "professional social inquiry" in the making of public policy. They laud the role "ordinary knowledge" based on "common sense, causal empiricism, or thoughtful speculation and analysis" can and should play in policy decisions (Lindblom and Cohen 1979: 24). However, Lindblom and Cohen are also keen on collective decision through social learning (which arguably underpinned many energy conservation efforts in the 1970s), interaction among individuals (be it through markets, bargaining, or voting), and random methods such as coin tossing, "reading the entrails of fowls," and "trial by water and fire" (Lindblom and Cohen 1979: 10). In short, anything goes—with the possible exception of excessive professional social inquiry, which can often generate too much noise in the system, not to mention expense. Professional social inquiry should not pretend to be conclusive or authoritative in a world of overwhelming complexity.

We now stand at the brink of the dissolution of the policy field. But the Lindblom and Cohen argument is casually empirical. It may indeed be the case that policy analysis as currently practiced and received has all the flaws they highlight. It does not follow that policy analysis must necessarily produce such results. Indeed, our argument suggests that many pieces of policy analysis are cast in a mistaken epistemological image. Lindblom and Cohen should give all policy analysts pause for reflection—and perhaps humility. But they fail to deliver a knockout blow.

CONCLUSION

Forensic policy analysis offers at least one major advance over positivism and piecemeal social engineering: it suffers no logical contradiction. Policy analysis as argument rests easily in a complex and dynamic world. Unfortunately, the forensic model is uncomfortably close to relativism's counsel of despair. While the case for relativism has not been carried by any of the authors discussed in this chapter, neither have we engineered any escape from its clutches. Possible exits are charted in the next chapter.

Chapter 11

From Relativism to
Critical Enlightenment

*T*HE SPECTERS of relativism and arbitrariness raised in the preceding chapter have yet to be banished. How can the relativism of frames be overcome to yield some defensible conception of rationality in policy analysis and public policy? Such a conception clearly must differ from the notions of reason in positivism and in piecemeal social engineering, both of which are uncomfortable with a plethora of frames. Perhaps some reconceptualization of rationality is required.

Our intent in this chapter is to investigate the idea that a common perspective shared by all the relevant stakeholders in a policy issue can be established—that is, that there can be rational consensus on a way of interpreting the world. The first epistemological category discussed in this chapter—*accommodation*—seeks to adjust the frames of policy analysts to those of responsible officials. The second—*critical policy analysis*—recommends instead communication and understanding that transcends the perspectives of analysts, officials, and other stakeholders. For all their differences, both orientations present a conception of policy analysis that is frame sensitive yet nonrelativistic.

ACCOMMODATING TRUTH TO POWER

One way to overcome disagreements among adherents of different frames in the policy field is through appeal to the frame or world view subscribed to by policy makers. Yet policy analysis that simply mimics the frame of responsible officials will at best provide intellectual gloss, at worst reinforce misconception. Thus proponents of adjudication of the content of policy analysis by policy makers recognize that it is an accommodation between the views of policy maker and analyst that should be sought. So analysts do indeed have something original and distinctive to bring to bear, but those who would be relevant must work in the context of a shared understanding.

Proponents of accommodation are sensitive to the frequency with which policy analysis is ignored by its intended audience. Barriers to communication between analysts and policy makers underlie the two-communities problem. Analysts are unwilling to sacrifice rigor and analytical standards for the timeliness and pertinence demanded by policy makers. Even the most conscientious policy makers may be faced with urgent, immediate decisions, which cannot await conclusive analysis let alone challenge from an unfamiliar frame.

Clearly, the term *two communities* is an oversimplification. There are many knowledge-based communities within government, and incommensurability across their world views can occur (see Hargrove 1980). Thus the British Treasury contains both monetarists and Keynesians. We have already stressed the variety of frames that can be held by policy analysts. Nonetheless, the general point is well taken: incommensurability between the world views of analyst and recipient can effectively block any policy analysis contributions. This point is corroborated by a vast literature on knowledge utilization in government, which generally uncovers a lack of any immediate and direct impact of analysis on policy. "Speaking truth to power," to use Wildavsky's (1979) term, is impossible if the pursuit of truth and power inhere in the different realms of the social scientist and policy practitioner.

The spheres of truth and power can be reconnected by the analyst addressing the political feasibility of his or her recommendations—especially through reference to the support or opposition of powerful actors. Such estimates may well enhance the likelihood of policy adoption and implementation. But acceptance of an analysis depends, too, on its intelligibility to the frames of policy makers.

Another way to reconnect truth and power would be to have policy analysts adopt a client's values as given and to build these values into analysis. Unfortunately, it is often the case that goals and values remain unstated by policy practitioners. Vagueness and ambiguity in goals can, indeed, be conducive to creation of a coalition in support of a policy. Moreover, practitioners often act first and then cast around for reasons to justify their actions (Palumbo and Nachmias 1983: 72–73). Think, for example, of the well-publicized Head Start experience: upon evaluation, the program looked bad, hence its supporters looked for other goals to justify it, a decision process consistent with the garbage can model discussed in chapter 5. Thus the prescription "take the policy maker's values as given, and then look for means to achieve them" is itself insensitive to political reality.

A recognition of the problematic nature of the goals and values of policy makers need not rule out value accommodation; the analyst might simply have to convince the audience that it does in fact subscribe to the value system that backs a policy proposal. An equally arduous procedure is proposed by Rohr (1976), who suggests that analysts and public administrators should study and accommodate themselves to the "regime values" of the polity in which they operate (in the U.S. case, Rohr believes Supreme Court decisions are especially instructive).

Yet successful convergence on a set of values shared by practitioners and analysts does not guarantee full accommodation of frames. As Robinson (1982) notes in the context of debates on energy policy, partisans of competing frames can subscribe to common values. To take another example, analysts and other stakeholders in macroeconomic policy debates may be able to agree on goals of growth, stability, and high employment (perhaps even on trade-offs between these values), yet still adhere to different and incompatible economic theories. Full accommodation requires an adjustment between the frames of stakeholders and analysts in their entirety, not just in their normative components.

At one extreme, adjustment through accommodation simply requires the analyst to adopt the frame provided by an organizational environment. This environment can perform many of the functions of a paradigm within a scientific community: it can control access to information, define the puzzles for which solutions are needed, and stipulate the kinds of answers acceptable. Clearly, many policy analysts working within government agencies do undergo accommodation of just this sort (see Meltsner 1976). A substantial literature suggests that an analyst who would be heard should define problems, goals, methods, and possible solutions in terms acceptable in the organizational environment. In this vein, Palumbo and Nachmias (1983: 73) suggest that one role for the evaluator is to search for interests served by an organization's actions in order to justify these actions after the fact. Such "loyalist" endeavors may increase the esteem policy makers accord to analysts.

A less extreme version of accommodation seeks shared understanding between analysts and other organizational inhabitants, while pursuing the distinctive contribution that analysis can make. One effort to bridge the gap between program managers and analysts is evaluability assessment (see Wholey 1983). Evaluability assessment has its origins in a rejection of the traditional style of program evaluation in the U.S. federal government, in which outsiders pass terminate-or-continue summary judgments. Given that these analyses often work with unrealistic goals and expectations, their results are typically macronegative, and hence potentially devastating. In the context of the demise of the Great Society programs of the 1960s, Aaron (1978: 159) points out that systematic evaluation "corrodes the kind of simple truths on which political movements are built."

Evaluability assessment promises a middle way between simple faith and sweeping condemnation. Analysts and managers work together to develop problem definitions, goals, and realistic success indicators. The purpose of evaluation is to improve program performance, rather than to decide on termination or continuance. The actual evaluation methodology need not depart substantially from more traditional approaches. Evaluability assessment has been applied—according to its proponents, with some success—in a wide variety of settings, but especially in the U.S. Department of Health and Human Services. The evaluability assessment approach, while it departs substantially from simple adoption of an organizational frame, still addresses itself to the perspective and needs of program management. Proponents of accommodation have generated two further kinds of practical procedure. The first suggests that analysts should strive to formulate umbrella metaphors under which both analysts and policy makers can shelter. The function of such metaphors is to induce analysts and policy makers to open up or expand their frames of reference, at least to the point where they can tell intelligible stories to each other. Illustrative here are Dror's urging of a "fuzzy gambling" metaphor for cardinal policy choices, and a "crazy states" metaphor for national security policy.

In the former metaphor, he asks that policy makers and analysts imagine the setting as if it were "an unstable casino, where not playing is itself a game with high odds against the player; where the rules of the game, their mixes of chance and skill, and the payoffs change in unpredictable ways during the gambling itself; where unforeseeable forms of external 'wild cards' may appear suddenly . . . and where health and life of oneself and one's loved ones may be at stake, sometimes without knowing it." (Dror 1983: 9; see also Dror 1984b, 1985). In the latter metaphor, he asks policy makers and analysts to recognize that some strategic actors engage in "seemingly irrational behavior" (Dror 1971c: xiv). Treatment of these actors as reasonable and relations with them as manageable through the normal means of statecraft is bound to fail. Of course, the shared metaphor will only work to the extent that policy makers are disposed to engage in dialogue.

The second procedure stresses the pertinence of qualitative and ethnographic methods (especially participant observation) in helping policy analysts sense the frames of policy makers and how situations, alternatives, and policy consequences are interpreted in terms of these frames. Neither procedure is intended to replace other methods, but simply to help analysts focus methods and report results in relevant and persuasive ways.

While this orientation does not guarantee agreement on specific policies, accommodation is clearly attractive in that it helps get analysis demanded, read, and heard by government organizations. Thus Palumbo and Nachmias (1983) want to elevate accommodation to the status of a "new paradigm" for evaluation research.

THE ACCOMMODATING POTENTIAL OF FRAMES

Accommodationists are generally catholic in their methodological tastes. So Patton (1984:10) argues that policy analysis methods cannot be judged good or bad in the abstract, but only in particular contexts for their use. Nevertheless, adoption of an accommodationist perspective on policy analysis and political practice can effectively sort the frames we discussed in part 2. This orientation rules out welfare economics, public choice, most optimistic information-processing procedures, political philosophy, and—less conclusively—group social structure. Accommodationists are much happier with individual social structure, decision analysis, and especially pessimistic information processing.

A rejection of public choice is perhaps most striking. Public choice generally condemns political structures, especially bureaucratic ones, rather than seeking accommodation with them. Political institutions are treated as variables by public choice analysts, and the motivations of their inhabitants as thoroughly untrustworthy. Political philosophy has as little respect for the established institutional division of policy-making capabilities as public choice, and hence would make accommodationists equally uneasy.

While Leman and Nelson (1981: 105–06) suggest that the policy-oriented economist should "think like a manager," welfare economists tend to be sufficiently confident of the power of their approach to regard the approval of outsiders (such as government officials) as superfluous. Economic advocacy can run against the political grain—for example, when it rails against pork barrel policy making.

Optimistic information-processing procedures tend to be thoroughly insensitive to political factors. So, for example, cybernetics would want to reprogram public organizations. One could imagine an accommodation between optimistic analysts and high-level policy makers, but similar accommodation at more junior levels is unlikely. The only exception here is decision analysis, which of course seeks explicit accommodation to the value and probability judgments of public officials (if not to their total frame of reference).

The group strand of social structure is inconsistent with accommodation inasmuch as its practitioners frequently end up championing the interests of some disadvantaged group against an established power structure. In contrast, the individual strand can be accommodating as long as it forgets its roots in sociological theory and confines itself to atheoretical application of procedures, such as experimentation.

Accommodationists would probably reserve their strongest approval for pessimistic information-gathering approaches. Incrementalism, especially, is highly attuned to the political and bureaucratic status quo. Indeed, incrementalists such as Wildavsky (1966) who commend the idea of "political rationality" see maintenance of that status quo as the primary task of public policy.

AGAINST ACCOMMODATION

Accommodating truth to power results in a feasible kind of policy analysis. Hence a critique can question only the necessity and intrinsic desirability of this orientation.

The major justification for accommodation is the supposed two-communities problem, which may in fact be nonexistent. Weiss (1980) refers to the typical pattern of policy research utilization in terms of "knowledge creep" or "enlightenment," through which the cumulative weight of social science findings can gradually permeate—and help determine—the frames of policy makers. Thus social science may be used even as social scientists are unaware of the fact (Knorr 1980). If indeed knowledge creep is the predominant means for the translation of social science knowledge into policy, then accommodation to the frames of policy makers would cut off enlightenment at its source.

Frames embedded in organizational perspectives often leave much to be desired. A bureaucratic organization is quite capable of generating a parochial and pathological outlook. Allison's (1971) account of the actions of organizations in the 1962 Cuban missile crisis is a clear warning here. Despite explicit direction from above, the organizations of the U.S. military persisted in following their own fixed routines, rational in the light of each organization's misinterpretation of the problems at hand. Policy disasters attributable to organizations clinging to inappropriate frames are legion. The faith of the French military command in the Maginot Line in 1939 constitutes only the most extreme example.

Accommodation highlights some deep questions about the ethical orientation of policy analysis. Lasswell's (1970) question—Must science serve power?—is especially pertinent. Lasswell himself answered in the negative, believing that science in the service of power could only exacerbate the gap between the power of the few and the powerlessness of the many. As Campbell (1982: 335) puts it in reiterating his case for critical rationalism in policy analysis, "An established power structure with the ability to employ applied social scientists, the machinery of social science, and control over the means of dissemination produces an unfair status quo bias in the mass production of belief assertions from the applied social sciences."

As an epistemological category that fits the behavior of many policy analysts within bureaucracies, the accommodationist view of policy analysis makes obvious sense. But when this orientation prevails, the knowledge and prescriptions that policy analysis produces are not particularly different from those available and accepted in its absence. What we are left with is making truth safe for power. Serving power—not dispersing it, or countervailing it, or criticizing it—is where avidly pursued accommodation leads us.

FROM ACCOMMODATION TO
CRITICAL INTERCHANGE

It should be apparent by now that there is nothing defensible about consensus as such in the interactions of policy analysts and stakeholders. However, consensus need not be merely accommodating. Based on a reflective and critical interchange among analysts and actors, consensus can be more or less rational. Such a conception of policy analysis owes much to critical theory (of which Habermas is the leading contemporary exponent), though terms such as emancipatory, discursive, hermeneutic, dialectical, practical discourse, transactional, and open communications may also be found in the literature. This orientation can also be found in the conception of policy sciences pervading the work of Lasswell. We do not mean to suggest an identity between the views of Habermas and Lasswell, and we note some substantial differences below. Nevertheless, both take a fundamentally psychoanalytic perspective on the relationship between the social scientist and the broader society, one that seeks to improve the "patient's" ability to lead a satisfying and humane life. We term the approach rooted in these two sources *critical policy analysis*, which should not be confused with the Popperian critical rationalism underlying piecemeal social engineering. Neither should it be equated with particular critical theories directed toward the liberation of a specific oppressed group, such as feminism, dependencia, or liberation theology.

The critical model diverges from accommodation most fundamentally in its recognition that real-world policy debate can suffer what Habermas (1970a) calls "systematically distorted communication" and Lasswell terms "symbol manipulation" (see also Edelman 1977). Critical policy analysis devotes itself to the elimination of distortion, which can occur through suppression, debasement, or deception.

Suppression occurs whenever any normative position, frame of reference, or argument is excluded from debate or (more likely) denied equal access. Note, for example, how hard it is to argue for innovations in the American political system if they are stigmatized as socialist, or in the Soviet system as capitalist. The elites in any social system generally have a clear interest in suppressing challenges to their dominance. Yet suppression need not be overt or deliberate. It occurs, too, whenever a category of people lacks the resources and skills to participate effectively in debate. Technical jargon (perhaps rooted in one of our frames of reference) may effectively exclude those who are not cognoscenti. Bureaucratic organizations are particularly adept at this kind of exclusion (see Hummel 1982: 152–61). Intrinsically meaningless concepts, such as the "useful life of housing stock," can be reified by such means, and come to shape public policy.

Debasement is the devaluation of information through practices such as surreptitiously slanting evidence or misusing social science methodologies. Debasement of political language can result from the efforts of opinion pollsters, political consultants, and superficial or sensational journalism. Less spectacularly, debasement may be mere noise in the system, resulting from political posturing, routine production of excessive information, or inappropriate policy analysis.

Deliberate deception is perhaps rarer than suppression or debasement. Think, though, of the deliberately misleading projections of future U.S. government revenues and expenditures. Some of the less scrupulous practitioners of advocacy research in the policy process take a rather cavalier attitude toward the veracity of the information backing their arguments. For example, an oil company may circulate photographs of smiling caribou happily migrating under the trans-Alaska pipeline—failing to point out that all the animals in the picture are males, females being afraid of the obstacle.

CRITICAL THEORY

Critical policy analysis has one source in critical theory, as we have already noted. Critical theory believes social science should serve what Habermas calls an "emancipatory" interest: the improvement of human existence through increased awareness on the part of individuals as political actors. Habermas berates contemporary social science for pursuing a "technical" interest in manipulation of society from above. A technical interest finds clear expression in positivist, piecemeal social engineering, and in accommodating conceptions of policy analysis.

A critical theory is grounded in the investigator's conception of the felt needs and deprivations of a group of individuals. There is a clear resemblance here to interpretive (phenomenological) social science, which accounts for social reality in terms of people acting in particular contexts in pursuit of their goals. In contrast to positivist social science, the interpretive approach attempts to understand social phenomena in terms of the logic of particular situations.[1]

Critical theory does not stop with interpretation but instead strives also to uncover the influences that, unknown to the individuals involved, are distorting their beliefs and actions. So, for example, individuals may be unaware of political socialization that promotes their support of an unequal social order.

The truly distinct feature of a critical theory is its fundamental practical intent. A theory must be intelligible in terms of the felt needs and deprivations of the individuals to whom it is addressed. In this way, it should make individuals reflect upon their situation in a new light, stripped of illusions and misconceptions. A critical theory is not validated through statistical tests but through action by the targeted individuals based on their new self-understanding.[2]

Critical theory commends, then, a continuous interchange of ideas, interpretations, and criticisms between social scientists and other political actors. Unconstrained discussion is attained most fully in what Habermas calls the "ideal speech situation." This situation imposes no restrictions on who may participate, what kinds of arguments can be advanced, and the duration of discussions. The only resource actors have at their disposal is argument, and the only authority is that of the better argument. All actors should have equal degrees of "communicative competence" (Habermas 1970b).

In this happy state, all decisions would be arrived at

---

1. We choose not to discuss interpretive epistemology here because few applications of this theory of knowledge have been made in the policy field, and—more important—it is hard to see how an interpretive approach could suffice for policy analysis. Interpretive social science is in itself descriptive rather than evaluative or critical (see Bernstein 1976; 167–69). Hence no allowance is made for any social science contributions to the situation under analysis, other than nay-saying warnings about what will not work in a particular context. Banfield's (1970) account of the futility of antipoverty policy is a good example of this kind of work. Given the impossibility of any more positive contribution, interpretive policy analysis cannot exist (see Dryzek 1982: 322).

2. There is a clear parallel with the psychoanalytic encounter here. This analogy is developed at length by Habermas himself, who sees an idealized conception of psychoanalysis as the model discipline for the social sciences.

through consensus. But that consensus does not represent sub-mission to the frame of a dominant actor, or compromise be-tween special interests. Instead, the consensus is rationally grounded and transcends the relativism of particular analyti-cal frames. Competing arguments from different frames could be compared and assessed on the basis of their reflective accep-tance by political actors. So Fisher and Ury (1981: 84–98) note that agreement in negotiations is facilitated if pursued through reference to an "objective criterion" (generalizable interest) in-dependent of the special interest of each party to a dispute. Such a consensus would of course also demolish divisions between the two communities, for, as Dunn (1982: 295) notes, the distinction between scientific and ordinary knowledge loses its force when interchange is truly open and critical. Theoretical knowledge requires the validation of nonexperts.

Critical theory is dismissed by its opponents—and some of its friends—as irrelevant and abstract theorizing; the ideal speech situation is believed to be an unattainable construct. Before moving beyond this dismissal, we address the other source of critical policy analysis—Lasswell.

THE POLITICS OF PREVENTION

Lasswell would agree with Habermas that the raison d'etre of the social sciences is to improve human existence: "We are concerned with the progressive democratization of mankind" (Lasswell 1948a: 221). His intent is also emancipatory: "No democracy is even approximately genuine until men realize that men *can* be free" (Lasswell and McDougal 1943: 225). Lasswell (1961) doubts, though, that increased awareness suf-fices to achieve any dramatic improvements. The reason is that elites, like the poor, will always be with us. Unequal distributions of wealth, safety, and deference will persist. The challenge, then, is to create and maintain a cadre of public policy specialists to "keep alive the pluralism of authority and control that prevents the absolutization of political power" (Lasswell 1980: 533). But the policy sciences have failed if they boil down to increasing the "competitive strength of an elite based on a vocabulary of footnotes, ques-tionnaires, and conditioned responses against an elite based on a vocabulary of poison gas, property, and family prestige" (Lasswell 1965: 15).

The kind of theory appropriate to this view lies far closer to critical theory than to positivism or falsificationism. The starting points are the motivations and resources that determine what people will do in particular situations. Motivations are not always conscious; for example, Lasswell (1930) argues that the political behavior of elected officials stems largely from personal needs displaced to the public sector. Elites must be well understood in terms of their social origins, special skills, personal traits, attitudes, sustaining assets, and recruitment patterns.

The accompanying emphasis on context takes the Lasswellian approach beyond psychiatry writ onto the public sector. It is context that determines the range of choices open to elites and citizens and the consequences that will follow from these choices. Key elements of context include economic organization, division of labor, prevailing technology, modes of political and social control, the nature and distribution of instruments of coercion, level of mass insecurity, and the focus of attention of political participants (based on key symbols).

The Lasswellian approach shares with critical theory a fundamental practical intent to improve the human condition with respect to freedom from coercion, want, indignity, and manipulation. The project is more limited than critical theory: policy scientists can do little to help society attain utopia, but they can do much to avoid dystopia. Lasswell's politics of prevention would have analysts anticipate factors likely to threaten the freedoms mentioned above sufficiently in advance of their ripening to forestall them by prescribing appropriate courses of action. An early warning of this sort appears in Lasswell's (1948b) own anticipation in the 1930s of the emergence of the "garrison state." Such warnings should function as self-denying prophecies, triggers for acts that prevent the unwanted future.

The Lasswellian world is pervaded by self-interest and—to make matters worse—by the illusion that self-interest is tantamount to the public interest. The chances of piercing these illusions can be improved in two ways. First, policy scientists must be committed to a "self-consciously analytical, descriptive mode of discourse" (Lasswell 1965: 14). This commitment requires that policy scientists resemble psychiatric clinicians in their need for extraordinary self-understanding. Otherwise, there is little likelihood of their fulfilling the injunctions to be aloof *and* empathetic, to hold membership of an elite *and* remain fundamentally sceptical of elite motives.

The second procedure recommended by Lasswell for piercing illusion is systematized in the idea of a "decision seminar" (Lasswell 1960; Brewer 1975). Participants are placed in an information-rich environment and must make explicit forecasts and prescriptions, observing and learning from the outcomes. Substantial consensus concerning the context of policy and the factors entering successful and disappointing forecasts and prescriptions should eventually emerge. The seminar promotes interaction among people representative of the range of pertinent interests in an issue and imposes no artificial conformity or compromise.

Whatever the differences between Habermas and Lasswell, they have received identical treatment from the policy analysis mainstream. Both have been dismissed as rarefied, abstract, and hence irrelevant. We suggest that this negative verdict merits reconsideration, especially in the light of the reservations we expressed in previous chapters on the alternatives. We therefore turn now to the concrete implications of critical policy analysis.

CRITICAL POLICY ANALYSIS

Perhaps the best means of demonstrating the nature and possibility of critical policy analysis is through extension of the forensic model discussed in the previous chapter. The methodological works of Dunn and Fischer are instructive here, inasmuch as both straddle the forensic-critical divide.

Dunn proposes an avowedly critical transactional model of policy analysis: knowledge is "transacted by negotiating the truth, cogency, and relevance of knowledge claims" (Dunn 1982: 306). In its bare essentials, transaction is merely forensic, allowing assumptions to be exposed and the logical structure of argument to be dismembered and criticized point by point (in exactly the manner discussed in chapter 10). However, Dunn also wants the clash of frames to stimulate critical self-reflection on the part of adherents of particular frames. Further, his test for adequate knowledge is thoroughly critical: "knowledge adequacy is certified by assumptions about the consequences of such knowledge in emancipating individuals and collectivities from unexamined or tacit beliefs that impede the realization of human potential" (Dunn 1982: 315). Unfortunately, this restatement of critical theory's emancipatory intent does not follow from Dunn's model. Something more is required, as we shall see below.

Recognizing that no ultimate test of the adequacy of a normative position is possible, but that most interesting policy issues feature multiple and conflicting values, Fischer (1980) proposes an "informal logic of practical discourse" for policy analysis. Under such a logic, a policy or normative principle can be justified by good reasons, or arguments, rather than by proof. Fischer himself sets his study in the context of Habermas's critical theory. However, he believes too that resolution of a policy issue should be sought primarily through reference to consistency with any established value systems, on the grounds that higher, more abstract normative matters are beyond the day-to-day concerns of practicing policy analysts (Fischer 1980: 165). The trouble here is that arguments might be made within a "systematically distorted" consensus on values. Fischer's methodology can be accommodating just as easily as it can be critical. Again, an extra ingredient is required to make the approach critical.

Fischer (in common with Dunn) leaves open the grounds on which a policy argument is persuasive and to whom it is persuasive. An argument might convince only oppressors. Or persuasion might be sought through dishonest means such as emotion—as in much contemporary advocacy research. It might even be the case that the rules of discourse elaborated so carefully by Dunn, Fischer, Hambrick (1974) and MacRae (1976) are intelligible only to individuals well trained in philosophy and social science and hence actually impede the cooperative discussion of the open-communications ideal. In sum: "good reasons" arguments are needed in the critical model—but they do not of themselves guarantee a critical model, since they can also occur outside it.

The missing ingredient here is the widespread and effective competent participation in policy debate called for by critical theory. The practical task of the critical policy analyst is not, then, simply to propound arguments within an interactive decision process but also to advance that process toward the open-communication ideal. To this end, Forester (1983: 55–59) proposes that policy analysts need communicative ethics (to accompany their privileged initial command of information and arguments) and the capability to direct the attention of other actors. Ethical policy analysts would point out false hopes and expectations, encourage dialogue and criticism by disseminating information and questions, counteract noise emanating from or circulating within bureaucracies, offer suggestions for action, and expose unwarranted exercise of political power. In short: the analyst should work to eliminate systematically distorted communication.

Competent participation grafted onto practical discourse would set the scene for critical policy analysis. In more detail, a critical methodology would combine the following elements.

Dialectics

A complex system can always be interpreted from a variety of perspectives; key differences in assumptions (especially about values and the nature of the problem at hand) therefore need to be exposed, discussed, disputed, and—if possible— reconciled. Dunn, Mitroff, and Deutsch (1981) stress this point in arguing that evaluation research should proceed in system-dialectical fashion, making use of multiple observers, information sources, theories, and methods. More limited suggestions along these lines include quasi-judicial proposals for competitive advocacy briefs and the interrogation of positions (George 1980; Mason 1969).

Any such clash of viewpoints or frames can cast the analyst in the role of critic of existing policy practice. In order to stimulate reflection among stakeholders, the analyst can engineer a confrontation between the social science frames of reference at his fingertips and the frameworks or implicit theories (including their normative components) held by other actors (Dryzek 1982: 322).

Equalization of Capabilities

A clash of frameworks confined to the powerful might simply make these people cling to their frameworks of privilege with renewed vigor. Critical policy analysis can rectify potential imbalance here by promoting policies that would equalize the distribution of power. Such policies include promotion of effective participation and access to the means for holding elites to account. Additional possibilities involve access to legal redress (for example, through legal aid) and higher education (Nielsen 1983) or even direct subsidy of disadvantaged actors to enable them to more effectively pursue political action. In this role, the policy analyst is simply an egalitarian social reformer.

A second means of overcoming imbalance is more pertinent to the role of policy analyst as such. Large corporations, government bureaucracies, national interest groups, and professional associations are highly organized and have the resources to hire skilled and persuasive advocates. Community organizations, small businesses, and the poor typically come off worse even in a forum of formal equality of access (such as a legislative hearing, court case, project review, public hearing, or special commission). Policy analysis can act as an antidote to such inequality by educating participants to the ways of the policy process, by sponsoring informal networks, and by directing attention to key issues.

One kind of capability requiring equalization concerns access to information—especially if we are indeed entering the "information age." Thus Lasswell (1980) stresses the need for freedom of information about the activities of large organizations, independence of the media from government, and widespread access to mass communications. Barber (1984) makes some suggestions for wider dissemination of high-quality information about policy and politics as part of his program for "strong democracy." His proposals range from reduced postal rates for political publications (especially low-circulation ones) to a public "civic communications cooperative," which would oversee the political use of telecommunications media, currently in the hands of people whose first concern is private profit. The critical potential of interactive information technology is explored at length by Luke and White (1985). The obvious danger of such technology is degeneration into a trivialized "push button democracy," which is why Barber believes responsible public oversight is necessary (Lasswell's comments about media independence notwithstanding). Such innovations only make sense as part of a wider program of participatory political reform.

Holistic Experimentation

Traditional piecemeal experimentation requires some policy maker operating on a treatment group. Obviously, such a relationship is unacceptable in critical policy analysis; yet, imperfect information still requires some form of systematic trial and test. Holistic experimentation resembles Lasswell's (1963: 95–122) idea of prototyping, the participatory and self-guiding development of a social community. No effort is made to apply statistical (or any other) controls, for generalization of results to any larger population is irrelevant. Hence replicability is not required, and all energies can be devoted to success in the case at hand. Treatment can be adjusted as expedient throughout the experiment. But even to speak of treatment is inappropriate, for there is no fundamental divide between experimenters and subjects. Experimental success is promoted by active participation; hence all individuals can be involved in the process of experimental design. As a practical matter, any target population is less likely to subvert a policy if it accepts the meaning and legitimacy of the action (Jennings 1983: 34–35).[3]

Institutional Innovation

Systematically distorted communication exists in markets through advertising, in bureaucracy as a result of hierarchy and organizational culture, in legal systems due to the formalization required by rules of admissibility, and in politics due to the demands of electoral strategy and power politics. Criti-

---

3. Contrary to Popper's (1972) contention, holistic experimentation clearly need not involve authoritarian central planning.

cal policy analysts might therefore devote attention to the design of institutions like (1) mediation; (2) broad-scale discursive exercises such as the U.S. National Coal Policy Project,
which brought together environmentalists and industry representatives (McFarland 1984); and (3) regulatory negotiation,
which seeks to replace administrative fiat with reasoned consensus in the development of government regulations. Such
institutions are currently in vogue as an alternative to more
traditional adversarial forms of conflict resolution. Clearly,
they are far more conducive to the exercise of critical reason
about the ends and means of policy than institutions where
political strategizing is supreme (see Amy 1983; Dryzek and
Hunter 1987).

In the interests of incremental institutional redesign, it is
worth noting that seemingly limited policy choices can affect
the well-being of institutions (Elkin 1983), the vitality of a
culture or community (Jennings 1983: 28), or the degree of
openness in political communication. So, for example, policies restricting the export of technology might effectively limit
the proliferation of high-technology weapons systems; but
such policies are unattractive in terms of the suspicion, detailed oversight, and secrecy they promote. Similarly, a garrison state, purportedly defending freedom, may by its very essence undermine freedom; and a worker's state, ostensibly run
by and for the workers, may in fact oppress them and foster
inequality.

THE CRITICAL STANDING OF FRAMES

Critical policy analysis can pass some clear judgments on
the frames discussed in part 2. Most strikingly, welfare economics, public choice, and individual social structure merit
condemnation because each embodies a technical interest in
manipulation and control of systems from above. Public
choice seeks manipulation of institutions rather than policy
content or the attributes of individuals, but it regards individual motivation as narrowly self-interested and certainly beyond the reach of critical reason. Welfare economics would
merit further disapproval to the degree of its capacity to impose a language of monetary costs and benefits on the policy

process. This imposition constitutes systematic trivialization and distortion of political discourse.

The group strand of social structure has long been home to more critical pursuits. Thus Myrdal (1944: liii), in his classic study of race relations in the United States, tried "to ascertain social reality as it is" by investigating the (systematically distorted) "doctrines, ideologies, values, and beliefs" creating this reality: "The interrelations between the material facts and peoples' valuations of and beliefs about those facts are precisely what makes the Negro a social problem." Practitioners of this strand can even commend emancipation strategies. The work of Piven and Cloward (1971) exposes the ways welfare policy keeps the poor in their place and also describes how grassroots protest might improve matters.

Critical policy analysts should regard many applications of the information-processing approach with distaste, inasmuch as these applications seek control and programming of human social systems. Such work generally takes off from servomechanism and computer analogies and is home to assertions of the sort that it is appropriate to treat "politics . . . as a component of management" (Volkov 1979: 5). More generally, rationalistic techniques clearly embody an interest in technical control. Incrementalist information-processing pursuits are also unattractive, because they are tied to perpetuation of the political status quo.

On the other hand, critical policy analysts may find some aspects of the information-processing approach attractive. Accounts of garbage can and bureaucratic decision making portray government in terms that should make citizens sceptical about the uses of power. Contentions that elites know best or that government pursues the public interest can thereby lose unwarranted credibility. Optimistic proposals that link new information technology with information diffusion, alternative media, and easy political organization could merit serious, if cautious, consideration.

Critical policy analysis would welcome the reflective and critical aspects of political philosophy. However, it would be sceptical of any attempts by philosophers to legislate morality for others, or to impose institutional designs, or to portray society in radically individualist terms. And the utilitarian strand of political philosophy would merit condemnation for the same reasons as welfare economics: it trivializes political discourse by treating it in terms of preference, to the exclusion of questions about collective human development.

The point to stress here is that the critical policy analyst could make use of facets of particular frames of reference but could not be a partisan of any of them.

A CRITIQUE OF CRITICAL POLICY ANALYSIS

Critical policy analysis has yet to be institutionalized to the extent of positivism, piecemeal social engineering, or accommodation. Moreover, applications to date have been limited in one or another of two ways. First, they have addressed policy areas with an identifiable target population—such as health, urban policy, social welfare, and education. Second, forays into other areas, such as foreign policy or institutional change, have been limited to dealing with small pieces of the puzzle, such as propaganda analysis and the succession of elites.

We have established that critical policy analysis is not an inherently sterile enterprise. However, it may still want practicality inasmuch as the approach requires huge effort on the part of policy analysts and other stakeholders in an issue. Like socialism, critical theory and Lasswellian policy science may look fine on paper but in practice may demand "too many meetings." Critical policy analysis (in common with piecemeal social engineering) is an extremely ambitious undertaking, requiring nothing less than a wholesale reconstruction of political institutions and public life. Though incremental steps may be possible along this road, it is by no means certain that the introduction of small doses of open communications and developmental constructs into a political system suffering systematically distorted communication and "presentmindedness" on a gigantic scale will significantly improve matters.

Perhaps the most fundamental criticism that can be leveled at critical policy analysis is that its pursuit of rational normative consensus is inconsistent with the dominant political tradition in the Western world—liberalism. Liberalism holds that a multiplicity of frames and normative stances is not only inevitable but positively desirable (see Paris and Reynolds 1983: 196). One is tempted to say: so much the worse for liberalism. But this is not the place to enter the classical debates of normative political theory.

Part Four

Choice

Chapter 12

Reasoned Selection

A QUESTION OF JUDGMENT

*T*HE EPISTEMOLOGICAL investigations of part 3 can help make sense of the proliferation of frames of reference in the policy field. These theories of knowledge give us a way of comparing the capabilities of different frames and of reaching summary judgments about their qualities. In the best (or at least simplest) of all worlds, we could construct a standings table, ranking frames of reference. The table would also possess a cutoff point, below which an approach is thoroughly rejected. This determination would identify the frames of reference meriting a place in the policy analyst's tool kit.

Unfortunately, epistemology is not decisive. There is no single correct philosophy of science, social science, or policy analysis but rather several competing perspectives. Each perspective yields a somewhat different judgment on the comparative capabilities of our various frames. The judgments of the epistemologies are summarized in table 1. Clearly, forensic and eclectic orientations are liberal and forgiving in their judgments; critical policy analysis, positivism, and accommodation are harsh and unyielding.

At this juncture, we advise the reader to consider which epistemology he or she finds most persuasive and hence determine his or her conception of the appropriate role of policy analysis. The reader can then proceed to make technical judgments accordingly. Clearly, none of the theories of knowledge discussed in part 3 is beyond criticism—while none is without redeeming qualities. We ourselves have made some summary judgments about the relative attractiveness of the various theories.

TABLE 1

Frames of Reference in the Light of Theories of Knowledge

Frame of reference	POS	PSE	ECL	FOR	REL	ACC	CRI
Welfare economics	+	−	−	?	−	− −	− −
Public choice	+ +	− −	−	?	−	− −	− −
Individual social structure	?	+	+ +	+	−	+	− −
Group social structure	− −	− −	+	+ +	−	− −	+ +
Optimistic information processing	?	+ +	+	+	−	− −	?
Pessimistic information processing	− −	+ +	+	+	+ +	+ +	?
Political philosophy	− −	?	+	+ +	?	− −	?

Note: Theories of knowledge are   Symbols in the cells are
  POS: positivism   + + strong approval
  PSE: piecemeal social engineering   + weak approval
  ECL: eclecticism   ? equivocal or mixed
  FOR: forensic   − weak disapproval
  REL: relativism   − − strong disapproval
  ACC: accommodationist
  CRI: critical policy analysis

We rejected a positivist conception of policy analysis on the grounds of its contradictions of agency, unverifiable theories of intervention, and self-negating knowledge production. Relativism and accommodation also merit rejection—not so much because they involve the dissolution of the policy field as because their counsels of despair and conformism cut off intellectual enlightenment at source. More positively, we find piecemeal social engineering, forensic, and critical epistemologies to be far more defensible—though each of these has major question marks against it.

These epistemological judgments set us apart from the policy field's mainstream (which is, as mainstreams go, somewhat diverse). One strand in mainstream opinion (for example, Lynn 1980: 6) would base policy analysis on an uneasy amalgam of positivism (a hammer to hit any nail) and accommodation (to ensure that institutionally fashionable hammers hit politically acceptable nails). Policy analysis constricted by the corsetry of positivism or the self-censorship of accommodation is tame policy analysis. The policy field really is of little significance if it is treated primarily as "normal science," calculating techniques used selectively in ways palatable to the prevailing distributions of power and interest. Tame analysis of this sort conserves the status quo.

When all is said and done, variety in both epistemological orientations and technical frames of reference survives the winnowing of part 3. Let us now consider some ways around this difficulty. We discuss (and dismiss) several ways proposed by others and then articulate our own preferred stance.

ALTERNATIVES TO ONCE-AND-FOR-ALL COMPARISON

Anything (or Nothing) Goes

Relativists would tell us that the difficulty we have identified is just a particular manifestation of the general impossibility of making rational choices among frames of reference. To relativists, any frame is as good as any other. Their position—the diametric opposite of those seeking once-and-for-all comparative judgment—was discussed at length in chapter 10. The reasons for rejecting relativism stated in that chapter still hold. In short, relativism dispenses not only with the ambitions of the policy field but also with rationality in policy choice. Policy outcomes are left to some invisible hand. Some observers (for example, Braybrooke and Lindblom 1963) suggest that democratic political systems do indeed possess effective invisible hands. However, the efficacy of political invisible hands breaks down if there is imperfect access to and communication within the political system in question, if there are long time lags or irreversibilities in the effects of policies, and if there is substantial complexity in the environment of policy (see Dryzek 1983b: 348–49).

Unfortunately, it is exactly the most critical policy issues that tend to exhibit compartmentalized information, manipulated communication, temporally distant visible consequences, effects that are hard to erase, and interference across the boundaries between institutions and between policies. A wiring diagram of the central issues facing a polity would therefore look like a Rube Goldberg machine. The outputs of any one subsystem influence (often in bizzare and tortuous ways) the inputs to other subsystems, in turn affecting the outputs of the latter. A policy arena in which everything is connected to everything else promotes self-perpetuating chaos or actions that do nothing more than cancel each other out (for example, 1970s U.S. energy policies to simultaneously regulate prices and promote conservation). Nothing approaching a stable equilibrium can result unless the external factors influencing the system—and to which the system may be trying to respond—effectively stand still. Consider, for example, U.S. trade policy in the 1970s and early 1980s. A refugee from this policy arena informed one of us that his best preparatory reading would have been Franz Kafka's *The Trial*.

The "anything goes" position amounts to indifference about the intellectual inputs to policy choice. If one is thereby led to despair of an effective approach emerging, little would be lost by dispensing with the policy field entirely, along with its component approaches. A position of "nothing goes" is the logical extreme of "anything goes." Policy would rely totally on invisible hands, which we have just dismissed as most feeble when most needed.

Build a Paradigm

Analysts who have taken to heart Kuhn's (1962) account of the development of scientific disciplines would interpret the diversity we have described as evidence of the immature, preparadigm, state-of-the-policy field. On this interpretation, we should take a step down the scientific road by developing a single paradigm, recognized and enforced by practitioners. Such a course would support intellectual conformity to produce the trappings of "normal science." (For an attempted application to the policy field, see Schneider, Stevens, and Tornatzky 1982.) This kind of movement would occur if one of the approaches we have discussed—or one we have missed—were to vanquish its opposition. Alternatively, elements of the various approaches might converge on some common assumptions, theories, and methods. Brunner (1984: 5) seems to believe convergence of this sort is already occurring, especially with respect to conceptualization of the elements of the policy process.

Our own view is less sanguine, given the deep differences

that persist even among those who do indeed agree that policy starts with problem recognition and initiation and moves through selection and implementation to evaluation and (perhaps) termination. Further, more recent accounts of the progress of social science disciplines suggest that attempts to converge on a single paradigm may actually impede progress (Ball 1976; Dryzek 1986). Reifying a single paradigm in the policy field could shrink the problem-solving power currently dispersed through a variety of approaches. Judging from past experience, a likely result of any such attempt would leave those concerned with policy analysis defensively striving for elusive success but despairing of ever achieving it. After this process goes on for several decades—and it has—policy analysts and their observers may begin to doubt the worth of the enterprise. Like the famous stage sailor Mr. Roberts, they may feel condemned to cruise from tedium to ennui (with an occasional excursion to dèjá vu).

Use Everything

Cognizant of diversity of perspectives on any given policy issue, some broad-minded individuals suggest the solution lies in interdisciplinary teams of analysts. In our language, each team would consist of representatives of a variety of technical frames. The minimum ostensible benefit would be that each member can make up for the blind spots of one or more of the others. The maximum conceivable benefit would be some remarkable fusion of perspectives, in which the whole exceeds the sum of its parts. But there is no guarantee that the members of the team will act in statesmanlike fashion. Far more likely is withdrawal into parochial perspectives and analytical preferences. If that happens, fusion and synergy are in reality nothing more than a shared staple or dust jacket. Alternatively, one or more practitioners may attempt to force an approach on the rest of the team, or "sell" it to the uncommitted. Or there might ensue only a chaotic babble of tongues (imagine the likely outcome of an encounter of all our Smoketown protagonists).

The "use everything" procedure makes sense only if encounter between the partisans of various frames is structured to produce clarification and synthesis—as in the dialectical approaches discussed in chapters 10 and 11. The process might prove time consuming, and there is no guarantee that all the relevant perspectives would be represented (or even identified). Participants might not gain any recognition or reward from their respective professional fraternities. Nevertheless, this strategy has the virtue of allowing for combination of the positive contributions of several approaches, while shaking out what is irrelevant and unhelpful.

SELECTION IN CONTEXT

Unlike the selection methods discussed in the previous section, our preferred procedure requires selection among approaches in context. Each of the various approaches we have discussed facilitates the pursuit of some values rather than others and can be fruitfully applied only in a specific range of contexts. Policy problems can exist in a wide variety of settings, and any given approach will apply in only a limited number of these settings. It would therefore be undesirable to reduce the current range of available approaches in the policy field; indeed, even more might be desirable. This recognition is not tantamount to advocating letting a hundred flowers bloom in a thousand contexts. But it does suggest that different occasions demand different flowers and arrangements. A good procedure for selection would specify rules to help one decide when an approach has more to offer than its alternatives.

From this perspective, policy analysis must be sensitive to the kinds of values each approach addresses, the kinds of social problems each can comprehend, and the other aspects of context each demands. For example, welfare economics is most appropriate to budgetary resource-allocation decisions, when efficiency is at issue. Pessimistic information processing is best suited to an essentially well-functioning political system experiencing only mild political conflict. Public choice applies only to formal institutional analysis and design.

The contingent quality of the judgments we reached in the comparative dissections of part 2 appears inescapable once we recognize the facts of life of contextual variation in public policy. First, policy processes vary in their number of participants, degree of partisan conflict, and tightness of coupling.

Hence the capabilities an approach ascribes to the policy process may be plausible in some cases, implausible in others. Second, it is entirely conceivable that an approach may be applicable to only a limited subset of policy choices—perhaps to those pertaining to process rather than content or to strategic choices within the mission area of a single bureaucracy rather than within the overall scope of a government. Hence the policy applicability of the same approach may be great in some cases, nonexistent in others. For example, the individual strand of the social structural approach has empirical relevance only with regard to essentially private goods—goods that can be measured as they accrue differentially to individuals. This strand has little to say about situations involving supply of public goods, which allow for little or no variation across individuals.

The general point here is that the capabilities ascribed to an approach depend heavily on the context of its intended use. Equally important, many of the approaches we have discussed make some very stringent demands on the character of that context. Such demands can be made by both epistemologies and technical approaches.

The context required by each of our technical approaches— at least if it is to be applied authoritatively rather than heuristically, forensically, or dialectically—is highly specific. Our discussion here is brief, as it reiterates points developed more fully in chapters 2 through 6.

1. Welfare economics requires a static environment, high control, little political conflict (high conflict means economic judgments will not be accepted by those whose interests are thereby slighted), minimal uncertainty about the effects of policy, substantial prescience as to the monetary costs and benefits of each policy alternative, a predetermined agenda of policy alternatives (unless stock solutions like a system of standards and charges for pollution control are wheeled out), a receptive bureaucratic audience, and a dominant market order in which the effects of policy are felt (otherwise, costs and benefits are hard to compute).

2. Public choice requires metapolicy on the political agenda, great control on the part of some actor (to secure

metapolicy), the absence of any strong informal power structure, rough consensus on process values, stable preferences, and a highly static environment (one in which the essential nature of the social problems facing a collective choice mechanism does not change).

3. Individual social structure demands rough consensus on values, high control, low uncertainty, a static environment (such that experiments may be replicated), rapid feedback, low complexity (so that identified causal relationships are valid), and minimal "public good" elements in the ends of policy.

4. Group social structure is less demanding than the individual strand, but it does require the existence of groups, actual or latent conflict among them, and unequal distribution of some good.

5. Optimistic information processing needs high control, consensus on values, muted political conflict, metapolicy capabilities, good feedback, an environment of no more than moderate complexity (if problems are too complex, they cannot easily be decomposed), and stability in the process of policy.

6. Pessimistic information processing is less demanding. However, it does require rapid feedback, reasonable simplicity in problem structure, and the absence of pressures for radical change in the policy process. These modest requirements reflect the modest ambitions of pessimistic information processing practitioners.

7. Political philosophy requires a classic conscience issue on the policy agenda, a minimum of linkage across policy issues, an absence of feasibility constraints, and no difficult technical questions concerning appropriate means to ends.

The ineluctable conclusion here is that, with one or two minor exceptions, the authoritative application of any of our technical approaches requires a set of circumstances that will never be met fully. Authoritative and comprehensively applicable single-framework policy analysis is generally beyond our grasp. We must be content with Lasswell's classic description of the policy sciences as "contextual, multi-method, and problem-oriented."

Epistemologies also make demands upon context. (Again, the brevity of our discussion here is accounted for by the fuller development of these points in chapters 8 through 11.)

1. Positivism requires an essentially static environment, constant or recurrent policy problems (rather than truly novel ones), high control over its environment on the part of the policy process, and consensus on values.
2. The requirements of piecemeal social engineering are similar to those of positivism, though it allows for a slightly more complex and dynamic environment. However, social problems in this environment must be well structured and decomposable, and the environment itself must be conducive to the generation of unambiguous feedback signals about the effects of policy.
3. Accommodation (and, to a lesser extent, eclectic policy analysis) demands high control, minimal political conflict, and an underlying consensus on values.
4. Forensic and critical policy analysis place comparatively modest demands on context, other than that control be weak and that stakeholders in the policy process be willing to devote large amounts of their time and energy to a discursive process. The modesty of the demands they place on context may be one of the strongest points in favor of forensic and critical approaches. We return to this point below.

The general point here is that attention to context is vital. We build on this insight in chapter 13.

A FINAL VISIT TO SMOKE VALLEY

Two years into her five-year contract as executive director of the Smoke Valley Air Quality Commission, life is not going smoothly for Gloria Meander. Her relationship with the commissioners is still cordial, her staff is very supportive, and she is well regarded among Smoke Valley civic, business, and labor leaders. It is becoming apparent, though, that Smoke Valley air is not getting any cleaner. Some of the more radical members of the local chapter of Friends of the Environment (FOE) are annoyed with the complacency they see in the SVAQC, and they instigate a campaign of criticism. FOE makes an alliance with PUMP and CARP, who see precious little benefit flowing in their direction from SVAQC decisions, despite their places on the commission's advisory board (whose meetings are by now badly attended and generally ignored). It has been a quiet year for news in the valley, so several local journalists join the campaign. Intellectual criticism of the SVAQC—some of which begins to be directed at Meander personally—comes from the Camelot School and Smoke Valley University Sociology Department, where disgruntled academics are still smarting from what they regard as unwarranted rejection of their various policy analyses.

Meander decides to get these people off her back. One way to accomplish this, she reasons, is to undertake an external review of the air quality issue. Her own staff analysts are not really credible, for they are closely tied to the SVAQC structure and are known for their loyalty to Meander. Most of the local academics in policy-related disciplines are still thoroughly estranged from the SVAQC and could be expected to produce too critical an appraisal for Meander's liking. Hence she casts her eyes further afield, and sees to it that the commission offers a contract to two policy analysts she knows from her graduate school days: professors Beaver and Kayak, who now work at faraway universities of modest repute. In Meander's eyes, Beaver and Kayak have several desirable qualities. First, they are not partisans of any of the analytical frameworks that contested—and lost—in Smoke Valley air pollution policy analysis in the previous four years. Second, they reside far away from the Smoketown area and have no local influence. And third, they combine at least a minimum of intellectual credibility and low rates of pay.

For once Meander may have miscalculated. She has not been paying attention to intellectual developments in the policy field since she left her position at Smoke Valley University. In particular, she is unaware that Beaver and Kayak have been working on a book on the underpinnings of the field. Knowing Meander's proclivities, Beaver and Kayak neglect to

inform her of their current research. They regard their Smoketown assignment as a golden opportunity to test some of their
ideas about the basis of policy analysis and the prospects for
reasoned policy design.

Meander conceives of the Beaver-Kayak review as simply a
means to help put out immediate fires, and hence she is characteristically vague in specifying the terms of their assignment. This ambiguity gives Beaver and Kayak considerable
latitude.

Our two analysts reason that the last thing Smoketown
needs is still another piece of single-framework policy analysis
to add to the existing analytical confusion. But they do need to
discover what went wrong with all the studies undertaken previously, as a prelude to doing better. To this end, they collect all
the written (published and unpublished) materials produced by
the Camelot team, the public choice group, Smoke Valley University sociologists, George Hamburger and his assistants, the
political philosophy seminar, and the Meander regime. Their
examination of this written material is supplemented by interviews with the analytical principals. Professor Uteil declines a
meeting on the grounds that the Camelot analysis remains correct and authoritative as written and needs no further explica-
tion. The public choice group has now splintered, but several of
its members agree to discuss their analysis, hoping that their
own newly modified (but increasingly disparate) ideas for institutional redesign can find an audience. The Smoke Valley University Sociology Department arrives en masse at the Beaver-
Kayak office suite, full of new ideas for analysis and thrilled to
get another opportunity to put a foot in the public policy door.
George Hamburger, now chief executive officer of Calvin R.
Giant, seeks a hefty fee for his renewed services, which proves
beyond the Beaver-Kayak budget. He also suggests that Giant is
well suited to take over the entire renewed analytical effort—if
suitably compensated.

After reviewing all the various pieces of analysis, Beaver
and Kayak dismiss each as of highly limited utility. Each is
clearly insensitive to one or more dimensions of the context of
policy choice and the values at issue. This insensitivity is still
more acute when it comes to the present, changed context and
value milieu. Thus Beaver and Kayak decide to make a fresh

analytical start. They receive Meander's cautious approval to proceed, though by now she is becoming suspicious of their motives. Hence she assigns one of her trusted assistants to liaise with them. For their part, Beaver and Kayak leave open the possibility that one or more of the previously applied analytical frameworks could reenter the picture at some later stage in their analysis.

For the first step in their reanalysis, Beaver and Kayak contemplate the values now at issue in Smoketown air pollution policy. They find multiple and conflicting values held by the relevant stakeholders. Friends of the Environment and the newly formed Citizens' League Against Smoke Pollution (CLASP) attach intrinsic value to clean air and are also highly concerned about the effect of air pollution on human health. Their concerns are shared—if to a less intense degree—by many ordinary Smoke Valley residents. PUMP and WALO remain committed to their redistributional goals. An economic recovery has made the Silicon Smoke Industrial Park less crucial to the Valley's future, hence the Chamber of Commerce is now more solidly against costly measures for the sake of clean air. The Smoketown City Council is now polarized: some of its younger members want a high-technology environmentally clean future for the valley, others are more concerned with retaining smokestack industry. The SVAQC bureaucracy under Meander seems to be concerned above all with its own budget, though some of its more idealistic members are disgruntled with the commission's do-nothing attitude. Beaver and Kayak suggest that two underlying dimensions of value have been missed by nearly all the stakeholders: the ecological integrity of Smoke Valley and (following Camelot and public choice) economic efficiency.

Clearly, substantial dissensus on values characterizes the air pollution case. Rather than sidestep this issue, Beaver and Kayak suggest the establishment of a forum for the structured but free discussion of these issues. Membership in this forum will technically be open to all concerned parties, though a number of invitations will be extended to key actors. So, for example, an invitation will be sent to Professor Uteil, who could argue the case for economic efficiency. Beaver and Kayak will themselves participate selectively in the proceedings, though the forum will initially be overseen by an expert in mediation. The outcome of these discussions cannot be foreseen; some consensus on which subsequent actions could be based might emerge—but there is no guarantee.

Next, Beaver and Kayak consider the context of their own analytical effort. This context is defined, first of all, by substantial complexity and uncertainty. The ramifications of various pollutants in the environment and their ultimate effects on the various values held by stakeholders in the issue cannot easily be charted. Pollutants interact with each other and with natural forces in variable and unpredictable ways. There may be some potential for feedback to ameliorate uncertainty and complexity, though intangibility of some of the values and the pervasive sleeper effects of certain kinds of pollutants may frustrate effective feedback. Certainly, an improved system of environmental monitoring and information presentation would help here, and some aspects of the Hamburger plan might be worth reviving. However, any such system would generate information only on technical questions of pollutant concentration. The impact on the real and perceived interests of the various stakeholders would not be captured by such means, still less changes in general values such as economic efficiency and ecological integrity.

The context is also characterized by weak control. The SVAQC is buffeted by a variety of political forces. Under Meander's sway, it has not sought to escape these constraints and assert a more forceful role. Hence the prospect for effective innovation in policy content seems poor. The context is, however, reasonably stable—the principal actors have coalesced into a fairly well-defined set, with changes such as that occasioned by the formation of CLASP now rare. But the potential audience for policy analysis is diverse and extensive, for there is widespread dissatisfaction with SVAQC performance.

The setting facing the Beaver-Kayak analysis may therefore be characterized in terms of high complexity and uncertainty, moderate feedback potential, weak control, substantial stability, and a broad audience. Clearly, none of the technical approaches applied so far to air pollution in Smoke Valley fits this context precisely—with the one exception of Meander's pessimistic information processing. Unfortunately, the latter approach has yielded results unacceptable in terms of some widely held values at issue.

Beaver and Kayak issue a preliminary report with three recommendations. First, a discursive forum should be established, in which partisans of different positions can participate. Second, the development of analytical approaches relevant to the context of Smoketown air quality issue should be funded. They recognize that the SVAQC may be unwilling to fund this second effort, and that the Hustle Thyme Foundation may be a more appropriate source of financial support. Third, some specific analytical procedures should be followed, based on the ground already covered. These procedures range from problem interpretation to the crafting, development, and assessment of policy alternatives in context. Such procedures should be sensitive to any value consensus achieved, and they should draw upon existing or novel technical approaches where pertinent. The discursive forum should be retained as a check on these latter steps.

These developments are too much for Meander, who pulls out all the stops to frustrate what now looks increasingly like a direct threat to her own authority and to the cozy relationship she has established with the commissioners and many Smoketown notables. Meander meets individually with the commissioners and convinces them that the report should be buried. One of them is quoted to the effect that "nobody elected Beaver and Kayak." Meander finds some unexpected allies in the Camelot School, the remnants of the public choice group, and Hamburger, who all regard the Beaver-Kayak report as both superfluous and a threat to their technical credibility. More sympathetic reactions to the report come from several media anti-SVAQC campaigners, FOE and CLASP, and some of the more enlightened members of the Chamber of Commerce. PUMP and WALO swallow their misgivings and agree to participate in the New Smoke Forum. And some SVAQC staff members see the report as providing an opportunity to actually begin attacking the roots of the pollution problem. Local politicians sense a bandwagon, and despite Meander's frantic lobbying, several of them announce their support for reopening the air quality issue.

Sensing she has lost this round, Meander suppresses her

ire and allows the renewed analytical effort to proceed. She thinks she will be able to co-opt or derail the analysis at some future time, but for now regards it as politic to go along. And who knows, there may just be something in what her old colleagues Beaver and Kayak have to offer. For Gloria is beginning to tire of presiding over a bureaucracy that does not actually accomplish anything . . .

Chapter 13

Toward Policy Design

Our EXPLORATION of major frames of reference and knowledge orientations leaves us dissatisfied with three commonly recommended stances for policy analysis. One attributes correctness to a single technical approach. A second would leave public policy to those who "do it" as a historical and institutional legacy. A third would compile a multicourse menu of dishes from several frames and epistemologies in the interests of a balanced diet. We believe there is a fourth position, falling under the rubric of *policy design*, which offers both a way to cope with the problems discussed in the previous chapter and the most promising direction for the future of the policy field.

Policy design has some similarities to design in architecture (Perlmutter 1965) and engineering (Bobrow 1972: 25–30). Design in each of these cases pursues values by recommending purposeful activities specific to time and place. Each stresses context sensitivity, the application of tools in pursuit of values, and a special focus on factors open to change by human agents.

However, one should not read too much into these commonalities. In engineering and architecture one generally finds a static environment, simple goals, readily decomposable problems, little conflict over values, hardly any partisan political conflict, and high control over the object being designed (see Alexander 1964; Simon 1981). Policy design, in contrast, may face a fluid environment, goals that are complex and often obscure, problems not amenable to decomposition into independent and manageable chunks, parties riven by conflicts of values and interests, uncertainty, and fragmented control. In the light of these rather severe problems, it is unsurprising that sporadic policy design efforts have stopped far short of a fully articulated set of strategies for the would-be policy designer.

Design is the creation of an actionable form to promote valued outcomes in a particular context. It is the emphasis on clarified values and context sensitivity that promises amelioration of the problems discussed in the previous chapter. We now turn to the three central elements of design: values, context, and the creation of form (which can apply to both the content and process of policy).

ADDRESS VALUES

In addressing values in policy design, one might begin with vague desiderata—peace, prosperity, equality, and the like. But one should not be content with such bland sentiments— value clarification needs to be pursued to the point where it provides guidance to the creation and assessment of actionable forms. The relevant values need to be formulated in operational and socially comprehensible form, which in turn involves three dimensions. The first is timing: when should the end be sought, and for how long should it be maintained? The second is amount: how much is enough? Sometimes more of a value will always be better. On other occasions, there will be thresholds of satisfaction. The third is priority: how important are the values relative to one another? It is rare that any alternative promises to satisfy all relevant values. Priority judgments are needed to distinguish between more and less attractive trade-offs (Bobrow 1974).

Occasionally, the values sought through public policy are few in number, simple, unambiguous, static, and uncontroversial. More often, they are multiple, complex, ambiguous, fluid, and controversial. In the former case, policy design can resemble engineering and architecture. Policy analysts would simply apply the technical perspective embodying the values in question. Thus welfare economics embodies allocative efficiency, group social structure addresses the well-being of particular groups in society, and Kantian political philosophy is responsive to individual rights. Alternatively, technical approaches for which value specification is arbitrary (such as optimistic information processing and piecemeal social engineering) can be brought into play. But even in this tractable set of cases, any choice of technical approach should remain tentative pending consideration of the context in which policy will take effect.

Such procedures will not suffice in the more frequent cases where goals and values are troublesome. Some means for coping with unstable and conflicting goals is required. Of the approaches we have discussed, only the forensic and critical epistemologies are capable of this task in anticipatory fashion. Incremental information processing can address conflicting values but only through the give and take of political interaction as a policy process unfolds. These three approaches can help meet an essential requirement (if design is to be more than an academic exercise): consensus on values—at the beginning of the design process, or in the course of stipulating context, or concurrent with the unfolding of policy process or content forms. Value consensus need not be reached prior to design, but such consensus must be attained at some point during the design process—perhaps stimulated by the design activity itself. Consensus need not be perfect or universal among those affected by a proposal, but those whose consent is required for its realization must at least be indifferent to the emergent shared value position.

Capture Context

The success or failure of any (designed) policy depends crucially on context. Context here can be of two kinds. One is the milieu (external to the policy process) within which policy will take effect. The other is the policy process within which designers and others are pursuing the adoption and implementation of policies. The pertinent context is something the analyst just has to live with, regardless of the obstacles it presents to the achievement of valued outcomes. Reality is a given, not mutable in the interests of seductive assumptions about the capabilities of a particular analytical approach.

While we do not have a definitive and exhaustive scheme

for classifying contexts, the following five dimensions strike us as having an important bearing on the kinds of policy analysis and design that can be pursued.

Complexity and Uncertainty

Complexity refers to the number and variety of elements and interactions in the environment of a decision system (see Weaver 1948). Substantial complexity means that the effects of any particular decision or policy can be modified, magnified, or nullified as they ramify through the environment. Accordingly, there is considerable uncertainty before (and after) the fact as to what might (or did) happen. The consequences of an action are unpredictable because the milieu cannot be comprehended at the requisite level of detail. It becomes impossible to establish reliable cause-and-effect mechanisms, to estimate temporal leads and lags, and to engage in any defensible decomposition into analytically distinct subsystems. These limits on predictability become especially acute when the valued outcomes sought and the proposed means to those outcomes involve radical departure from the status quo. Any designer assuming clarity and predictability under such circumstances is indeed utopian.

Feedback Potential

Complexity and uncertainty can be ameliorated by good feedback. Feedback is simply information about the effects of past choices, which a system can use to inform its subsequent choices. Feedback is potentially useful here to the extent that it is timely, clear, accurate, and comprehensive. Timeliness means that feedback is received before the implications of an action become irreversible. Clarity refers to the extent to which feedback has unambiguous implications for ensuing choices. Accuracy is the degree to which the information received really does pertain to the effects of previous actions. Comprehensiveness means that effects on the whole range of pertinent values are reported.

This list suggests that feedback potential can vary substantially. Feedback quality can depend upon the tangibility of the values involved, the degree of difficulty in identifying cause-and-effect relationships, and the interests and capabilities of the providers of feedback. Feedback potential is especially high when complexity and uncertainty are but moderate, when the outcomes sought and the milieu in which they are pursued are historically familiar, and when the pertinent effects have readily identifiable harbingers. Good feedback is unlikely when critical members of the system are motivated to distort or downplay bad news, which might be taken as indicative of poor judgment in prior policy selection. Finally, the quality of feedback and policy based upon it depend crucially on the responsiveness of those who receive the feedback.

Control

Control is the degree to which a single actor (or small group of actors) can ensure that a form is executed faithfully to its design. Quintessential control is rare—perhaps nonexistent—in public policy. The factors obstructing control include partisan conflict, semiautonomous implementing bureaucracies, garbage can tendencies in the policy process, and acts of nature (the weather, for example, for agricultural policy). Policies resting on assumptions of strong and concentrated control may be actionable only on paper; if so, their adoption is but a hollow victory for their designers. It should be noted that complexity and weak feedback can undercut control; both make it hard to induce others to do what a particular form expects of them.

Stability

The actors and interests involved in a policy issue may form a well-defined and constant set. On the other hand, it is entirely possible that actors may move among choice opportunities in unpredictable fashion (as they do in loosely coupled garbage can models). Instability of this sort means that the same issue can attract different sets of actors each time it arises. Sources of instability include turnover and reassignment of office holders; competition for elite and mass attention; the issue attention cycle, involving shifts from general indifference to fear to optimism about solutions (Downs 1972); and, less obviously, political factors such as changes in economic structures. For an example of the last kind of instability, consider how a policy design constructed in 1973 for ensuring reliability in U.S. oil imports for the 1983–93 decade would have gone astray if it concentrated on OPEC suppliers only and missed the rise of non-OPEC oil exporters. Even when the actors in an issue area are stable over time, their interests may not be. Take the example of U.S. trade policy: the same large firms continue to matter, but with a decline in their competitiveness in foreign markets their preference may change from free trade to protection at home and government sponsorship abroad.

Audience

While we reject the idea that policy analysis should accommodate itself to the prevailing distribution of policy-making capabilities, it remains true that the analyst or designer must be sensitive to the perceptions and interests of those who need to be galvanized into action by any policy proposal. These people constitute part of the analyst's context within the policy process; collectively, they are the analyst's audience. The character of this audience can vary, depending, for example, on whether the analyst is an employee of a particular bureaucracy, or a staff member of a public interest group.

In contrast to the first four dimensions of context, the analyst may have some latitude in selecting his or her audience. But even given this latitude, the proclivities of the chosen audience are ignored at the analyst's peril. For example, if the analyst is an employee of the audience, he or she "must have some understanding of how the organization actually functions, of who has power, of who has information, and of the incentives to which people with power and information respond" (Lynn 1980: 17). "The analyst-as-craftsman cannot define the 'problem' to be addressed . . . without taking into account the perceptions of the audience for the analysis" (Lynn 1980: 14). Thus attention needs to be paid to the cognitive style and tastes of the audience. If the audience has an appetite for precise numerical information, value precision, and synoptic reasoning, then welfare economics, public choice, decision analysis, and optimistic information processing will be attractive to it. If, in contrast, the audience is allergic to numbers, acquiesces in normative ambiguity, and prefers a minimum of decision commitments, then incremental information processing will be far more palatable. The point here is not that policy designers should end up at the same place as the audience; but that designers must begin there.

SELECT APPROPRIATE APPROACHES

With the captured context in mind, one can then go through the various technical approaches to see which can fit this context—bearing in mind, of course, how one has chosen to deal with the prior question of values. To illustrate: suppose that the policy issue at hand features consensus on values, moderate complexity, high feedback potential, high control, and stable actors and interests. One might then reasonably apply piecemeal social engineering, individual social structure, and synoptic information processing.

An appropriate approach addresses the relevant values and the factors that, given the context, determine policy results. Thus the approach must be amenable to contextually appropriate reasoning about the impact, adoption, and implementation of policy alternatives.[1] The trouble is that each approach can pursue this reasoning only in limited ways, which in turn limits the relevance of the approach to the case at hand. The Smoke Valley stories provide cautionary illustrations of the ways in which particular frames can impose values and assume a context far different from that actually operating.

Even if one avoids insensitive application of a frame of the sort engaged in by some of our Smoke Valley analysts, the fit between context and frame will still usually be less than perfect, which means that the analyst needs to be a craftsperson rather than a robot in judging the degree of acceptable imper-

---

1. These three forms of reasoning may be summarized as follows. Impact reasoning begins with the assumption that a policy alternative really will be adopted and implemented; it then proceeds to stipulate what must happen for the policy to do well in terms of the pertinent values. For example, what behaviors and in whom must the policy trigger? Adoption reasoning clarifies who must support, consent to, or acquiesce in actions. Adoption reasoning also addresses why actors will or will not do what adoption requires. Implementation reasoning addresses the identity, willingness, and capabilities of those who will carry out policy and the authority, information, and resources they need.

fection and how approaches may be bent to fit the circumstances at hand.

This last suggestion may disappoint those looking for a precise policy design cookbook. Any such cookbook would contain a collectively exhaustive and mutually exclusive taxonomy of contexts and values, together with the procedures to be followed in each category in that taxonomy. A skilled and attentive cook could then guarantee success. Such recipes cannot easily be written for two reasons.

First, there is a danger of taxonomic proliferation. If there are just two possible positions on each of the five dimensions outlined above, then we get thirty-two (two to the power five) categories of context. If—as seems likely—there are more than two positions, the possibilites multiply. A taxonomy with large numbers of cells can soon become too cumbersome for ready use, except for optimistic information processors with their computer-based decision aids.

Second, we suspect that there are some categories of context in which none of the currently available technical approaches (or epistemologies) are applicable or defensible. For example, a situation of profound uncertainty, high complexity, dissensus on values, no feedback, weak control, great instability, and an audience interested only in simple solutions that reduce current anxiety has little hope for appropriate policy design. Some might argue for a second-best solution here— apply the approach with the best fit, even if it is not very comfortable. Such a solution would, we believe, reflect badly on the whole idea of policy design. Far better to use such situations to advance the foundations of policy design by exploring and developing approaches, with these gaps in our current set of tools in mind. The less the summed capabilities of our approaches can cope with the range of conceivable contexts, the less should we expect from designed policy.

In passing, we should note one superficially beguiling strategy for messy contexts. This strategy involves looking to some technical expertise—be it natural science or social science—to convert an intractable political issue into a technically manageable one. In one sense, this is a counsel of despair. More important, it will rarely work: in complex and controversial policy issues, the natural science experts disagree among themselves as much as political actors do (see our comments on natural science in chapter 8).

APPLY THE APPROPRIATE APPROACHES

Assuming there does exist one or more approaches both appropriate to the captured context and consistent with the perspective on values adopted, one can proceed to use these approaches to perform or assist in the following operations.

Interpretation of the problem and performance goals

To illustrate, welfare economics interprets problems in terms of market failure and performance in terms of efficiency. Group social structure interprets problems in terms of inequality of distribution and outcomes in terms of equity.

Identification and Collection of Needed Information

Information processing calls for data on the search and interpretation attributes of individuals and organizations. Group social structure requires information about the characteristics and holdings of categories within populations. Decision analysis leads one to inquire into the utility functions of political leadership.

Invention and Stipulation of Policy Alternatives

Some approaches possess a stock of standard policy instruments. Thus welfare economics has quasi-market incentive mechanisms; public choice has an inventory of institutional arrangements; and optimistic information processing stresses the application of generic man-machine combinations. On the other hand, there is nothing to stop a broader search for policy alternatives, whether or not the approach one is utilizing possesses a ready stock of instruments of its own. Here, one can make use of analogy (across different policy areas), history (alternatives applied in the past), the current political agenda, parallel cases (policies adopted by other governments), or even creativity. The latter, contrary to common wisdom, can be taught and systematized (see, for example, de Bono 1970).

Policy alternatives can be closed and mechanistic or can leave substantial latitude for specification in the course of their pursuit. Mechanistic policy alternatives can contain substantial numbers of "if . . . then" statements. The degree of detail appropriate depends on the context.

There is no good rule to tell exactly when one has a satisfactory set of policy alternatives. The following rule of thumb may sometimes be helpful. One alternative will correspond to current practice. A second will provide for no purposeful action. At least one more will consist of purposeful actions not currently followed. Thus some effort is made to control for the pervasive inertia of the public sector and for the assumption that doing something necessarily helps. Innovative policy alternatives are made to compete with both previous practice and "hands off" alternatives. A "new" policy must then have something more than freshness to commend it.

Assessment and Comparison of Policy Alternatives

All the approaches we discussed in part 2 possess methods for the assessment and comparison of policy alternatives. The judgments resulting from the application of any of these methods will apply only to a given context. Correspondingly, if context has been improperly characterized, an approach will yield misleading judgments about the quality of policy alternatives. Hence the operation of judging the relative and absolute merits of policy alternatives provides a useful check on the accuracy with which context has been captured. If predicted results are implausible, then perhaps context needs to be reexamined.

Assessment and comparison of alternatives involve a common set of basic questions. What is the best result an alternative can produce in terms of valued outcomes? What is the worst? How likely is each? What is the range of probable error in these judgments? How uncertain are the results? To what extent will an alternative yield clear and prompt feedback? Is an alternative robust (that is, capable of doing well across a wide range of future conditions and developments), or is it fragile (easily derailed if the future does not unfold according to expectations)? Finally, how clear or murky is the promise of competing alternatives? This last question bears on the extent to which a superior policy alternative can be clearly identified.

Assessment and comparison may well reopen the issue of inventing and stipulating policy alternatives. The point here is that a set of options should not be cast in concrete and then mechanically assessed. Instead, proposed policy alternatives can be treated as open to modification, testing, and perhaps replacement in a process of convergence on good choices (see, for example, Quade 1982: 111–13).

Construction of Arguments

The process of policy design sketched here is not mechanical and linear. Rather, it is a recursive process, in which the latter stages can both advance upon and reopen earlier phases. Conflicting values and perspectives, instability, and weak control often necessitate this recursiveness. The design orientation proposed here is a means for coping with this reality while still generating policy-applicable knowledge. Design often involves the construction of arguments, including arguments about the appropriateness of any approach to the problem at hand. The objective here is to improve the quality of debate, as proposals, frameworks, and their adherents confront one another in the policy arena.

If policy design is to contribute to such systematic argument, it will often need a discursive, critical aspect. Ideally, the resulting clash of views will produce a synthesis, in the classic dialectical sense of an improvement over both thesis and antithesis.

This posture may imply a modest role for the individual policy analyst, but it does face up to the obvious imperfections of all the approaches we have discussed in this volume as they face the realities of public policy. No single frame can provide all the answers in the polyglot of contexts and value positions characterizing the arena of public policy, even within the confines of particular policy issue areas. Policy design of the kind we commend is catalytic rather than authoritative: it involves no dictates to apparently lesser mortals among political elites and publics. This stance is consistent with the idea of critical policy analysis—under which frames are to be used rather than believed or routinely applied.

There is a clear implication here for the education and skills policy analysts should acquire. If they are to be parties to a constructive, critical dialogue, they need a good grasp of several approaches, rather than a technical mastery of one. But a broader repertoire will not substitute for the ability to discern normative issues and to grasp political context. The combination of these attributes offers the prospect of morally sensitive, politically realistic, and sound analysis—and thus of improved policy dialogue. This combination may seem a tall order; but the record of more constricted analytical approaches to public policy is distinctly unimpressive.

Bibliographical Notes

CHAPTER 2. WELFARE ECONOMICS

Anderson et al. (1977), Baumol and Oates (1975), Dales (1968), Dorfman and Dorfman (1977), Kneese and Schultze (1975), and Ridker and Henning (1971) apply welfare economics principles to environmental policy. Kelman (1981) provides a critique. Some general formulations central to welfare economics and intended to buttress its policy applications have been developed by Bator (1957, 1958), Baumol (1977), Dorfman (1969), Freeman (1977), Haveman and Weisbrod (1975), Krutilla (1967), Margolis (1977), Musgrave (1969), Weisbrod (1968), and Zeckhauser (1974). Useful applications can be found in Amacher, Tollison, and Willett (1976), Enthoven and Smith (1971), Haveman and Margolis (1977), Hitch and McKean (1965), Mishan (1973), Stokey and Zeckhauser (1978), and Sugden and Williams (1978). Critiques of the approach or its elements are provided by Diesing (1962), Elkin (1983), Goldfarb (1975), Leman and Nelson (1981), Page (1977), Tribe (1972, 1973), and Wildavsky (1966). Tribe, Diesing, Wildavsky, and Elkin believe political health is a better guide to policy than economic health. While economically based, Lerner (1944) offers an alternative to mainstream reasoning on equity and efficiency.

CHAPTER 3. PUBLIC CHOICE

The general foundations of public choice are developed in Arrow (1963), Mueller (1979), Olson (1965), Riker (1962), Riker and Ordeshook (1973), and Sen (1970, 1972). Empirical support for public choice assumptions is yielded by Gist and Hill (1981) and Sterne, Rabushka, and Scott (1972). Advocacy of the public choice approach to policy analysis can be found in Blair and Maser (1978), Mitchell and Mitchell (1986), Ostrom and Ostrom (1971), Tullock (1979), and Tullock and Wagner (1978). Russell (1979) constitutes a progress report on empirical applications. The case against bureaucracy and bureaucrats is presented by Niskanen (1971). Arguments for particular institutions and choice mechanisms can be found in Bish (1978), Black (1958), Buchanan and Tullock (1962), Coase (1960), Ferejohn, Forsythe, and Noll (1978), Haefele (1973), E. Ostrom (1971, 1973),

215

Schultze (1970), and Tiebout (1956). Supportive applications are made by Buchanan and Tullock (1974), Doron (1979), Hochman and Peterson (1974), Olson (1982), and Ricketts (1981). The approach is attacked by DeGregori (1974), Furniss (1978), Goldberg (1974), and Golembiewski (1977). Its limited treatment of institutions is exposed implicitly in the work of Edelman (1971, 1977) and Tribe (1976). Empirical doubts are raised by Christenson and Sachs (1980), Encarnation (1982), and Lovrich and Neiman (1984).

CHAPTER 4. SOCIAL STRUCTURE

Sociology and varieties of the social structure approach are addressed in Coleman (1971), Demerath, Larsen, and Schuessler (1975), Gouldner (1970), Lazarsfeld, Reitz, and Pasanella (1975), MacRae (1973), Menzies (1982), Rein (1976), and Scott and Shore (1979). Advocacy issues are a major concern of Bulmer (1983), Guillemin and Horowitz (1983), and Tallman (1976). Applications of the approach are made by Banfield (1970), Coleman (1966), Cone and Hayes (1980), Harrington (1962), Jencks (1972), A. Myrdal (1941), G. Myrdal (1944), Piven and Cloward (1971), and Titmuss (1971).

CHAPTER 5. INFORMATION PROCESSING

Major issues in information processing are presented and explored in the works of Lindblom, March, Simon, and their associates. This literature spans the incremental-rationalist debate, delves deeply into organizational behavior, and develops the brain, computer, and garbage can analogies. See Braybrooke and Lindblom (1963), Cohen, March, and Olsen (1972), Cyert and March (1963), Lindblom (1959, 1965, 1968, 1979), Lindblom and Cohen (1979), March (1978), March and Olsen (1976), March and Simon (1958), Newell and Simon (1972), and Simon (1957, 1960, 1969, 1978). The origins of cybernetics can be found in the writings of Wiener (1948, 1954) and its extension in Deutsch (1963) and Steinbruner (1974). Some intriguing Soviet views can be glimpsed in Afyansev and Melikhov (1979) and Sergiyev (1979).

Decision analysis is developed by Bell, Keeney, and Raiffa (1977), Keeney and Raiffa (1976), and Raiffa (1968). For illustrative applications, see Edwards, Guttentag, and Snapper (1975), Keeney (1973), and Ulvila and Snider (1980). Behavioral decision theory is assayed and illustrated in Slovic, Fischoff, and Lichtenstein (1977) and Tversky and Kahneman (1975). Applications of the incremental approach to public policy are made by Allison (1974), Crecine (1969),

Halperin (1974), Kanter (1975), Neustadt (1970), and Wildavsky (1974). Suggestions for closer approximation to optimistic information processing are provided by Berlin and Weiss (1977), George (1972, 1980), Janis and Mann (1977), and Mason (1969). Warnings against such attempts can be found in Bardach (1977), Biderman (1966), Brewer and Shubik (1979), Hargrove (1975), Perrow (1972), Pressman and Wildavsky (1973), Wildavsky (1966), and Wilensky (1967).

CHAPTER 6. POLITICAL PHILOSOPHY

Gunnell (1983) surveys political philosophy as both a subfield of political science and an interdisciplinary endeavor. The two contemporary nonutilitarian classics in political philosophy are Nozick (1974) and Rawls (1971). Other recent attempts at grand theorizing include those of Ackerman (1980) and Fried (1978). A debate of the pros and cons of utilitarianism may be found in Smart and Williams (1973). Minority concerns for an ecological ethic are represented in Callicott (1979). Goodin (1982) connects theory with policy under a utilitarian banner. Specific policy applications may be found in Dworkin (1977), Fishkin (1983), Goodin (1985), Grey (1976), Shue (1980), and Walzer (1977). Two journals that promise more than they deliver in terms of policy applications are *Philosophy and Public Affairs* and *Ethics*.

CHAPTER 8. POSITIVISM

The proponents of positivism for the policy field include Anderson (1979), Dye (1976, 1984), Eulau (1977), Nachmias (1979), and Ranney (1968). In political science specifically, policy-oriented postbehavioralists include Easton (1969) and Falco (1973). The critics of positivist policy analysis include Brunner (1982), Fay (1975), Paris and Reynolds (1983), Rein (1976), and Tribe (1972). Kuhn (1962) and Popper (1959) are critical of positivist conceptions of natural science. Von Wright (1971) makes additional criticisms of positivism in the social sciences.

CHAPTER 9. PIECEMEAL SOCIAL ENGINEERING

The most consistent and effective advocate of piecemeal social engineering is Popper (see especially Popper, 1972), though he shows no concern for the policy field per se. Avowed Popperians in the policy field include Campbell (1969), the high priest of social experimentation. A more recent convert is Dror (1984a), who commends a "modified critical rationalism" to policy analysis. Prominent exponents of social experimentation in public policy also include Campbell and Ross (1968), Campbell and Stanley (1963), Cook and Campbell (1979), and Rivlin (1971). Some good examples of policy experimentation may be found in Freeman and Solomon (1981). Wilson (1983) commends an experimental approach to policy against violent crime. Discontent with the experimental approach to policy evaluation is expressed by Edwards, Guttentag, and Snapper (1975) and Phillips (1976), and more widely detected by Palumbo and Nachmias (1983).

CHAPTER 10. FROM RATIONALITY TO RELATIVISM

Frame-sensitive inquiry owes much to Kuhn (1962). Lakatos (1970) and Popper (1970) attempt to portray Kuhn as a relativist. Kuhn (1970) demurs. The leading contemporary avowed relativist is Feyerabend (1975, 1978).

What we term eclectic policy analysis is sketched by Landau (1977) and Rein (1976, 1983). Rein also has sympathies with a forensic approach, though more truly forensic strategies are developed by Brown (1976), Dunn (1981), Hambrick (1974), Paris and Reynolds (1983), and Rivlin (1973). The more systematic work in this idiom reflects Toulmin's (1958) analysis of the logical structure of argument. Lindblom and Cohen (1979) offer perhaps the most powerful relativist conception of policy analysis.

CHAPTER 11. FROM RELATIVISM TO CRITICAL ENLIGHTENMENT

Beginning with works relevant to our discussion of accommodation, political feasibility analysis is addressed by Allison (1974), Behn (1981), and Meltsner (1972). Caplan (1979), Caplan, Morrison, and Stambaugh (1975), Chelimsky (1982), and Weiss (1977, 1980) contemplate problems of knowledge utilization in policy making. On the prospects for accommodation, see especially H. Margolis (1973), Meltsner (1976), and Wholey (1983). House and Coleman (1980), Levine and Williams (1971), and Palumbo and Nachmias (1983) all suggest the analyst locate his or her tasks in the appropriate political or organizational environment.

In critical policy analysis, basic works include Habermas (1971, 1973b, and 1984), although Fay (1975: 92–110) offers a clearer and more accessible account of critical theory. Habermas (1973a) and Mc-

Carthy (1978) discuss the "ideal speech situation." The many pertinent works of Lasswell include Lasswell (1930, 1948a, 1960, 1961, 1965, 1980) and Lasswell and McDougal (1943). An outline of "interpretive" social science may be found in von Wright (1971). Ahonen (1983) and Edelman (1977) provide studies of systematically distorted communication in policy debate. The essential idea of holistic experimentation is sketched by Mitroff and Blankenship (1973), and discussed as prototyping by Holmberg, Dobyns, et al. (1962) and Lasswell (1963: 95–122). Contemporary critical policy analysts include Dallmayr (1981), Dunn (1982), Dunn, Mitroff, and Deutsch (1981), and Forester (1981, 1983). Examples of critical policy analysis are harder to come by. Two good examples of analysis designed to provide critical dialogue are G. Myrdal (1944) and Titmuss (1974). Berger (1977) is a summary report on a policy process involving extensive informed participation and communicative ethics. Applications of the Lasswellian approach in analysis of propaganda and elite succession may be found in Lasswell (1927), Lasswell and Blumenstock (1939), Lasswell, Lietes, et al. (1949), Lasswell, Lerner, and Pool (1952), and Lasswell, Lerner, and Rothwell (1952).

CHAPTER 13. TOWARD POLICY DESIGN

The idea of design has found some expression in the policy analysis and organizational theory literature. To Miller (1984; following Simon 1981) "design science" is any area of inquiry that helps to create the objects it studies. To Linder and Peters (1984) and Salamon (1981), design's central concern is with the capabilities of the various policy instruments government has at its disposal. E. Alexander (1982) views design as the invention of policy alternatives. For Bobrow (1974: 9), the objective of the policy field is the production of designs thought of as "blueprints for purposeful action." Dryzek (1983b) considers design to be the process of inventing, developing, and fine tuning a course of action. Social arrangements—both formal and informal—have sometimes been treated as constructs to be assembled for a particular purpose (Thompson 1966), based on a recognition that collections of elements in private and public institutions can vary in the extent to which they serve valued purposes (Downs 1967).

Bibliography

AARON, Henry J. 1978. *Politics and the Professors: The Great Society in Perspective.* Washington, D.C.: Brookings.

ACKERMAN, Bruce A. 1980. *Social Justice in the Liberal State.* New Haven: Yale University Press.

ACKERMAN, Bruce A., Susan Rose-Ackerman, James W. Sawyer, Jr., and Dale W. Henderson. 1974. *The Uncertain Search for Environmental Quality.* New York: Free Press.

ACTON, H. B. 1963. "Negative Utilitarianism." *Proceedings of the Aristotelian Society* 37 (supplement): 83–94.

AFYANSEV, Sergei, and Sergei Melikhov. 1979. "Modal Concepts of the Foreign Policy Decision Making Process." In *Political Theory and Political Practice,* ed. Soviet Political Science Association, 148–57. Moscow: U.S.S.R. Academy of Sciences.

AHONEN, Pertti. 1983. *Public Policy Evaluation as Discourse.* Helsinki: Finnish Political Science Association.

ALEXANDER, Christopher. 1964. *Notes on the Synthesis of Form.* Cambridge: Harvard University Press.

———. 1965. "A City Is Not a Tree." *Architectural Forum* 122 (1) and (2): 58–61 and 58–62.

ALEXANDER, Ernest A. 1982. "Design in the Decision-Making Process." *Policy Sciences* 14:279–92.

ALFORD, Robert A. 1975. "Ideological Filters and Bureaucratic Responses in Interpreting Research: Community Planning and Poverty." In *Social Policy and Sociology,* ed. N. J. Demerath III, Otto Larsen, and Karl F. Schuessler, 25–36. New York: Academic

ALLISON, Graham T. 1971. *Essence of Decision: Explaining the Cuban Missile Crisis.* Boston: Little, Brown.

———. 1974. "Implementation Analysis." In *Benefit Cost and Policy Analysis,* ed. Richard Zeckhauser et al., 369–91. Chicago: Aldine.

AMACHER, Ryan C., Robert D. Tollison, and Thomas D. Willett, eds. 1976. *The Economic Approach to Public Policy: Selected Readings.* Ithaca: Cornell University Press.

AMY, Douglas James. 1983. "Environmental Mediation: An Alternative Approach to Policy Stalements." *Policy Sciences* 15:345–65.

ANDERSON, Frederick R., et al. 1977. *Environmental Improvement Through Economic Incentives.* Baltimore: Johns Hopkins University Press for Resources for the Future.

221

ANDERSON, James E. 1979. *Public Policy-Making*, 2d ed. New York: Holt, Rinehart, and Winston.

ARROW, Kenneth J. 1963. *Social Choice and Individual Values*, 2d ed. New Haven: Yale University Press.

ASHBY, W. Ross. 1963. *An Introduction to Cybernetics*. New York: Wiley.

AXELROD, Robert M. 1976. *Structure of Decision: The Cognitive Maps of Political Elites*. Princeton: Princeton University Press.

――――. 1977. "The Medical Metaphor." *American Journal of Political Science* 21:430–32.

BADIA, P., A. Haber, and R. Runyon, eds. 1970. *Research Problems in Psychology*. Reading: Addison-Wesley.

BAILEY, F., and R. T. Holt. 1971. "The Analysis of Governmental Structures in Urban Systems." In *Proceedings of the Joint National Conference on Major Systems*. Anaheim, California, October.

BALL, Terence. 1976. "From Paradigms to Research Programs: Toward a Post-Kuhnian Political Science." *American Journal of Political Science* 20:151–77.

――――. 1984. "Marxian Science and Positivist Politics." In *After Marx*, ed. Terence Ball and James Farr, 235–60. New York: Cambridge University Press.

BANFIELD, Edward C. 1970. *The Unheavenly City*. Boston: Little, Brown.

BARBER, Benjamin. 1984. *Strong Democracy: Participatory Politics for a New Age*. Berkeley: University of California Press.

BARDACH, Eugene. 1977. *The Implementation Game*. Cambridge: MIT Press.

BATOR, Francis M. 1957. "The Simple Analytics of Welfare Maximization." *American Economic Review* 47:22–59.

――――. 1958. "The Anatomy of Market Failure." *Quarterly Journal of Economics* 72:351–79.

BAUMOL, William J. 1977. "On the Discount Rate for Public Projects." In *Public Expenditure and Policy Analysis*, ed., Robert H. Haveman and Julius Margolis, 161–79, 2d ed. Chicago: Rand McNally.

BAUMOL, William J., and Wallace E. Oates. 1975. *The Theory of Environmental Policy*. Englewood Cliffs: Prentice-Hall.

BEHN, R. D. 1981. "Policy Analysis and Policy Politics." *Policy Analysis* 7:199–226.

BELL, David E., Ralph L. Keeney, and Howard Raiffa, eds. 1977. *Conflicting Objectives in Decisions*. New York: Wiley.

BERGER, Thomas R. 1977. *Northern Frontier, Northern Homeland: Report of the Mackenzie Valley Pipeline Inquiry*. Toronto: James Lorimer.

BERLIN, Victor N., and Roland G. Weiss. 1977. "The Role of Evaluation Systems in the Government. Policy and Program Change: A Cybernetic Approach." In Institute for Electronic and Electrical Engineering, Proceedings, International Conference on Cybernetics and Society.

BERNSTEIN, Richard J. 1976. The Restructuring of Social and Political Theory. Philadelphia: University of Pennsylvania Press.

BIDERMAN, Albert D. 1966. "Social Indicators and Goals." In Social Indicators, ed. Raymond A. Bauer, 68–153. Cambridge: MIT Press.

BISH, Robert L. 1975. "The Assumption of Knowledge in Policy Analysis." Policy Studies Journal 3:256–62.

———. 1978. "Intergovernmental Relations in the United States: Some Concepts and Implications from a Public Choice Perspective." In Intergovernmental Policy Making: Limits to Coordination and Central Control, ed. K. Hanf and F. W. Schapf, 19–36. Beverly Hills: Sage.

BLACK, Duncan. 1958. The Theory of Committees and Elections. Cambridge: Cambridge University Press.

BLAIR, John P., and Steven M. Maser. 1978. "A Reassessment of Axiomatic Models in Policy Studies." In Policy Analysis and Deductive Reasoning, ed. Gordon E. Tullock and Richard E. Wagner, 3–16. Lexington: Lexington Books.

BOBROW, Davis B. 1969. "Ecology of International Games." Peace Research Society (International) Papers 11:67–88.

———. 1972. International Relations: New Approaches. New York: Free Press.

———. 1974. Technology-Related International Outcomes: R and D Strategies to Induce Sound Public Policy. International Studies Occasional Paper 3. Pittsburgh: International Studies Association.

BOBROW, Davis B., and Robert P. Stoker. 1981. "Evaluation of Foreign Policy." In Cumulation in International Relations Research, ed. P. Terrence Hopmann, Dina A. Zinnes, and J. David Singer, 99–132. University of Denver Monograph Series in World Affairs, vol. 18, book 3.

BRANDON, William P. 1984. "Public Policy as the Continuation of Moral Philosophy by Other Means." Policy Studies Review 4:60–70.

BRAYBROOKE, David, and Charles E. Lindblom. 1963. A Strategy of Decision: Policy Evaluation as a Social Process. New York: Free Press.

BRENNAN, G., and J. M. Buchanan. 1977. "Towards a Tax Constitution for Leviathan." Journal of Public Economics 8:255–73.

BREWER, Garry D. 1975. "Dealing with Complex Social Problems: The Potential of the 'Decision Seminar.' " In *Political Development and Change: A Policy Approach*, ed. Garry D. Brewer and Ronald D. Brunner, 439–61. New York: Free Press.

BREWER, Garry D., and Peter Deleon. 1983. *The Foundations of Policy Analysis*. Homewood: Dorsey.

BREWER, Garry D., and Martin Shubik. 1979. *The War Game*. Cambridge: Harvard University Press.

BROWN, Peter. 1976. "Ethics and Policy Research." *Policy Analysis* 2:325–40.

BRUNNER, Ronald D. 1982. "The Policy Sciences as Science." *Policy Sciences* 15:115–35.

———. 1984. "Editorial: Integrating Knowledge and Action." *Policy Sciences* 17:3–12.

BRUNNER, Ronald D., and Garry D. Brewer. 1971. *Organized Complexity*. New York: Free Press.

BUCHANAN, James M., and Gordon Tullock. 1962. *The Calculus of Consent: Logical Foundations of Constitutional Democracy*. Ann Arbor: University of Michigan Press.

———. 1974. "Polluters' Profits and Political Response: Direct Controls versus Taxes." *American Economic Review* 65:139–47.

BUCKLEY, W., T. Burns, and L. D. Meeker. 1974. "Structural Resolutions of Collective Action Problems." *Behavioral Sciences* 19:277–97.

BULMER, Martin. 1983. "The British Tradition of Social Administration: Moral Concerns at the Expense of Scientific Rigor." In *Ethics, the Social Sciences, and Policy Analysis*, ed. Daniel Callahan and Bruce Jennings, 161–85. New York: Plenum.

CAIN, Glen G., and Harold G. Watts. 1972. "Problems in Making Policy Inferences from the Coleman Report." In *Evaluating Social Programs*, ed. Peter H. Rossi and Walter Williams, 73–95. New York: Seminar.

CALLICOTT, J. Baird. 1979. "Elements of an Environmental Ethic: Moral Considerability and the Biotic Universe." *Environmental Ethics* 1:71–82.

CAMPBELL, Donald T. 1969. "Reforms as Experiments." *American Psychologist* 24:409–29.

———. 1982. "Experiments as Arguments." *Knowledge: Creation, Diffusion, Utilization* 3:327–37.

CAMPBELL, Donald T., and H. L. Ross. 1968. "The Connecticut Crackdown on Speeding." *Law and Society Review* 3:33–53.

CAMPBELL, Donald T., and Julian C. Stanley. 1963. *Experimental and Quasiexperimental Designs for Research*. Chicago: Rand McNally.

CAPLAN, Nathan. 1979. "The Two-Communities Theory and Knowledge Utilization." *American Behavioral Scientist* 22:459–70.

CAPLAN, Nathan, Andrea Morrison, and Russell J. Stambaugh. 1975. *The Use of Social Science in Policy Decisions at the National Level.* Ann Arbor: Institute for Social Research.

CHELIMSKY, Eleanor. 1982. "Making Evaluation Relevant to Congressional Needs." *GAO Review* 17:22–27.

CHRISTENSON, James A., and Carolyn E. Sachs. 1980. "The Impact of Government Size and Number of Administrative Units on the Quality of Government Services." *Administrative Science Quarterly* 25:89–101.

COASE, R. H. 1960. "The Problem of Social Cost." *Journal of Law and Economics* 3:1–44.

COHEN, M. D., J. G. March, and J. P. Olsen. 1972. "A Garbage Can Model of Organizational Choice." *Administrative Science Quarterly* 17:1–25.

COLEMAN, James S. 1966. *Equality of Educational Opportunity.* Washington, D.C.: U.S. Department of Health, Education, and Welfare.

————. 1971. *Resources for Social Change.* New York: Wiley.

————. 1972. "Reply to Cain and Watts." In *Evaluating Social Programs,* ed. Peter H. Rossi and Walter Williams, 97–107. New York: Seminar.

————. 1975. "Integration, Yes; Busing, No." Interview by W. Goodman, *New York Times Magazine,* August: 10–11.

COMMONER, Barry. 1972. *The Closing Circle.* New York: Bantam.

CONE, John D., and Steven C. Hayes. 1980. *Environmental Problems/Behavioral Solutions.* Monterey: Brooks/Cole.

COOK, T. D. and D. T. Campbell. 1979. *Quasi-Experimentation: Design and Analysis for Field Settings.* Boston: Houghton Mifflin.

CRANDALL, Robert W., and Lester P. Lave, eds. 1981. *The Scientific Basis of Health and Safety Regulation.* Washington, D.C.: Brookings.

CRECINE, John P. 1969. *Governmental Problem Solving: A Computer Simulation of Municipal Budgeting.* Chicago: Rand McNally.

————. 1982. "Information Processing Approaches to Political Science." Mimeo.

CYERT, Richard, and James G. March. 1963. *A Behavioral Theory of the Firm.* Englewood Cliffs: Prentice-Hall.

DALES, J. M. 1968. *Pollution, Property, and Prices.* Toronto: University of Toronto Press.

DALLMAYR, Fred R. 1981. "Critical Theory and Public Policy." *Policy Studies Journal* 9:522–34.

DE BONO, Edward. 1970. *Lateral Thinking: Creativity Step by Step.* New York: Harper and Row.

DEGREGORI, Thomas R. 1974. "Caveat Emptor: A Critique of the Emerging Paradigm of Public Choice." *Administration and Society* 6:205–28.

DEMERATH, N. J., III, Otto Larsen, and Karl F. Schuessler, eds. 1975. *Social Policy and Sociology*. New York: Academic.

DEUTSCH, Karl W. 1953. *Nationalism and Social Communication: An Inquiry into the Foundations of Nationality*. Cambridge: MIT Press.

———. 1963. *The Nerves of Government: Models of Political Communication and Control*. New York: Free Press.

DIESING, Paul. 1962. *Reason in Society*. Urbana: University of Illinois Press.

DORFMAN, Robert. 1969. "An Economic Interpretation of Optimal Control Theory." *American Economic Review* 59:817–31.

DORFMAN, Robert, and Nancy S. Dorfman. 1977. *The Economics of the Environment*, 2d ed. New York: Norton.

DORON, Gideon. 1979. *The Smoking Paradox*. Cambridge: Abt.

DOUGLAS, Mary, and Aaron Wildavsky. 1982. *Risk and Culture: An Essay on the Selection of Technological and Environmental Dangers*. Berkeley and Los Angeles: University of California Press.

DOWNS, Anthony. 1967. *Inside Bureaucracy*. Boston: Little, Brown.

———. 1972. "Up and Down with Ecology—The 'Issue-Attention' Cycle." *Public Interest* 28:38–50.

DROR, Yehezkel. 1964. "The Barriers Facing Policy Science." *American Behavioral Scientist* 7 (5): 3–7.

———. 1971a. *Design for Policy Sciences*. New York: American Elsevier.

———. 1971b. *Ventures in Policy Sciences: Concepts and Applications*. New York: American Elsevier.

———. 1971c. *Crazy States: A Counterconventional Strategic Problem*. Lexington: Heath.

———. 1976. "Some Features of a Meta-Model for Policy Studies." In *Problems of Theory in Policy Analysis*, ed. Phillip M. Gregg, 51–61. Lexington: Lexington Books.

———. 1983. "Policy-Gambling: A Preliminary Explanation." *Policy Studies Journal* 12:9–13.

———. 1984a. "On Becoming More of a Policy Scientist." *Policy Studies Review* 4:13–21.

———. 1984b. "Workshop in Advanced Policy Analysis: Policymaking as Fuzzy Gambling." Paper presented at the Annual Meeting of the American Political Science Association.

———. 1985. *Policy Making Under Adversity*. New Brunswick: Transaction.

DRYZEK, John S. 1982. "Policy Analysis as a Hermenuetic Activity."
Policy Sciences 14:309–29.
———. 1983a. *Conflict and Choice in Resource Management: The
Case of Alaska.* Boulder: Westview.
———. 1983b. "Don't Toss Coins in Garbage Cans: A Prologue to
Policy Design." *Journal of Public Policy* 3:345–68.
———. 1986. "The Progress of Political Science." *Journal of Politics*
48:301–20.
DRYZEK, John S., and Robert E. Goodin. 1986. "Risk-Sharing and Social Justice: The Motivational Foundations of the Post-War Welfare State." *British Journal of Political Science* 16:1–34.
DRYZEK, John S., and Susan Hunter. 1987. "Environmental Mediation
for International Problems." *International Studies Quarterly* 31.
DUNN, William N. 1981. *Public Policy Analysis: An Introduction.*
Englewood Cliffs: Prentice-Hall.
———. 1982. "Reforms as Arguments." *Knowledge: Creation, Diffu-
sion, Utilization* 3:293–326.
DUNN, William N., Ian I. Mitroff, and Stuart Jay Deutsch. 1981. "The
Obsolescence of Evaluation Research." *Evaluation and Program
Planning* 4:207–18.
DWORKIN, Ronald. 1977. *Taking Rights Seriously.* Cambridge: Har-
vard University Press.
DYE, Thomas R. 1976. *Policy Analysis: What Governments Do, Why
They Do It, and What Difference it Makes.* University, Ala.: Uni-
versity of Alabama Press.
———. 1984. *Understanding Public Policy*, 5th ed. Englewood Cliffs:
Prentice-Hall.
EASTON, David. 1969. "The New Revolution in Political Science."
American Political Science Review 63:1051–61.
EDELMAN, Murray. 1971. *Politics as Symbolic Action.* New York:
Academic.
———. 1977. *Political Language: Words that Succeed and Policies
that Fail.* New York: Academic.
EDWARDS, Ward, Marcia Guttentag, and Kurt Snapper. 1975. "A Deci-
sion Theoretic Approach to Evaluation Research." In *Handbook
of Evaluation Research*, vol. 1, ed. Elmer N. Streuning and Mar-
cia Guttentag, 139–81. Beverly Hills: Sage.
ELKIN, Stephen L. 1974. "Political Science and the Analysis of Public
Policy." *Public Policy* 22:399–422.
———. 1983. "Economic and Political Rationality." Paper presented
at the Midwestern Political Science Association Meeting.
ENCARNATION, Dennis J. 1982. "William Niskanen on Bureaucratic
Responsiveness: An Empirical Analysis and a Theoretical Refor-

mulation." Paper presented at the American Political Science Association Convention.

ENTHOVEN, Alan C., and K. Wayne Smith. 1971. *How Much Is Enough: Shaping the Defense Program, 1961–69.* New York: Harper and Row.

EULAU, Heinz. 1977. "The Interventionist Synthesis." *American Journal of Political Science* 21:419–23.

EULAU, Heinz, and Kenneth Prewitt. 1973. *Labyrinths of Democracy.* Indianapolis: Bobbs-Merrill.

FALCO, Maria J. 1973. *Truth and Meaning in Political Science.* Columbus: Charles E. Merrill.

FARR, James. 1985. "Situational Analysis: Explanation in Political Science." *Journal of Politics* 47:1085–107.

FAY, Brian. 1975. *Social Theory and Political Practice.* London: Allen and Unwin.

FEREJOHN, John A., Robert Forsythe, and Roger G. Noll. 1978. "An Experimental Analysis of Decision-Making Procedures for Discrete Public Goods: A Case Study of a Problem in Institutional Design." In *Research in Experimental Economics,* vol. 1, ed. Vernon L. Smith. Greenwich: JAI.

FEYERABEND, Paul. 1975. *Against Method: Outline of an Anarchistic Theory of Knowledge.* London: New Left.

———. 1978. *Science in a Free Society.* London: New Left.

FIORINA, Morris P. 1981. "Congressional Control of the Bureaucracy: A Mismatch of Incentives and Capabilities." In *Congress Reconsidered,* ed. Lawrence C. Dodd and Bruce I. Oppenheimer, 2d ed., 332–48. Washington, D.C.: Congressional Quarterly Press.

FISCHER, Frank. 1980. *Politics, Values, and Public Policy: The Problem of Methodology.* Boulder: Westview.

FISHER, Roger, and William Ury. 1981. *Getting to Yes.* Boston: Houghton Mifflin.

FISHKIN, James S. 1983. *Justice, Equal Opportunity, and the Family.* New Haven: Yale University Press.

FORESTER, John. 1981. "Questioning and Organizing Attention: Toward a Critical Theory of Planning and Administrative Practice." *Administration and Society* 13:161–205.

———. 1983. "What Analysts Do." In *Values, Ethics, and the Practice of Policy Analysis,* ed. William N. Dunn, 47–62. Lexington: Lexington Books.

FORRESTER, Jay W. 1971. *World Dynamics.* Cambridge: Wright-Allen.

FREEMAN, A. Myrick, III. 1977. "Project Design and Evaluation with Multiple Objectives." In *Public Expenditure and Policy Analysis,* ed. Robert H. Haveman and Julius Margolis, 2d ed., 239–56. Chicago: Rand McNally.

FREEMAN, Harold, and Ann Solomon, eds. 1981. *Evaluation Studies Review Annual*, vol. 6. Beverly Hills: Sage.

FREY, Bruno S., et al. 1984. "Consensus and Dissension Among Economists: An Empirical Inquiry." *American Economic Review* 74:986–94.

FRIED, Charles L. 1978. *Right and Wrong*. Cambridge: Harvard University Press.

FRIEDMAN, Milton. 1953. *Essays in Positive Economics*. Chicago: University of Chicago Press.

FRIEDMAN, Milton, and Rose Friedman. 1979. *Free to Choose*. New York: Harcourt, Brace, Jovanovich.

———. 1984. *Tyranny of the Status Quo*. New York: Harcourt, Brace, Jovanovich.

FROHLICH, Norman, Thomas Hunt, Joe Oppenheimer, and R. Harrison Wagner. 1975. "Individual Contributions for Public Goods." *Journal of Conflict Resolution* 19:310–29.

FROHLICH, Norman, and Joe A. Oppenheimer. 1978. *Modern Political Economy*. Englewood Cliffs: Prentice-Hall.

FURNISS, Norman. 1978. "The Political Implications of the Public Choice–Property Rights School." *American Political Science Review* 72:399–410.

GEORGE, Alexander L. 1972. "The Case for Multiple Advocacy in Making Foreign Policy." *American Political Science Review* 66:751–85.

———. 1980. *Presidential Decisionmaking in Foreign Policy: The Effective Use of Information and Advice*. Boulder: Westview.

GEORGESCU-ROEGEN, Nicholas. 1954. "Choice, Expectations, and Measurability." *Quarterly Journal of Economics* 68:503–34.

GIST, John R., and R. Carter Hill. 1981. "The Economics of Choice in the Allocation of Federal Grants: An Empirical Test." *Public Choice* 36:63–73.

GOLDBERG, Victor P. 1974. "Public Choice–Property Rights." *Journal of Economic Issues* 8:555–79.

GOLDFARB, Robert S. 1975. "Learning in Government Programs and the Usefulness of Cost-Benefit Analysis: Lessons from Manpower and Urban Renewal History." *Policy Sciences* 6:281–99.

GOLEMBIEWSKI, Robert T. 1977. "A Critique of 'Democratic Administration' and its Supporting Ideation." *American Political Science Review* 71:1488–507.

GOODIN, Robert E. 1982. *Political Theory and Public Policy*. Chicago: University of Chicago Press.

————. 1985. *Protecting the Vulnerable: A Re-analysis of our Social Responsibilities*. Chicago: University of Chicago Press.

GOODIN, Robert, and Ilmar Waldner. 1979. "Thinking Big, Thinking Small, and Not Thinking at All." *Public Policy* 27:1–24.

GOULDNER, Alvin W. 1970. *The Coming Crisis of Western Sociology*. New York: Basic.

GREENBERG, George D., Jeffrey A. Miller, Lawrence B. Mohr, and Bruce C. Vladeck. 1977. "Developing Public Policy Theory: Perspectives from Empirical Research." *American Political Science Review* 71:1532–43.

GREY, Thomas C. 1976. "Property and Need: The Welfare State and Theories of Distributive Justice." *Stanford Law Review* 28:877–902.

GUILLEMIN, Jeanne, and Irving Louis Horowitz. 1983. "Social Research and Political Advocacy: New Stages and Old Problems in Integrating Science and Values." In *Ethics, the Social Sciences, and Policy Analysis*, ed. Daniel Callahan and Bruce Jennings, 187–211. New York: Plenum.

GUNNELL, John G. 1983. "Political Theory: The Evolution of a Sub-Field." In *Political Science: The State of the Discipline*, ed. Ada W. Finifter, 3–45. Washington, D.C.: American Political Science Association.

HABERMAS, Jurgen. 1970a. "On Systematically Distorted Communication." *Inquiry* 13:205–18.

————. 1970b. "Towards a Theory of Communicative Competence." *Inquiry* 13:360–75.

————. 1971. *Knowledge and Human Interests*. Boston: Beacon.

————. 1973a. *Legitimation Crisis*. Boston: Beacon.

————. 1973b. *Theory and Practice*. Boston: Beacon.

————. 1984. *The Theory of Communicative Action I: Reason and the Rationalization of Society*. Boston: Beacon.

HAEFELE, Edwin T. 1973. *Representative Government and Environmental Management*. Baltimore: Johns Hopkins University Press for Resources for the Future.

HALPERIN, Morton H. 1974. *Bureaucratic Politics and Foreign Policy*. Washington, D.C.: Brookings.

HAMBRICK, Ralph S., Jr. 1974. "A Guide for the Analysis of Policy Arguments." *Policy Sciences* 5:469–78.

HANNAN, Michael T., Nancy Brandon Tuma, and Lyle P. Groeneveld. 1977. "Income and Marital Events: Evidence from an Income Maintenance Experiment." *American Journal of Sociology* 82:1186–211.

HARDIN, Garrett. 1968. "The Tragedy of the Commons." *Science* 162:1243–48.

HARGROVE, Erwin C. 1975. *The Missing Link*. Washington, D.C.: Urban Institute.

———. 1980. "The Bureaucratic Politics of Evaluation." *Public Administration Review* 40:151–59.

HARRINGTON, Michael. 1962. *The Other America: Poverty in the United States*. New York: Macmillan.

HARSANYI, J. C. 1955. "Cardinal Welfare, Individualistic Ethics, and Interpersonal Comparisons of Utility." *Journal of Political Economy* 63:309–21.

———. 1969. "Rational-Choice Models of Political Behavior vs. Functionalist and Conformist Theories." *World Politics* 21:513–38.

HART, H. L. A. 1979. "Between Utility and Rights." In *The Idea of Freedom: Essays in Honour of Isaiah Berlin*, ed. Alan Ryan, 77–98. Oxford: Oxford University Press.

HAVEMAN, Robert H., and Julius Margolis. 1977. *Public Expenditure and Policy Analysis*, 2d ed. Chicago: Rand McNally.

HAVEMAN, Robert H., and Burton A. Weisbrod. 1975. "Defining Benefits of Public Programs: Some Guidance for Policy Analysts." *Policy Analysis* 1:169–96.

HAWKINS, Robert B. 1973. *Public Benefits from Public Choice: A Program to Reform and Revitalize Local Government in California, Increase Local Government Costs and Services, and Finance the Ability of the Public to Determine the Scope and Impact of Government Plans and Programs*. Report to the Governor of California. Sacramento.

HIRSCHMAN, Albert O. 1970. "The Search for Paradigms as a Hindrance to Understanding." *World Politics* 22:329–43.

HITCH, Charles J., and Roland N. McKean. 1965. *The Economics of Defense in the Nuclear Age*. Cambridge: Harvard University Press.

HOCHMAN, Harold M., and George E. Peterson, eds. 1974. *Redistribution Through Public Choice*. New York: Columbia University Press.

HOLMBERG, A. R., H. F. Dobyns, et al. 1962. "Community and Regional Development: The Cornell-Peru Experiment." *Human Organization* 21:108–24.

HOUSE, Peter, and Joseph Coleman. 1980. "Realities of Public Policy Analysis." In *Improving Policy Analysis*, ed. Stuart S. Nagel, 183–99. Beverly Hills: Sage.

HUMMEL, Ralph P. 1982. *The Bureaucratic Experience*, 2d ed. New York: St. Martin's.

HUNTER, Douglas E. 1984. *Political/Military Applications of Bayesian Analysis*. Boulder: Westview.

INBAR, Michael. 1979. *Routine Decision-Making*. Beverly Hills: Sage.

International Association for the Evaluation of Educational Achievement. 1973. *Stockholm Report*. Stockholm: IAEEA.

JACOBSON, Gary C. 1980. *Money in Congressional Elections*. New Haven: Yale University Press.

JAMES, Roger. 1980. *Return to Reason: Popper's Thought in Public Life*. Shepton Mallet: Open Books.

JANIS, Irving L., and Leon Mann. 1977. *Decision-Making*. New York: Free Press.

JENCKS, Christopher. 1972. *Inequality: A Reassessment of the Effect of Family and Schooling in America*. New York: Basic.

JENNINGS, Bruce. 1983. "Interpretive Social Science and Policy Analysis." In *Ethics, the Social Sciences, and Policy Analysis*, ed. Daniel Callahan and Bruce Jennings, 3–35. New York: Plenum.

KANTER, Arnold. 1975. *Defense Politics*. Chicago: University of Chicago Press.

KEARL, J. R., Clayne Pope, Gordon Whiting, and Larry Wimmer. 1979. "What Economists Think." *American Economic Review, Papers and Proceedings* 69:28–37.

KEENEY, R. L. 1973. "A Decision Analysis with Multiple Objectives: The Mexico City Airport." *Bell Journal of Economic and Management Science* 4:101–17.

KEENEY, Ralph L., and Howard Raiffa. 1976. *Decision Making with Multiple Objectives: Preferences and Value Tradeoffs*. New York: Wiley.

KELMAN, Steven. 1981. *What Price Incentives? Economists and the Environment*. Boston: Auburn House.

KEYNES, J. M. 1936. *The General Theory of Employment, Interest, and Money*. London: Macmillan.

KNEESE, Allen V., and Charles L. Schultze. 1975. *Pollution, Prices, and Public Policy*. Washington, D.C.: Brookings.

KNORR, Karin Dagmar. 1980. "The Gap Between Knowledge and Policy." In *Improving Policy Analysis*, ed. Stuart S. Nagel, 219–33. Beverly Hills: Sage.

KRUTILLA, John. 1967. "Conservation Reconsidered." *American Economic Review* 57:777–86.

KUHN, Thomas S. 1962. *The Structure of Scientific Revolutions*. Chicago: University of Chicago Press.

———. 1970. "Reflections on My Critics." In *Criticism and the Growth of Knowledge*, ed. Imre Lakatos and Alan Musgrave, 231–78. Cambridge: Cambridge University Press.

LAKATOS, Imre. 1970. "Falsification and the Methodology of Scientific Research Programmes." In *Criticism and the Growth of*

Knowledge, ed. Imre Lakatos and Alan Musgrave, 91–196. Cambridge: Cambridge University Press.

LANDAU, Martin. 1977. "The Proper Domain of Policy Analysis." *American Journal of Political Science* 21:423–27.

LA PORTE, Todd R., ed. 1975. *Organized Social Complexity: Challenges to Politics and Policy.* Princeton: Princeton University Press.

LASLETT, Peter, ed. 1956. *Philosophy, Politics, and Society.* Oxford: Basil Blackwell.

LASSWELL, Harold D. 1927. *Propaganda Technique in the Great War.* New York: Knopf.

———. 1930. *Psychopathology and Politics.* Chicago: University of Chicago Press.

———. 1948a. *Power and Personality.* New York: Norton.

———. 1948b. *The Analysis of Political Behavior: An Empirical Approach.* London: Kegan Paul, Trench, Tubner.

———. 1951. "The Policy Orientation." In *The Policy Sciences: Recent Developments in Scope and Methods,* ed. Daniel Lerner and Harold D. Lasswell, 3–15. Stanford: Stanford University Press.

———. 1960. "The Technique of Decision Seminars." *Midwest Journal of Political Science* 4:213–36.

———. 1961. *Politics: Who Gets What, When, and How.* Cleveland: World.

———. 1963. *The Future of Political Science.* New York: Atherton.

———. 1965. *World Politics and Personal Insecurity.* New York: Free Press.

———. 1970. "Must Science Serve Power?" *American Psychologist* 25:117–23.

———. 1980. "Must Science Serve Power?" (3–15) and "The Future of World Communication and Propaganda" (516–34). In *Propaganda and Communication in World History,* vol. 3, ed. Harold D. Lasswell, Daniel Lerner, and Hans Speier. Honolulu: University Press of Hawaii.

LASSWELL, Harold, and Dorothy Blumenstock. 1939. *World Revolutionary Propaganda.* New York: Knopf.

LASSWELL, Harold D., Daniel Lerner, and Ithiel De Sola Pool. 1952. *The Comparative Study of Symbols.* Stanford: Stanford University Press.

LASSWELL, Harold D., Daniel Lerner, and C. Easton Rothwell. 1952. *The Comparative Study of Elites.* Stanford: Stanford University Press.

LASSWELL, Harold, Nathan Lietes, et al. 1949. *The Language of Politics: Quantitative Semantics.* New York: Stewart.

234 BIBLIOGRAPHY

LASSWELL, Harold D., and Myres S. McDougel. 1943. "Legal Education and Public Policy." *Yale Law Journal* 52:203–95.

LAUDAN, Larry. 1977. *Progress and Its Problems: Towards a Theory of Scientific Growth.* Berkeley and Los Angeles: University of California Press.

LAVE, Lester B., and Eugene P. Seskin. 1977. *Air Pollution and Human Health.* Baltimore: Johns Hopkins University Press for Resources for the Future.

LAZARSFELD, Paul F., Jeffrey G. Reitz, and Ann K. Pasanella. 1975. *An Introduction to Applied Sociology.* New York: Elsevier.

LEMAN, Christopher K., and Robert H. Nelson. 1981. "Ten Commandments for Policy Economists." *Journal of Policy Analysis and Management* 1:97–117.

LERNER, Abba. 1944. *The Economics of Control: Principles of Welfare Economics.* New York: Macmillan.

LERNER, Daniel, and Harold D. Lasswell. eds. 1951. *The Policy Sciences: Recent Developments in Scope and Methods.* Stanford: Stanford University Press.

LEVINE, Robert A., and A. P. Williams. 1971. *Making Evaluation Effective.* Santa Monica: RAND Corporation (R-7888-HEW/CMU).

LINDBLOM, Charles E. 1959. "The Science of Muddling Through." *Public Administration Review* 19:79–88.

———. 1965. *The Intelligence of Democracy: Decision Making Through Mutual Adjustment.* New York: Free Press.

———. 1968. *The Policy Making Process.* Englewood Cliffs: Prentice-Hall.

———. 1979. "Still Muddling: Not Yet Through." *Public Administration Review* 39:517–26.

LINDBLOM, Charles E., and David K. Cohen. 1979. *Usable Knowledge.* New Haven: Yale University Press.

LINDER, Stephen H., and B. Guy Peters. 1984. "From Social Theory to Policy Design." *Journal of Public Policy* 4:237–59.

LOVINS, Amory B. 1977. *Soft Energy Paths: Toward a Durable Peace.* New York: Harper and Row.

LOVRICH, Nicholas P., and Max Neiman. 1984. *Public Choice Theory in Public Administration: An Annotated Bibliography.* New York: Garland.

LUKE, Timothy W., and Stephen K. White. 1985. "Critical Theory, The Informational Revolution, and an Ecological Modernity." In *Critical Theory and Public Life,* ed. John Forester, 22–53. Cambridge: MIT Press.

LYNN, Laurence E., Jr. 1980. *Designing Public Policy: A Casebook on the Role of Policy Analysis.* Santa Monica: Goodyear.

McADAMS, John. 1984. "The Anti-Policy Analysts." *Policy Studies Journal* 13:91–101.

McCARTHY, Thomas. 1978. *The Critical Theory of Jurgen Habermas.* Cambridge: MIT Press.

McFARLAND, Andrew. 1984. "An Experiment in Regulatory Negotiation: The National Coal Policy Project." Paper presented at the Annual Meeting of the Western Political Science Association.

MacRAE, Duncan, Jr. 1973. "Sociology in Policy Analysis." *Policy Studies Journal* 2:4–7.

———. 1976. *The Social Function of Social Science.* New Haven: Yale University Press.

MARCH, James G. 1972. "Model Bias in Social Action." *Review of Educational Research* 42:413–29.

———. 1978. "Bounded Rationality, Ambiguity and the Engineering of Choice." *Bell Journal of Economic and Management Science* 9:587–608.

MARCH, James G., and Johan P. Olsen. 1976. *Ambiguity and Choice in Organisations.* Bergen: Universitetsforlaget.

MARCH, James G., and Herbert A. Simon. 1958. *Organizations.* New York: Wiley.

MARGOLIS, Howard. 1973. *Technical Advice on Policy Issues.* Sage Administrative and Policy Studies Series, vol. 1. Beverly Hills: Sage.

MARGOLIS, Julius. 1977. "Shadow Prices for Incorrect or Nonexistent Market Values." In *Public Expenditures and Policy Analysis*, ed. Robert H. Haveman and Julius Margolis, 2d ed., 204–20. Chicago: Rand McNally.

MASON, Richard O. 1969. "A Dialectical Approach to Strategic Planning." *Management Science* 15:B403–B14.

MASTERMAN, Margaret. 1970. "The Nature of a Paradigm." In *Criticism and the Growth of Knowledge*, ed. Imre Lakatos and Alan Musgrave, 59–89. Cambridge: Cambridge University Press.

MELTSNER, Arnold J. 1972. "Political Feasibility and Policy Analysis." *Public Administration Review* 32:859–67.

———. 1976. *Policy Analysts in the Bureaucracy.* Berkeley and Los Angeles: University of California Press.

MENZIES, Ken. 1982. *Sociological Theory in Use.* London: Routledge and Kegan Paul.

MIHRAM, G. Arthur. 1977. "On 'Systems Science' and Cybernetics: Proposals for Unifying Science and Government." In Institute for Electronic and Electrical Engineering, *Proceedings, International Conference on Cybernetics and Society*, 26–32.

MILLER, Trudi C. 1984. "Conclusion: A Design Science Perspective."

In *Public Sector Performance: A Conceptual Turning Point*, ed. Trudi C. Miller, 251–68. Baltimore: Johns Hopkins University Press.

MISHAN, E. J. 1973. *Economics for Social Decisions*. New York: Praeger.

MITCHELL, Joyce C., and William C. Mitchell. 1986. "Policy Analysis: The Elementary Uses of Efficiency." In *Research in Public Policy Analysis and Management*, ed. Stuart S. Nagel, 3:175–92. Greenwich: JAI.

MITROFF, Ian I., and L. Vaughn Blankenship. 1973. "On the Methodology of the Holistic Experiment: An Approach to the Conceptualization of Large-Scale Social Experiments." *Technological Forecasting and Social Change* 4:339–53.

MUELLER, Dennis C. 1979. *Public Choice*. Cambridge: Cambridge University Press.

MUSGRAVE, R. A. 1969. "Cost-Benefit Analysis and the Theory of Public Finance." *Journal of Economic Literature* 7:797–806.

MYRDAL, Alva. 1941. *Nation and Family: The Swedish Experiment in Democratic Family and Population Policy*. New York: Harper.

MYRDAL, Gunnar. 1944. *An American Dilemma: The Negro Problem and Modern Democracy*. New York: Harper.

NACHMIAS, David. 1979. *Public Policy Evaluation: Approaches and Methods*. New York: St. Martin's.

———. 1980. *The Practice of Policy Evaluation*. New York: St. Martin's.

NEUSTADT, Richard E. 1970. *Alliance Politics*. New York: Columbia University Press.

NEWELL, Allen, and Herbert A. Simon. 1972. *Human Problem-Solving*. Englewood Cliffs: Prentice-Hall.

NIELSEN, Kai. 1983. "Emancipatory Social Science and Social Critique." In *Ethics, the Social Sciences, and Policy Analysis*, ed. Daniel Callahan and Bruce Jennings, 113–57. New York: Plenum.

NISKANEN, William A., Jr. 1971. *Bureaucracy and Representative Government*. Chicago: Aldine-Atherton.

NOZICK, Robert. 1974. *Anarchy, State, and Utopia*. New York: Basic.

OLSON, Mancur. 1965. *The Logic of Collective Action*. Cambridge: Harvard University Press.

———. 1982. *The Rise and Decline of Nations*. New Haven: Yale University Press.

OSTROM, Elinor. 1971. "Institutional Arrangements and the Measurement of Policy Consequences: Applications to Evaluating Policy Performance." *Urban Affairs Quarterly* 6:447–75.

———. 1973. "The Need for Multiple Indicators in Measuring the Output of Public Agencies." *Policy Studies Journal* 2:85–92.

OSTROM, Vincent, and Elinor Ostrom. 1971. "Public Choice: A Different Approach to the Study of Public Administration." *Public Administration Review* 31:203–16.

PAGE, Talbot. 1977. *Conservation and Economic Efficiency.* Baltimore: Johns Hopkins University Press for Resources for the Future.

PALUMBO, Dennis J., and David Nachmias. 1983. "The Preconditions for Successful Evaluation: Is There an Ideal Paradigm?" *Policy Sciences* 16:67–79.

PARIS, David C., and James F. Reynolds. 1983. *The Logic of Policy Inquiry.* New York: Longman.

PATTON, Michael Q. 1984. "Sneetches, Zax, and Empty Pants: Alternative Approaches to Evaluation." Paper presented at the Meeting of the California Postsecondary Conference on Education.

PELTZMAN, Sam. 1975. "The Effects of Automobile Safety Regulation." *Journal of Political Economy* 83:677–725.

PERLMUTTER, Howard V. 1965. *Toward a Theory and Practice of Social Architecture.* Tavistock Pamphlet 12. London: Tavistock.

PERROW, Charles. 1972. *Complex Organizations: A Critical Essay.* Glenview: Scott Foresman.

PHILLIPS, D. C. 1976. "Forty Years On: Anti-Naturalism, and Problems of Social Experiment and Piecemeal Social Reform." *Inquiry* 19:403–25.

PIVEN, Frances Fox, and Richard A. Cloward. 1971. *Regulating the Poor: The Functions of Public Welfare.* New York: Random House.

———. 1982. *The New Class War: Reagan's Attack on the Welfare State and Its Consequences.* New York: Random House.

POPPER, Karl. 1959. *The Logic of Scientific Discovery.* London: Heinemann.

———. 1963. *The Open Society and Its Enemies.* Princeton: Princeton University Press.

———. 1970. "Normal Science and Its Dangers." In *Criticism and the Growth of Knowledge,* ed. Imre Lakatos and Alan Musgrave, 51–58. Cambridge: Cambridge University Press.

———. 1972. *The Poverty of Historicism,* rev. ed. London: Routledge and Kegan Paul.

POSNER, Richard. 1972. *Economic Analysis of the Law.* Boston: Little, Brown.

PRESSMAN, Jeffrey, and Aaron Wildavsky. 1973. *Implementation.* Berkeley and Los Angeles: University of California Press.

QUADE, E. S. 1982. *Analysis for Public Decisions*, 2d ed. New York: North Holland.

RAIFFA, Howard. 1968. *Decision Analysis: Introductory Lectures on Choices Under Uncertainty.* Reading: Addison-Wesley.

RANNEY, Austin, ed. 1968. *Political Science and Public Policy.* Chicago: Markham.

RAWLS, John. 1951. "Outline of a Decision Procedure for Ethics." *Philosophical Review* 60:177–97.

———. 1971. *A Theory of Justice.* Cambridge: Harvard University Press.

REIN, Martin. 1976. *Social Science and Public Policy.* Harmondsworth: Penguin.

———. 1983. "Value-Critical Policy Analysis." In *Ethics, The Social Sciences, and Policy Analysis,* ed. Daniel Callahan and Bruce Jennings, 83–111. New York: Plenum.

REISS, ALBERT J., JR. 1975. "Inappropriate Theories and Inadequate Methods as Policy Plagues: Self-Reported Delinquency and the Law." In *Social Policy and Sociology,* ed. N. J. Demerath III, Otto Larsen, and Karl F. Schuessler, 211–22. New York: Academic.

RICKETTS, Martin. 1981. "Housing Policy: Towards a Public Choice Perspective." *Journal of Public Policy* 1:501–22.

RIDKER, R. G., and J. A. Henning. 1971. "The Determinants of Residential Property Values with Special Reference to Air Pollution." *Review of Economics and Statistics* 53:246–57.

RIKER, William. 1962. *The Theory of Political Coalitions.* New Haven: Yale University Press.

RIKER, William H., and Peter C. Ordeshook. 1973. *An Introduction to Positive Political Theory.* Englewood Cliffs: Prentice-Hall.

RIVLIN, Alice M. 1971. *Systematic Thinking for Social Action.* Washington, D.C.: Brookings.

———. 1973. "Forensic Social Science." In *Perspectives on Inequality.* Cambridge: Harvard Educational Review Reprint Series 8.

ROBINSON, John Bridger. 1982. "Apples and Horned Toads: On the Framework-Determined Nature of the Energy Debate." *Policy Sciences* 15:23–45.

ROHR, John. 1976. "The Study of Ethics in the Public Administration Curriculum." *Public Administration Review* 36:398–406.

ROUTLEY, Richard, and Val Routley. 1978. "Nuclear Energy and Obligations to the Future." *Inquiry* 21:133–79.

RUSSELL, Clifford S., ed. 1979. *Collective Decision Making: Applications from Public Choice Theory.* Baltimore: Johns Hopkins University Press for Resources for the Future.

SALAMON, Lester M. 1981. "Rethinking Management: Third-Party Government and the Changing Forms of Government Actions." *Public Policy* 24:255–75.

SCHNEIDER, Janet A., Nancy J. Stevens, and Louis G. Tornatzky. 1982. "Policy Research and Analysis: An Empirical Profile, 1975–1980." *Policy Sciences* 15:99–114.

SCHULMAN, Paul R. 1975. "Nonincremental Policy Making: Notes Toward an Alternative Paradigm." *American Political Science Review* 69:1354–70.

SCHULTZE, Charles L. 1968. *The Politics and Economics of Public Spending.* Washington, D.C.: Brookings.

———. 1970. "The Role of Incentives, Penalties and Rewards in Attaining Effective Policy." In *Public Expenditure and Policy Analysis,* ed. Robert H. Haveman and Julius Margolis, 145–72. Chicago: Markham.

SCOTT, Robert A., and Arnold R. Shore. 1979. *Why Sociology Does Not Apply.* New York: Elsevier.

SEN, Amartya K. 1970. *Collective Choice and Social Welfare.* San Francisco: Holden Bay.

———. 1972. *On Economic Inequality.* Oxford: Clarendon.

SERGIYEV, Artemy. 1979. "Methodological Problems of Quantitative Analysis and Simulation of Socio-Political Systems." In *Political Theory and Political Practice,* ed. Soviet Political Sciences Association, 134–47. Moscow: U.S.S.R. Academy of Sciences.

SHUE, Henry. 1980. *Basic Rights: Subsistence, Affluence, and U.S. Foreign Policy.* Princeton: Princeton University Press.

SIKORA, R. I., and Brian Barry, eds. 1978. *Obligations to Future Generations.* Philadelphia: Temple University Press.

SIMON, Herbert A. 1957. *Models of Man.* New York: Wiley.

———. 1960. *The New Science of Management Decision.* New York: Harper and Row.

———. 1969. *The Sciences of the Artificial.* Cambridge: MIT Press.

———. 1978. "On How to Decide What to Do." *Bell Journal of Economic and Management Science* 9:494–507.

———. 1981. *The Sciences of the Artificial,* 2d ed. Cambridge: MIT Press.

SLOVIC, Paul, Baruch Fischoff, and Sarah Lichtenstein. 1977. "Behavioral Decision Theory." *Annual Review of Psychology* 28:1–39.

SMART, J. J. C., and Bernard Williams. 1973. *Utilitarianism: For and Against.* Cambridge: Cambridge University Press.

STEINBRUNER, John D. 1974. *The Cybernetic Theory of Decision: New Dimensions of Political Analysis.* Princeton: Princeton University Press.

STERNE, Richard S., Alvin Rabushka, and Helen A. Scott. 1972. "Serving the Elderly: An Illustration of the Niskanen Effect." *Public Choice* 13:81–90.

STOKEY, Edith, and Richard Zeckhauser. 1978. *A Primer for Policy Analysis*. New York: Norton.

STONE, Christopher D. 1972. "Should Trees Have Standing? Toward Legal Rights for Natural Objects." *Southern California Law Review* 45:450–501.

SUGDEN, Robert, and Alan Williams. 1978. *The Principles of Practical Cost-Benefit Analysis*. Oxford: Oxford University Press.

TALLMAN, Irving. 1976. *Passion, Action and Politics: A Perspective on Social Problems and Social Problem Solving*. San Francisco: Freeman.

THOMPSON, James D., ed. 1966. *Approaches to Organizational Design*. Pittsburgh: University of Pittsburgh Press.

THOMPSON, Judith Jarvis. 1971. "A Defense of Abortion." *Philosophy and Public Affairs* 1:47–66.

TIEBOUT, Charles M. 1956. "A Pure Theory of Local Expenditures." *Journal of Political Economy* 64:416–24.

TITMUSS, Richard M. 1971. *The Gift Relationship: From Human Blood to Social Policy*. London: Allen and Unwin.

———. 1974. *Social Policy: An Introduction*. New York: Pantheon.

TOMKINS, Mark E. 1979. "The Role of Information in Policy Analysis." Mimeo.

TOULMIN, Stephen. 1958. *The Uses of Argument*. Cambridge: Cambridge University Press.

TRIBE, Laurence H. 1972. "Policy Science: Analysis or Ideology?" *Philosophy and Public Affairs* 2:66–110.

———. 1973. "Technology Assessment and the Fourth Discontinuity: The Limits of Instrumental Rationality." *Southern California Law Review* 46:617–60.

———. 1976. "Ways Not to Think About Plastic Trees." In *When Values Conflict: Essays on Environmental Analysis, Discourse, and Decision*, ed. Laurence H. Tribe, Corinne S. Schelling, and John Voss, 61–92. Cambridge: Ballinger.

TRIBE, Laurence H., Corinne S. Schelling, and John Voss, eds. 1976. *When Values Conflict: Essays on Environmental Analysis, Discourse, and Decision*. Cambridge: Ballinger.

TULLOCK, Gordon. 1979. "Public Choice in Practice." In *Collective Decision Making: Applications from Public Choice Theory*, ed. Clifford S. Russell, 27–45. Baltimore: Johns Hopkins University Press for Resources for the Future.

TULLOCK, Gordon E., and Richard E. Wagner, eds. 1978. *Policy Analysis and Deductive Reasoning*. Lexington: Lexington Books.

TVERSKY, Amos, and Daniel Kahneman. 1975. "Judgment Under Uncertainty: Heuristics and Biases." In *Benefit-Cost and Policy Analysis 1974*, ed. Richard Zeckhauser, et al., 295–307. Chicago: Aldine.

ULVILA, Jacob W., and Warren D. Snider. 1980. "Negotiation of International Oil Tanker Standards: An Application of Multiattribute Value Theory." *Operations Research* 28:81–96.

VOLKOV, Leonid. 1979. "Standards of Political Behavior and Perfection of the Management and Administration of Developed Socialist Society." Paper presented at the 11th World Congress of the International Political Science Association, Moscow.

VON NEUMANN, J., and O. Morgenstern. 1947. *Theory of Games and Economic Behavior*, 2d ed. Princeton: Princeton University Press.

VON WRIGHT, Georg Henrik. 1971. *Explanation and Understanding*. Ithaca: Cornell University Press.

WALZER, Michael. 1977. *Just and Unjust Wars*. New York: Basic.

———. 1983. *Spheres of Justice: A Defense of Pluralism and Equality*. New York: Basic.

WEAVER, Warren. 1948. "Science and Complexity." *American Scientist* 36:536–44.

WEINBERG, Alvin. 1972. "Science and Trans-Science." *Minerva* 10:209–22.

WEISBROD, Burton A. 1968. "Income Redistribution Effects and Benefit-Cost Analysis." In *Problems in Public Expenditure Analysis*, ed. S. B. Chase, 177–209. Washington, D.C.: Brookings.

WEISS, Carol H., ed. 1977. *Using Social Research in Public Policy Making*. Lexington: Heath.

———. 1980. "Knowledge Creep and Decision Accretion." *Knowledge: Creation, Diffusion, Utilization* 1:381–404.

WHOLEY, Joseph S. 1983. *Evaluation and Effective Public Management*. Boston: Little, Brown.

WIENER, Norbert. 1948. *Cybernetics*. New York: Wiley.

———. 1954. *The Human Use of Human Beings*. Boston: Houghton Mifflin.

WILDAVSKY, Aaron. 1966. "The Political Economy of Efficiency." *Public Administration Review* 26:292–310.

———. 1974. *The Politics of the Budgetary Process*, 2d ed. Boston: Little, Brown.

———. 1979. *Speaking Truth to Power*. Boston: Little, Brown.

WILENSKY, Harold. 1967. *Organizational Intelligence*. New York: Basic.

WILLIAMS, Walter, and John W. Evans. 1969. "The Politics of Evaluation: The Case of Head Start." *Annals of the American Academy of Politial and Social Science* 385:118–32.

WILSON, James Q. 1983. *Thinking About Crime*, rev. ed. New York: Basic.

ZECKHAUSER, Richard. 1974. "Risk Spreading and Distribution." In *Redistribution Through Public Choice*, ed. Harold M. Hochman and George E. Peterson, 206–28. New York: Columbia University Press.

ZIMMERMAN, William. 1973. "Issue Area and Foreign-Policy Process: A Research Note in Search of a General Theory." *American Political Science Review* 67:1204–12.

Index

Pitt Series in Policy and Institutional Studies
Bert A. Rockman, Editor